Wool-Working. Two scenes, here (A), next page, (B); black-figure lekythos by the Amasis Painter"; from Athens, ca. 560 B.C. The painter, perhaps best known for his lively scenes of Dionysiac revel, gives a picture of everyday domesticity typical for the average woman of antiquity—Greek or Roman. In A, the woman on the right weighs balls of wool, the first step in the process of making cloth. The woman on the far left twists the washed raw wool into long strands called roves. Facing her (in B) is a woman using spindle, whorl, and distaff to make the yarn which will be used to weave the cloth on an upright loom (A). The finished product is folded and placed on a low stool in B. The making of wool was so much a part of what was expected of the ancient woman that even the emperor Augustus, the historian Suetonius tells us (*Aug.* 73), liked to wear clothing made for him by his sister, wife, daughter, and granddaughters. (The Metropolitan Museum of Art, Fletcher Fund, 1931)

Women
in Greece and Rome

Mary R. Lefkowitz
Maureen B. Fant

Samuel-Stevens
Toronto & Sarasota
1977

Aspects of Antiquity

Samuel Stevens Edition (U.S.)
Cloth: ISBN 0-89522-003-2
Paper: ISBN 0-89522-004-0

Samuel Stevens Edition (Canada)
Cloth: 0-88866-587-3
Paper: 0-88866-588-1

Library of Congress Catalogue Card Number 77-83159

Canadian Cataloguing in Publication Data

Main entry under title:

Women in Greece and Rome

Bibliography: p.
Includes index.
ISBN 0-88866-587-3 bd.   ISBN 0-88866-588-1 pa.

1. Women—Greece. 2. Women—Rome. I. Lefkowitz,
Mary R   II. Fant, Maureen B

HQ1134.W64   301.41'2'0938   C77-001362-7

cover design by Peter Maher

Printed and Bound in The United States of America

Samuel-Stevens, Publishers
554 Spadina Crescent
Toronto, Canada M5S 2J9
Samuel Stevens & Company
Box 3899
Sarasota, Florida 33578

For R. G. L., H. W. L.,
and J. C. F.

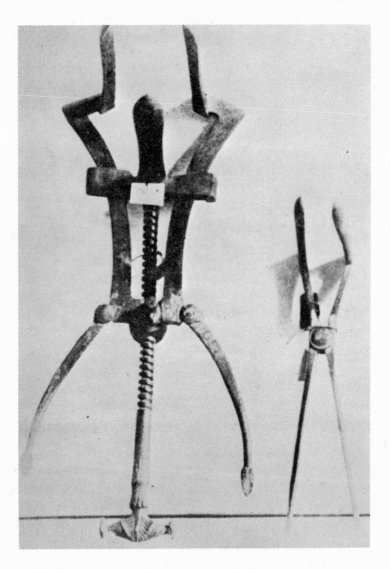

A Gynecological Instrument. Trivalve speculum; before 79 A.D. (found in the "House of the Surgeon," Pompeii). This kind of speculum was used through much of antiquity down to the seventh century A.D. The three blades are at right angles to the handles. The two upper blades, which can be opened and closed by adjusting the screw, are used to separate the labia of the vagina; the tongue in the center was used to raise a prolapsed bladder or cystocele, or, if inverted, to raise a prolapsed rectum, conditions caused by prolonged labor or frequent childbearing. (Museo Nazionale, Naples. From J. V. Ricci, "The Vaginal Speculum and its Modifications throughout the Ages," *Transactions of the Gynaecological Department of the City Hospital,* New York, 1948-49, fig. 1.)

Contents

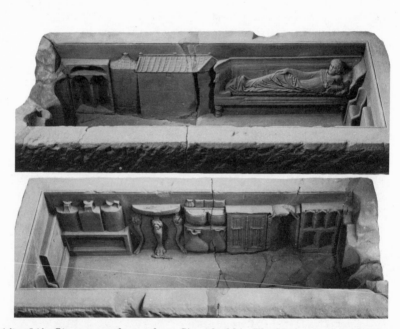

After Life. Stone sarcophagus from Simpelveld in The Netherlands; second or third century A.D. Though this piece is unique, it represents the widely held belief that the soul resides after death in the place of burial (cf. p. 104). The sarcophagus is carved with facsimiles of the material goods the deceased woman enjoyed in life, so that her soul might enjoy them after death. She is shown reclining on her funeral couch, surrounded by her furniture, storage jars, and bath house. (Rijksmuseum van Oudheden, Leiden)

Preface

Histories of the ancient world have traditionally been written without much reference to women. The ancients themselves set the pattern: wars and politics, not social or domestic affairs, claimed the chief attention of educated men. But the politics of today's world urge our reconsideration of past practice, and studies of other cultures offer promising new analytical approaches to evidence that had formerly been discounted or ignored. This book is intended to make accessible to people who do not know the ancient languages the kinds of materials on which historians of women in the ancient world must base their work.

A glance through the contents will reveal that the materials in this book are assembled from disparate sources, mostly the types of documents one does not expect to find in a "history" book. Yet such are the materials on which the modern historian must rely to produce a comprehensive history of women in antiquity. They offer a spectrum of opinions, some possibly representative and often persistently influential; and a record, scattered over space and time, of personal feelings, often, because they are spoken in the stress of bereavement or in the formality of legal documents, unrepresentative of the conditions that ordinarily characterized family life. General trends of attitudes towards women and impressions of their status in society emerge, but these too should be considered in the larger context of "men's" history. If, starting in the Hellenistic period, women appear to play a larger role in determining their own affairs and society's, it must be remembered that concomitant emphasis is given in contemporary documents and art to the achievements of ordinary *men*.

Many familiar texts, like Hesiod's story of Pandora, Aristotle's reflections on women, selections from Juvenal's sixth satire, are reproduced here for the reader's convenience. Other interesting documents, e.g., some of the papyrus letters and funerary inscriptions, are not available elsewhere in translation. Special effort has been made to include a representative selection of medical documents, including (for the first time in English) cures not consonant with conventional ideas of Greek enlightenment. Omitted from the book are literary texts (readily available in paperback) that should be read in their entirety, and also mythological documents, like stories of the Amazons and the legends in the first books of Livy. For supplementary lists of such materials see *A Sampler of Women's Studies* (Ann Arbor, 1972), p. 84, and the course outlines by K. Berman in *Classical World* 47 (1974) 213-220 and by S. K. Dickison in *Female Studies VII* (Old Westbury, 1973) 54-56. Every reader will want to consult S. Pomeroy's *Goddesses, Whores, Wives, and Slaves* (New York, 1975) with its comprehensive bibliography, and M. Arthur's critical annotated bibliography of work on women in antiquity in *Signs* 2.2 (1976) 382-403.

Assembling materials from diffuse and often recondite sources, from two cultures, covering a period of a thousand years, involves more knowledge and expertise than any two people can easily possess. Special thanks are due to Prof. Ann C. Sheffield of Barnard, whose collection of class readings provided helpful guidelines. We are grateful also for valuable suggestions to Profs. Marylin Arthur, Roger Bagnall, J. Clayton Fant, Ann Hanson, Michael Jameson, William Metcalf, to Drs. Bennett Simon and George S. Richardson, and to Prof. Naphtali Lewis for instructive criticism and insight.

The translation of Semonides is reprinted by permission of Hugh Lloyd-Jones, and of the new Archilochus fragment by John Van Sickle. Two of the Sulpicia poems first appeared in *Maine Times*.

Excerpts from the following have been reprinted with permission of the copyright holder. Harvard University Press and Loeb Classical Library: Aristotle, *On the Generation of Animals* (tr. A. L. Peck); Appian, *Civil War* (tr. H. White); Aulus Gellius, *Attic Nights* (tr. J. C. Rolfe); Callimachus, *Hymns and Epigrams* (tr. A. W. Mair); Celsus, *On Medicine* (tr. W. G. Spencer); Demosthenes, *Against Macartatus* (in *Private Orations* vol. V, tr. A. T. Murray); Dio Cassius, *Roman History* (tr. E. Cary); Diogenes Laertius, *Lives of Eminent Philosophers* (tr. R. D. Hicks); Seneca, *Moral Essays* (tr. J. W. Basore); *Select*

Papyri vol. I (tr. A. S. Hunt and C. C. Edgar); Plutarch, *Moralia* (tr. F. C. Babbitt and F. H. Sandbach).—Penguin Books, Ltd.: Apollonius of Rhodes, *Voyage of the Argo* (tr. E. V. Rieu), pp. 131-2, copyright © E. V. Rieu 1959, 1971; Herodotus, *The Histories* (tr. A. de Selincourt), p. 527, copyright © the Estate of Aubrey de Selincourt, 1957, A. R. Burn 1972; Sallust, *The Conspiracy of Catiline* (tr. S. A. Handford), pp. 192-3, copyright © S. A. Handford, 1963; *The Letters of the Younger Pliny* (tr. B. Radice), pp. 102-3, 126-7, 159, 161, 187-8, 197-8, 218, copyright © Betty Radice, 1963, 1969; Plato, *The Laws* (tr. T. J. Saunders), pp. 262-3, 293-5, 336-8, copyright © Trevor J. Saunders, 1970.— Oxford University Press: Irenaeus in W. Foerster, *Gnosis: A Selection of Gnostic Texts* (tr. R. M. Wilson); H. Musurillo, *Acts of the Christian Martyrs*; F. de Zulueta, *The Institutes of Gaius*, Part 1;—Cornell University Press: M. T. May, *Galen on the Usefulness of the Parts of the Body; Xenophon's Socratic Discourse* (tr. C. Lord).—Cambridge University Press: G. Milligan, *Selections from the Greek Papyri.*—MacDonald and Jane's: K. Freeman, *The Murder of Herodes and Other Trials from the Athenian Law Courts.*—University of Texas Press: *Ancient Roman Statutes.*—The Johns Hopkins University Press: Soranus, *Gynecology* (tr. O. Temkin).—Mrs. Frances Schwartz: *Hippocrates, On Intercourse and Pregnancy* (tr. T. H. Ellinger).—D. C. Heath: D. C. Munro, *A Source Book on Roman History.*— Random House, Inc.: R. Y. Hathorn, *The Basic Works of Cicero.* —Princeton University Press (Bollingen Series): Plato, *Timaeus* (tr. T. Taylor).—The University of Michigan Press: J. G. Winter, *Life and Letters in the Papyri.*—Columbia University Press: *Roman Civilization* vol. II (*ADA*, tr. N. Lewis and M. Reinhold). —Hakkert: two inscriptions from N. Lewis, *Greek Historical Documents: The Roman Principate.*—University of Illinois Press: R. Lattimore, *Themes in Greek and Latin Epitaphs.*— University of California Press: P. Friedländer and H. Hoffleit, *Epigrammata.*—AMS Press: A. J. Brock, *Greek Medicine.*

The translation of Aretaeus is F. Adams's; of Aristotle's *Politics*, B. Jowett's; of Plutarch's *Lives*, J. Dryden's; of Juvenal, L. Evans's (adapted); of Jerome, W. H. Fremantle's.

June 1977

Mary R. Lefkowitz
Maureen B. Fant
Wellesley College

List of Abbreviations

ADA	Regia Academia Italica, *Acta Divi Augusti*, Pars Prior (Rome, 1945).
AP	*Greek Anthology*, ed. W. R. Paton, Loeb Classical Library (Cambridge, Mass., 1916).
ARS	A. C. Johnson, P. R. Coleman-Norton, F. C. Bourne, *Ancient Roman Statutes* (Austin, Texas, 1961).
CIL	*Corpus Inscriptionum Latinarum* (Berlin, 1863-).
FH	P. Friedländer, with H. B. Hoffleit, *Epigrammata: Greek Inscriptions in Verse* (Berkeley, Calif., 1948).
FIRA	S. Riccobono *et al., Fontes Iuris Romani Antejustiniani,*[2] 3 vols. (Florence, 1940-1943).
GLP	*Select Papyri* III, ed. D. L. Page, Loeb Classical Library (Cambridge, Mass., 1941).
IG	*Inscriptiones Graecae* (Berlin, 1873-).
ILLRP	A. Degrassi, *Inscriptiones Latinae Liberae Rei Publicae*, vol. I[2] (Florence, 1965), vol II (1963).
ILS	H. Dessau, *Inscriptiones Latinae Selectae*, 3 vols. (Berlin, 1892-1916).
Kaibel	G. Kaibel, *Epigrammata Graeca ex lapidibus conlecta* (Berlin 1878).
P. Cattaoui	B. P. Grenfell and A. S. Hunt, "Papyrus Cattaoui," *Archiv für Papyrusforschung* 3 (1903-1906), 55 ff.
Peek	W. Peek, *Griechische Vers-Inschriften, I, Grab-epigramme* (Berlin, 1955).
P. Fam. Tebt.	B. A. van Gronigen, *Papyrologica Lugduno-Batava* (Leyden, 1950).
Pleket	H. W. Pleket, *Epigraphica II: Texts on the Social History of the Greek World* (Leyden, 1969).
SB	F. Preisigke, *et al., Sammelbuch griechischer Urkunden aus Agypten* (Strassburg, *et al.,* 1915 ff).
Syll.	W. Dittenberger, *Sylloge Inscriptionum Graecarum,*[3] 4 vols. (Leipzig, 1915-1924).
Thesleff	H. Thesleff, ed., *The Pythagorean Texts of the Hellenistic Period* (Abo, 1965).
UPZ	U. Wilcken, *Urkunden der Ptolemäerzeit (Altere Funde)* (Berlin-Leipzig, 1927 ff.).

Hermippus in his *Lives* attributes to Thales the story which other biographers tell about Socrates, namely, that Thales said there were three reasons he was grateful to Fortune: "first, that I was born a man and not an animal, second, that I was born a man and not a woman, and third, that I was born a Greek and not a foreigner."

(Diogenes Laertius, *Lives of Eminent Philosophers* I. 33)

Compare the saying of Rabbi Judah in the synagogue liturgy:

"Three blessings one must say daily: Blessed art thou who did not make me a gentile; Blessed art thou who did not make me a woman; Blessed art thou who did not make me a boor."[1]

Love-scene. Red-figure kylix (drinking cup); from Athens, ca. 460 B.C. One scholar makes the following observation about this kind of scene: "Vase-painting was noticeably affected by the homosexual ethos; painters sometimes depicted a naked woman with a male waist and hips, as if a woman's body was nothing but a young man's body plus breasts and minus external genitals, and in many of their pictures of heterosexual intercourse from the rear position the penis appears (whatever the painter's intention) to be penetrating the anus, not the vagina" (K. J. Dover, *Arethusa* 6 [1973] 66). The legends on the kylix say, "The girl is beautiful," and "Hold still!" (Courtesy, Museum of Fine Arts, Boston)

I. The Greek World

Dancer. Bronze statuette, ca. 200 B.C. Dance was a part of many aspects of Greek life: religion, theatre, and entertainment, of which women participated in all but theatre. For entertainment, professional dancers, usually slaves or prostitutes, performed. The violent, spiral movement so well suggested by this Hellenistic sculptor perhaps indicates that his woman is dancing in religious ecstasy. (Metropolitan Museum of Art, New York: Walter Baker Collection)

Hades Abducting Persephone. Fragment of a terracotta votive plaque; from the Greek city of Locri in Southern Italy, 470-460 B.C. For the myth of Persephone's marriage to Hades, god of the underworld, see pp. 92-96. The rape, or attempted rape, of a young woman by a non-human male—god or monster—is a leitmotif in Greek myth and art, found in such diverse pairings as Daphne and Apollo, a nymph and a satyr (sometimes lighthearted, often not), Lapith and Centaur. In art, the woman frequently has a passive, resigned gaze but indicates her fear and unwillingness by a gesture like Persephone's raised arms. (The Norbert Schimmel Collection)

The Marriage of Persephone. Terracotta votive tablet, from Locri in southern Italy; ca. 470-450 B.C. Because this tablet was found in a sanctuary of Persephone along with many similar reliefs illustrating episodes from her myth, it may be presumed that preparations for her wedding (bringing the wedding dress to the bride) are shown here. Robbed of its context, the piece could well appear to illustrate a mortal wedding. (Museo Nazionale, Reggio di Calabria; Soprintendenza di Archeologia della Calabria)

1. WOMEN'S LIVES—AS SEEN BY WOMEN

It is only fitting that the first speakers in a book about women should be women. Their words give some sense of the importance of women in women's lives, of the pleasures of owning and giving, of participating in festivals and in household games. But we must wait for men to tell us about the social, legal, and physical environments in which ancient women lived, since the course of women's lives, from birth to death, was set by men, fathers, husbands, brothers, uncles, by the male citizens by whom governments were formed and armies raised. It is men too who—selectively, we may presume—tell us most about women's achievements.

Aside from poetry, women's writing survives only in private letters written on papyrus, preserved, by an accident of nature, only from Hellenistic and Roman Egypt. Students of the ancient world are always acutely aware that only a fraction of the writings of antiquity have survived. Much of what remains was preserved because men in late antiquity and the Middle Ages felt it to have enduring value. It is then both logical and poignant that we should have so little of what women wrote. Surviving fragments and references in the work of male authors are tantalizing indications that the intellectual efforts of women were, at least occasionally, committed to writing.

That women in all periods of antiquity could write sophisticated verse indicates that at least some women were educated. But the fact that from all antiquity only a few female authors' names and a few fragments of their poetry survive suggests that such intellectual attainments were at best exceptional. If all women had gone to school and had been able to record what they felt about their world, a very different, and surely less self-congratulatory, picture of ancient life would have emerged. As it is, what little remains of women's writings offers eloquent testimony not so much of an informing literary inheritance, as of a potential never realized.

What the women poets say about themselves contrasts sharply in both diction and content with men poets' depictions of them. While men (e.g., below, note 4) portray them as particularly concerned with physical appearances and household details, women poets, especially the influential Sappho, concentrate on feelings and reactions to their environment. But even Sappho was remembered in antiquity less for the beauty of her verse than for her "sordid" emotional attachment to other females, an attachment which would have been acceptable between men.

A. SAPPHO

(Lesbos, sixth century B.C.)

Ode 1

Aphrodite on your intricate throne, immortal, daughter of Zeus, weaver of plots, I beg you, do not tame me with pain or my heart with anguish

but come here, as once before when I asked you, you heard my words from afar and listened, and left your father's golden house and came

you yoked your chariot, and lovely swift sparrows brought you, fast whirling over the dark earth from heaven through the midst of the bright air,

and soon they arrived. And you, o blessed goddess, smiled with your immortal face and asked why now did I suffer, and why did I call now,

and what did I most want in my maddened heart to have for myself. "Who now am I to persuade to your love, who, Sappho, has done you wrong? For if she flees, soon she'll pursue you, and if she won't take gifts, soon she'll give them, and if she won't love, soon she will love you, even if she doesn't want to."[2]

Come to me now again, release me from my cruel anxiety, accomplish all that my heart wants accomplished. You yourself join my battle.

Ode 31

The man seems to me strong as a god, the man who sits across from you and listens to your sweet talk nearby

and your lovely laughter—which, when I hear it, strikes fear in the heart in my breast. For whenever I glance at you, it seems that I can say nothing at all

but my tongue is broken in silence, and that instant a light fire rushes beneath my skin, I can no longer see anything in my eyes and my ears are thundering,

and cold sweat catches hold of me, and shuddering hunts me all over, and I am greener than grass, and I seem to myself to be little short of death

But all is endurable, since even a poor man . . . .[3]

Ode 16

Some would say an army of cavalry, others of infantry, others of ships, is the fairest thing on the dark earth, but I say it's whatever you're in love with

It's completely easy to make this clear to everyone, for Helen, who far surpassed other people in beauty, left behind the most aristocratic

of husbands and went to Troy. She sailed away, and did not remember at all her daughter or her beloved parents, but [Aphrodite] took her aside

(3 lines missing)

which makes me remember Anactoria[4] who is no longer near,
her lovely step and the brilliant glancing of her face I would
rather see than the Lydians' chariots of their infantry fighting
in all their armor.

Ode 94

The truth is, I wish I were dead. She left me, whispering often,
and she said this, "Oh what a cruel fate is ours, Sappho, yes,
I leave you against my will."

And I answered her: "Farewell, go and remember me, for you
know how we cared for you.

If you do remember, I want to remind you ... and were happy

... of violets ... you set beside me and with woven garlands made
of flowers around your soft neck

and with perfume, royal, rich ... you annointed yourself and
on soft beds you would drive out your passion

and then ... sanctuary ... was ... from which we were away ... "

Ode 96

... you, like a goddess renowned, in your song she took most joy

Now she is unique among Lydian women, as the moon once the
sun sets

stands out among all the stars, and her light grasps both the salt
sea and the flowering meadows

and fair dew flows forth, and soft roses and chervil and fragrant
melilot bloom.

Often as she goes out, she remembers gentle Atthis, and her
tender heart is eaten by grief ...

Ode 44
(The wedding of Hector and Andromache)

" ... Hector and his comrades are bringing a girl with curving
eyes from holy Thebes and ... Phakia, soft Andromache, in their
ships across the salt sea, many curved bands of gold and purple
robes and intricate playthings, countless silver cups and ivory."
So he spoke. And [Hector's] beloved father quickly got up, and
the story went out to his friends throughout the city [of Troy]
with its wide dancing places. Then the Trojan women led mules
to wheeled carts and a crowd of women came out, and also of ...
-ankled maidens, and separately the daughters of Priam and

men brought horses with chariots (unknown number of lines missing) ... and the sweet-sounding *aulos* was mixed with the noise of castanets, and the maidens shrilly sang a sacred song and the holy sound reached heaven ...... bowls and goblets ... perfume and cassia and incense were mixed and all the older women shouted out, and all the men cried out a fair loud song, calling on Paean, the far-shooter, the lyre player, to sing of Hector and Andromache, who were like gods....

B. CORINNA

(Tanagra in Boeotia, fifth century B.C.)

The Contest of Cithaeron and Helicon

This fragment from a much longer poem concentrates more on the feelings than on the tangible rewards of victory and defeat.

"...They hid the holy goddess' baby in a cave, a secret from Cronus the crooked-minded, when (his mother) blessed Rhea stole him away and won great honor from the immortals." So he sang. Straightway the Muses got the blessed gods to bring their voting pebbles to the golden bowls, and then all were counted. Cithaeron won more. Hermes came when he heard that he had won the victory, and the gods decorated him with wreaths, and there was joy in his heart. But Helicon was overcome by harsh grief...and he tore out a bare rock and from the height dashed it into countless stones.

Reflections on a woman poet

I blame shrill Myrtis, because—though a woman—she entered into rivalry with Pindar.

C. ERINNA

(Telos, fourth century B.C.)
GP III 120

A fragment of her 300-line poem *The Distaff*, which describes the games Baucis and the poem's speaker (Baucis' "Mother") played when they were little. Now the speaker is prevented by some unspecified religious scruple from attending Baucis' funeral.

Into the deep wave you [leaped] from white horses deliriously racing. I shouted, "no, stop, dear friend!" And you were a tortoise, bounding through the yard of the large court. These are the things I lament, poor Baucis, and weep for. These are the traces of you that lie burning, still warm, in my heart— the things we enjoyed then are now embers. We held our dolls in our rooms when we were little girls, pretending to be wives; we were happy. And at dawn your mother came, after she gave out shares of wool to her slave women, and called you about the salted meat. Ah, when we were little, what a fright Mormo⁵ gave us —her head had big ears, and she ran on all fours, and kept changing her faces.

But when you went to [your husband's] bed, then you forgot everything you had heard from your mother when you were a child, dear Baucis. Aphrodite made you forget.

So I weep for you, but I stay away from your funeral rites. My feet are not profane... from the house, nor can my eyes look on your corpse, and I cannot uncover my head and join the lamentation, but instead shame tears my cheeks....

Two Epigrams for Baucis
AP VII. 712, 710

I am the tomb of Baucis the bride. This stone has heard much lamentation. As you pass by, tell this to Death beneath the ground: "You are jealous, Death." As you look, the fine inscription on the tomb tells you of Baucis' savage fate: how her husband's father lighted her funeral pyre with the torches they carried while they sang to Hymenaeus, the marriage god. And you, Hymenaeus, transformed the wedding dances into cries of lamentation.

Stones, you are my Sirens. Sad urn, you hold my death, these few ashes. Tell all who pass by my tomb to greet me, be they from this city or another country: "the tomb holds a bride, my father called me Baucis, I came from Tenos," so they will know. And tell them that my friend Erinna inscribed this epigram on my tomb.

D. ANYTE

(Tegea, third century B.C.)

AP VII. 492, 490, 649, 486

We leave you, Miletus, dear homeland, because we refused unlawful sex to impious Gauls. We were three maidens, your citizens. Violent war with the Celts brought us to this fate. We did not wait for unholy union or marriage, but we found ourselves a protector in Death.

*

I weep for Antibia, a virgin. Many suitors wanted her and came to her father's house, because she was known for her beauty and cleverness. But deadly Fate sent all their hopes rolling away.[6]

*

Instead of a bridal bed and holy rites of marriage, your mother set here on your marble tomb a maiden, like you in size and in beauty, Thersis. So now we can speak to you although you are dead.

*

Often here on her daughter's tomb, Cleina in her sorrow cried for her dear child who died too soon, calling back Philaenis' soul. Before she could be married, she crossed the pale stream of Acheron.

E. NOSSIS

(Locri, third century B.C.)

AP VI. 265, 275, 273, 332, 604, 605

Sacred Hera— since you often come down from heaven to see Lacinion with its fragrant incense—take this linen cloth. Theophilis, daughter of Cleocha, and her noble daughter Nossis, wove it for you.

*

I think that Aphrodite will be happy to receive as an offering this band from Simaetha's hair, since it is intricate, and smells sweetly of the nectar that Aphrodite herself uses to annoint fair Adonis.

*

Artemis, goddess of Delos and bright Ortygia, set down your sacred bow in the Graces' laps, wash your skin clean in the Inopus, and come to Locri to deliver Alcetis from her hard labor pains.

*

Let's go to the temple of Aphrodite to see how her statue is intricately worked from gold. Polyarchis set it there, with the great wealth she won from her own body's fame.

*

This picture captures Thaumarete's form — how well he painted her looks and her beauty, her gentle eyes. If your little watch-dog saw you, he would wag his tail, and think that he saw the mistress of his house.[7]

*

This picture — the image she made of herself, Callo set here in blonde Aphrodite's house. How gently she stands there. See her charm blooming young. I greet her: there is no blemish at all in her life.

Women's Lives—as Seen by Men

A. EPITAPHS

Epitaphs preserve ideals more faithfully than historical fact, but as such constitute a record of models of approved public and private behavior in women's lives.

i. FH 138; Athens, fifth century B.C.

This dust conceals Archedice, daughter of that man who achieved the highest eminence of all those of his time in Greece, Hippias.[8] Though she was daughter, wife, sister, and mother of tyrants, she was not lifted up in spirit to the pitch of folly.

ii. FH 139; Chios, fifth century B.C.

Of a worthy wife this is the tomb—here, by the road that throngs with people—of Aspasia, who is dead; in response to her noble disposition Euopides set up this monument for her: she was his consort.

iii. Kaibel 609; Theater at Aquileia, third century B.C.

In the past she won resounding fame in many towns and many cities for her skill in all kinds of plays, mimes, and choruses, and (often) dances. But she did not die on the stage, this tenth Muse.
To Bassilla the actress Heracleides the skilled speaker and biographer set up this stone. Even though she is dead she will have the same honor she had in life, when she made her body "die" on the floor of the stage. This is what her fellow actors are saying to her: "Bassilla farewell, no one lives forever."

iv. Pleket 4; Sardes, first century B.C.

Inscription set up by the municipality, in honor of Menophila, daughter of Hermagenes.

This stone marks a woman of accomplishment and beauty. Who she is the Muses' inscriptions reveal: for you here in the stone is a carved lily and an alpha, a book and a basket, and with these a wreath. The book shows that you were wise, the wreath that you wore on your head shows that you were a leader; the letter alpha (i.e., the numeral one) that you were an only child; the basket is a sign of your orderly excellence; the flower shows the prime of your life, which Fate stole away. "Now I am empty dust." For such as you in death there are many—though you had neither husband nor parents—to whom you have left tears.

B. PRAISE OF ACCOMPLISHED WOMEN

i. Telesilla of Argos, poetess, fifth century B.C.
Plutarch, *The Bravery of Women* 245c-f.

Of all the deeds performed by women for the community none

is more famous than the struggle against Cleomenes for Argos, which the women carried out at the instigation of Telesilla the poetess. She, as they say, was the daughter of a famous house but sickly in body, and so she sent to the god to ask about health; and when an oracle was given her to cultivate the Muses, she followed the god's advice, and by devoting herself to poetry and music she was quickly relieved of her trouble, and was greatly admired by the women for her poetic art.

But when Cleomenes king of the Spartans, having slain many Argives... proceeded against the city, an impulsive daring, divinely inspired, came to the younger women to try, for their country's sake, to hold off the enemy. Under the lead of Telesilla they took up arms, and, taking their stand by the battlements, manned the walls all round, so that the enemy were amazed. The result was that they repulsed Cleomenes with great loss, and the other king, Demaratus, who managed to get inside ... they drove out. In this way the city was saved. The women who fell in the battle they buried close by the Argive Road, and to the survivors they granted the privilege of erecting a statute of Ares as a memorial of their surpassing valor. . . . On the anniversary of [the battle] they celebrate even to this day the "Festival of Impudence," at which they clothe the women in men's shirts and cloaks, and the men in women's robes and veils.

To repair the scarcity of men they did not unite the women with slaves, as Herodotus records, but with the best of their neighboring subjects, whom they made Argive citizens. It was reputed that the women showed disrespect and an intentional indifference to those husbands in their married relations from a feeling that they were underlings. Wherefore the Argives enacted a law, the one which says that married women having a beard must occupy the same bed with their husbands![9]

ii. Artemisia of Halicarnassus, the sea-captain
Herodotus, *Histories VIII*. 87

Halicarnassus, a city in Asia Minor, was an ally of Persia in the second war with Greece, at the battle of Salamis in 480 B.C.

I cannot give precise details of the part played in this battle by the various Greek or foreign contingents in the Persian fleet; I must, however, mention Artemisia, on account of an exploit which still further increased her reputation with Xerxes. At a stage in the battle when the Persian fleet had lost all semblance of order, Artemisia was chased by an Athenian trireme. As her ship happened to be closest to the enemy and there were other friendly ships just ahead of her, escape was impossible. In this awkward situation she hit on a plan which turned out greatly to her advantage: with the Athenian close on her tail she drove ahead with all possible speed and rammed one of her friends—a ship of Calynda, with Damasithymus, the Calyndian king, on board. I cannot say if she did this deliberately because of some quarrel she had had with this man while the fleet was in the Hellespont, or if it was just chance that that particular vessel was in her way; but in any case she rammed and sank her, and was lucky enough, as a result, to reap a double benefit. For the captain of the Athenian trireme, on seeing her ram an enemy, naturally supposed that her ship was a Greek one, or else a deserter which was fighting on the Greek side; so he abandoned the chase and turned to attack elsewhere. That, then, was one piece of luck—that she escaped with her life; the other was that, by the very act of doing an injury to the Persian fleet, she raised herself higher than ever in Xerxes' esteem. For the story goes that Xerxes, who was watching the battle, observed the incident, and that one of the bystanders remarked: "Do you see, my lord, how well Artemisia is fighting? She has sunk an enemy ship." Xerxes asked if they were sure it was really Artemisia, and was told that there was no doubt whatever—they knew her ensign well, and of course supposed that it was an enemy ship that had been sunk. She was, indeed, lucky in every way—not least in the fact that there were no survivors from the Calyndian ship to accuse her. Xerxes comment on what was told him is said to have been: "My men have turned into women, my women into men."

iii. Hipparchia of Maroneia, philosopher, fourth/third century B.C.
Diogenes Laertius VI. 96-98.

Hipparchia too, sister of Metrocles, was captured by their doctrines. Both of them were born at Maroneia.

She fell in love with the discourses and the life of [the philosopher] Crates, and would not pay attention to any of her suitors, their wealth, their high birth or their beauty. But to her Crates was everything. She used even to threaten her parents she would make away with herself, unless she were given in marriage to him. Crates therefore was implored by her parents to dissuade the girl, and did all he could, and at last, failing to persuade her, got up, took off his clothes before her face and said, "This is the bridegroom, here are his possessions; make your choice accordingly; for you will be no helpmeet of mine, unless you share my pursuits."

The girl chose and, adopting the same dress, went about with her husband and lived with him in public and went out to dinners with him. Accordingly she appeared at the banquet given by Lysimachus, and there put down Theodorus, known as the atheist, by means of the following sophism. Any action which would not be called wrong if done by Theodorus would not be called wrong if done by Hipparchia. Now Theodorus does no wrong when he strikes himself: therefore neither does Hipparchia do wrong when she strikes Theodorus. He had no reply wherewith to meet the argument, but tried to strip her of her cloak. But Hipparchia showed no sign of alarm or of the perturbation natural in a woman. And when he said to her: "Is this she, who quitting woof and warp and comb and loom?"[10] she replied, "It is I, Theodorus, but do you suppose that I have been ill advised about myself, if instead of wasting further time upon the loom I spent it in education?" These tales and countless others are told of the female philosopher.

iv. Polygnota of Thebes, harpist
Pleket 6; Delphi, 86 B.C.

The god. With good fortune. During the archonship of Habromachus, in the month Boucration, during the magistracy of Strategos, Cleon, Antiphilus, and Damon.

The city of Delphi has decreed: whereas Polygnota, daughter of Socrates, a Theban harpist resident in Delphi, at the appointed time of the fifteenth Pythian games, which could not be held on account of the present war, began on that very day and spent her time and competed at the request of the archons and the citizens for three days, and won the highest degree of respect, deserving the praise of Apollo and of the Theban people and of our city—she is awarded a crown and five hundred drachmas. With good fortune.

Voted: to commend Polygnota daughter of Socrates, the Theban, for her piety and reverence toward the god and for the range of her preparation and her art; to bestow on her and on her descendants the guest-friendship of the city, the right to

14

consult the oracle, the privileges of being heard first, of safety, of exemption from taxes, and of front seating at the games held by the city, the right of owning land and a house and all the other honors ordinarily awarded to other benefactors of the city; to invite her to the town hall for the public banquet; to defend her; and to offer sacrifice to Apollo. The god. With good fortune.

[In a succeeding paragraph similar honors are awarded also to her nephew Lycinus, who lived with her.]

C. COMPLAINTS

i. Hesiod, *Works and Days* 42-105, 695-705

Woman is given to man's representative Epimetheus ("Afterthinker") as punishment for his brother Prometheus' ("Forethinker") crimes against Zeus.

For the gods have hidden away and are hiding from men the means of life. If they weren't, you could easily work just for a day to get what would keep you for a year, even if you remained idle—you could put your rudder away over the fireplace, and the work of oxen and of toiling mules would disappear.

But Zeus hid the means of life because he was angry in his heart, because crooked-minded Prometheus deceived him. That is why he devised for men these miserable sorrows. Zeus had hidden fire. But Prometheus son of Iapetus stole it back for men, away from Zeus the Deviser; he hid it from Thunderer Zeus in a hollow reed.

So Zeus became angry at him and told him: "Son of Iapetus, since you can devise better than everyone, are you glad that you stole fire and tricked my mind? That theft will be a big pain for you and for men in the future, for I'll give them in return for the fire an evil which they can all enjoy in their hearts while putting their arms round an evil of their very own." So Zeus spoke, and laughed, father of god and men.

Zeus ordered famous Hephaestus to mix as fast as he could earth with water, and to put in it a human's voice and strength, and to make its face resemble a deathless goddess's, with the fair form of a virgin. And he ordered Athena to teach her her work, to weave on the intricate loom. And he ordered golden Aphrodite to shed grace on her head and cruel passion and worries that tire the limbs. And he commanded Hermes, slayer of Argos, to put in her a bitch's mind and a thieving heart. So Zeus spoke, and they obeyed Zeus son of Cronus, their lord.

Immediately the famous lame god Hephaestus molded from earth a thing like a modest virgin, acting on Zeus' orders. He put life in her and the grey-eyed goddess Athena put on her clothing. Around her goddesses, the Graces and queenly Persuasion, put golden bands on her skin, and the fair-haired Seasons crowned her with spring flowers. In her breast the Guide Hermes, slayer of Argos put lies, tricky speeches, and a thieving heart; he did this in accordance with Zeus' plans. Hermes, the gods' herald, put in her a voice, and they named this woman Pandora, because all [pantes] gods who live on Olympus gave her a gift [doron], a pain to men-who-eat-barley.

And when he had completed this steep trap from which there is no escape, Father Zeus sent famed Hermes, the gods' swift messenger, to Epimetheus, bringing this gift. Nor did Epimetheus think, as Prometheus had told him, not ever to accept a gift from Olympian Zeus but to send it right back again, so that it would not prove an evil for mortals. But he accepted it, and when he had taken the evil he understood what he'd done.

Before that the races of men had lived on the earth without evils and without harsh labor and cruel diseases which give men over to the Fates—for in evil times men grow old quickly. But the woman lifted in her hands the great lid from the jar and scattered these evils about—she devised miserable sorrows for men. Only Hope stayed there inside in her unbroken house beneath the rim of the jar. She did not fly out; before that the woman put back the lid of the jar, according to the plans of Zeus Aegis-holder, gatherer of clouds.

The other thousand miseries fly around among men. The earth is full of evils, and the sea is full of them. Diseases come to men in the day, and at night uninvited, bringing evils for mortals in silence, since Deviser Zeus took away their voices. So there is no way to escape the mind of Zeus.

Advice on how to live with women

Bring a wife to your house when you are the right age, not much less than thirty, and not much more. This is the right time for marriage. Your wife should be four years past puberty, and be married to you in the fifth. Marry a virgin, so you can

teach her good habits. The best one to marry is the girl who
lives near you; look over her in detail, so you don't marry one
who'll bring joy to your neighbors. For a man can win nothing
better than a good wife, and nothing more painful than a bad
one—a dinner-snatcher, who roasts her husband, strong as he
may be, without fire, and gives him over to a savage old age.

ii. Semonides of Amorgos, *On Women*

Although the context of this famous poem is lost, its use of animal and inani-
mate metaphors suggests that it was intended, like Aesop's fables, as social
satire; see H. Lloyd-Jones, *Females of the Species*. But it is important to note
that, as in Hesiod, good behavior is defined in terms of service to a woman's
husband, not by its intrinsic value to the society as a whole, or by a woman's
worth to other women or to herself.

In the beginning the god made the female mind separately.
One he made from a long-bristled sow. In her house everything
lies in disorder, smeared with mud, and rolls about the floor;
and she herself unwashed, in clothes unlaundered, sits by the
dungheap and grows fat. Another he made from a wicked vixen;
a woman who knows everything. No bad thing and no better
kind of thing is lost on her; for she often calls a good thing bad
and a bad thing good. Her attitude is never the same.
Another the Olympians molded out of earth, a stunted creature; you see, a woman like her knows nothing, bad or good. The
only work she understands is eating; and not even when the god
makes cruel winter weather does she feel the cold and draw a
stool near to the fire.
Another he made from a bitch, own daughter of her mother,
who wants to hear everything and know everything. She peers
everywhere and strays everywhere, always yapping, even if she
sees no human being. A man cannot stop her by threatening,
nor by losing his temper and knocking out her teeth with a
stone, nor with honeyed words, not even if she is sitting with
friends, but ceaselessly she keeps up a barking you can do
nothing with.
Another he made from the sea; she has two characters. One
day she smiles and is happy; a stranger who sees her in the
house will praise her, and say, 'There is no woman better than
this among all mankind, nor more beautiful.' But on another
day she is unbearable to look at or come near to; then she raves
so that you can't approach her, like a bitch over her pups, and
she shows herself ungentle and contrary to enemies and friends

alike. Just so the sea often stands without a tremor, harmless, a great delight to sailors, in the summer season; but often it raves, tossed about by thundering waves. It is the sea that such a woman most resembles in her temper; like the ocean, she has a changeful nature.

Another he made from an ash-gray ass that has suffered many blows; when compelled and scolded she puts up with everything, much against her will, and does her work to satisfaction. But meanwhile she munches in the back room all night and all day, and she munches by the hearth; and likewise when she comes to the act of love, she accepts any partner.

Another he made from a ferret, a miserable, wretched creature; nothing about her is beautiful or desirable, pleasing or lovable. She is mad for the bed of love, but she makes any man she has with her sick. She does great damage to neighbors by her thieving, and often eats up sacrifices left unburned.

Another was the offspring of a proud mare with a long mane. She pushes servile work and trouble on to others; she would never set her hand to a mill, nor pick up a sieve nor throw the dung out of the house, nor sit over the oven dodging the soot; she makes her husband acquainted with Necessity. She washes the dirt off herself twice, sometimes three times, every day; she rubs herself with scents, and always has her thick hair combed and garlanded with flowers. A woman like her is a fine sight for others, but for the man she belongs to she proves a plague, unless he is some tyrant or king [who takes pride in such objects].

Another is from a monkey; this is the biggest plague of all that Zeus has given to men. Her face is hideous; when a woman like her goes through the town, everyone laughs at her. She is short in the neck; she moves awkwardly; she has no bottom, and is all legs. Hard luck on the poor man who holds such a misery in his arms! She knows every trick and twist, just like a monkey; she does not mind being laughed at, and will do no one a good turn but considers, and spends the whole day planning, how she can do someone the worst possible harm.

Another is from a bee; the man who gets her is fortunate, for on her alone blame does not settle. She causes his property to grow and increase, and she grows old with a husband whom she loves and who loves her, the mother of a handsome and reputable family. She stands out among all women, and a godlike beauty plays about her. She takes no pleasure in sitting among women in places where they tell stories about love. Women like her are the best and most sensible whom Zeus bestows on men.

Zeus has contrived that all these tribes of women are with men and remain with them. Yes, this is the worst plague Zeus has made—women; if they seem to be some use to him who has them, it is to him especially that they prove a plague. The man who lives with a woman never goes through all his day in cheerfulness; he will not be quick to push out of his house Starvation, a housemate who is an enemy, a god who is against us. Just when a man most wishes to enjoy himself at home, through the dispensation of a god or the kindness of a man, she finds a way of finding fault with him and lifts her crest for battle. Yes, where there is a woman, men cannot even give hearty entertainment to a guest who has come to the house; and the very woman who seems most respectable is the one who turns out guilty of the worst atrocity; because while her husband is not looking... and the neighbors get pleasure in seeing how he too is mistaken. Each man will take care to praise his own wife and find fault with the other's; we do not realize that the fate of all of us is alike. Yes, this is the greatest plague that Zeus has made, and he has bound us to them with a fetter that cannot be broken. Because of this some have gone to Hades fighting for a woman....

iii. Hipponax of Ephesus, 68

The two days in a woman's life a man can best enjoy are when he marries her and when he carries her dead body to the grave.[11]

3. LAW

A. ATHENIAN FUNERAL LAW, *SYLL.* 1218.

Legislation frequently limited the expense, luxury, and amount of mourning at funerals. In practical terms, such laws also effectively restricted women's opportunities for gathering and self-expression. The following, from Ioulis on the island of Keos, dates from the late fifth century B.C. but is a copy of an earlier law.[12]

The laws concerning the departed.

The dead shall be buried as follows: in three or fewer white cloths—i.e. a spread, a shroud and a coverlet—the three worth not over a hundred drachmas. They shall carry him out on a simply-wrought bed and shall not cover the bier with the cloths. They shall take to the tomb not more than three choes of wine and not more than one chous of olive oil, and they shall carry away the (empty) jars. They shall carry the corpse covered, in silence all the way to the tomb. They shall perform the pre-burial sacrifice according to ancestral custom. They shall carry home from the tomb the bed and the spreads.

On the following day a free man shall sprinkle first the house with sea water, and then all the rooms with hyssop. When it has been sprinkled throughout, the house shall be cleansed and they shall offer sacrifices upon the hearth.

The women who go to the funeral shall not go away from the tomb before the men.

They shall not hold monthly services for the dead.

They shall not place a cup beneath the bed, nor pour out the water, nor carry the sweepings to the tomb.

Wherever a person dies, after the bed is carried out no women shall go to the house except those polluted (by the death); those polluted are mother, wife, sisters and daughters, in addition to these not more than five women, namely children of daughters and cousins, and no one else. The polluted shall be cleansed by washing... in poured water.

[The rest is lost.]

B. ARISTOTLE'S WILL, FOURTH CENTURY B.C.; DIOGENES LAERTIUS V. 11-16

Restriction of women's rights to own property and to determine the course of their own lives provides vivid illustrations of Athenian male society's estimation of women's capabilities and general value. In this document the speaker is Aristotle himself.

All will be well; but, in case anything should happen, Aristotle has made these dispositions. Antipater is to be executor in all matters and in general; but, until Nicanor shall arrive, Aristomenes, Timarchus, Hipparchus, Dioteles and (if he consent and if circumstances permit him) Theophrastus shall take charge as well of Herpyllis and the children as of the property. And when the girl shall be grown up she shall be given in marriage to

Nicanor; but if anything happen to the girl (which heaven forbid–and no such thing will happen) before her marriage, or
when she is married but before there are children, Nicanor shall
have full powers, both with regard to the child and with regard
to everything else, to administer in a manner worthy both of
himself and of us. Nicanor shall take charge of the girl and of
the boy Nicomachus as he shall think fit in all that concerns
them as if he were father and brother. And if anything should
happen to Nicanor (which heaven forbid!) either before he
marries the girl, or when he has married her but before there
are children, any arrangements that he may make shall be valid.
And if Theophrastus is willing to live with her, he shall have
the same rights as Nicanor. Otherwise, the executors in consultation with Antipater shall administer as regards the daughter
and the boy as seems to them to be best. The executors and
Nicanor, in memory of me and of the steady affection which
Herpyllis has borne towards me, shall take care of her in every
other respect and, if she desires to be married, shall see that she
be given to one not unworthy; and besides what she has already
received they shall give her a talent of silver out of the estate and
three handmaids whomsoever she shall choose besides the maid
she has at present and the man-servant Pyrrhaeus; and if she
chooses to remain at Chaleis, the lodge by the garden, if in Stagira, my father's house. Whichever of these two houses she
chooses, the executors shall furnish with such furniture as they
think proper and as Herpyllis herself may approve. Nicanor shall
take charge of the boy Myrmex, that he be taken to his own
friends in a manner worthy of me with the property of his which
we received. Ambraeis shall be given her freedom, and on my
daughter's marriage shall receive 500 drachmas and the maid
whom she now has. And to Thale shall be given, in addition to the
maid whom she has and who was bought, a thousand drachmas
and a maid. And Simon, in addition to the money before paid to
him towards another servant, shall either have a servant pur-
chased for him or receive a further sum of money. And Tycho,
Philo, Olympius and his child shall have their freedom when my
daughter is married. None of the servants who waited upon me
shall be sold but they shall continue to be employed; and when
they arrive at the proper age they shall have their freedom if they
deserve it. My executors shall see to it, when the images which
Gryllion has been commissioned to execute are finished, that they
be set up, namely that of Nicanor, that of Proxenus, which it was

my intention to have executed, and that of Nicanor's mother; also they shall set up the bust which has been executed of Arimnestus, to be a memorial of him seeing that he died childless, and shall dedicate my mother's statue to Demeter at Nemea or wherever they think best. And wherever they bury me, there the bones of Pythias shall be laid, in accordance with her own instructions. And to commemorate Nicanor's safe return, as I vowed on his behalf, they shall set up in Stagira stone statues of life size to Zeus and Athena the Saviors.

C. ATHENIAN LAWS ABOUT HEIRESSES

Demosthenes, *Against Macartatus* 51, 54.

Whenever a man dies without making a will, if he leaves female children his estate shall go with them, but if not, the persons herein mentioned shall be entitled to his property: if there be brothers by the same father, and if there be lawfully born sons of brothers, they shall take the share of the father. But if there are no brothers or sons of brothers, their descendants shall inherit it in like manner; but males and the sons of males shall take precedence, if they are of the same ancestors, even though they be more remote of kin. If there are no relatives on the father's side within the degree of children of cousins, those on the mother's side shall inherit in like manner. But if there shall be no relatives on either side within the degree mentioned, the nearest of kin on the father's side shall inherit. But no illegitimate child of either sex shall have the right of succession either to religious rites or civic privileges, from the time of the archonship of Euclides [403 B.C.].

In regard to all heiresses who are classified as Thetes,[13] if the nearest of kin does not wish to marry one, let him give her in marriage with a portion of five hundred drachmae, if he be of the class of Pentacosiomedimni, if of the class of Knights, with a portion of three hundred, and if of the class of Zeugitae, with one hundred and fifty, in addition to what is her own. If there are several kinsmen in the same degree of relationship, each one of them shall contribute to the portion of the heiress according to his due share. And if there be several heiresses, it shall not be necessary for a single kinsman to give in marriage more than one, but the next of kin shall in each case give her in marriage or marry her himself. And if the nearest of kin does not marry her or give her in marriage, the archon shall compel him either to marry her himself or give her in marriage. And if the archon shall not compel him, let him be fined a thousand drachmae, which are to be consecrate to Hera. And let any person who chooses denounce to the archon any person who disobeys this law.[14]

D. TRIALS FOR ADULTERY AND MURDER

(In each case only one side's argument survives and the verdict is unknown.)

i. Lysias, *On the Murder of Eratosthenes* 9-33, 37-50.

A husband who murdered his wife's lover, Eratosthenes, speaks in his own defence. Ca. 400 B.C.

Members of the jury: when I decided to marry and had brought a wife home, at first my attitude towards her was this: I did not wish to annoy her, but neither was she to have too much of her own way. I watched her as well as I could, and kept an eye on her as was proper. But later, after my child had been born, I came to trust her, and I handed all my possessions over to her, believing that this was the greatest possible proof of affection.

Well, members of the jury, in the beginning she was the best of women. She was a clever housewife, economical and exact in her management of everything. But then, my mother died; and her death has proved to be the source of all my troubles, because it was when my wife went to the funeral that this man Eratosthenes saw her; and as time went on, he was able to seduce her. He kept a look out for our maid who goes to market; and approaching her with his suggestions, he succeeded in corrupting her mistress.

Now first of all, gentlemen, I must explain that I have a small house which is divided into two—the men's quarters and the women's—each having the same space, the women upstairs and the men downstairs.

After the birth of my child, his mother nursed him; but I did not want her to run the risk of going downstairs every time she had to give him a bath, so I myself took over the upper storey, and let the women have the ground floor. And so it came about that by this time it was quite customary for my wife often to go downstairs and sleep with the child, so that she could give him the breast and stop him from crying.

This went on for a long while, and I had not the slightest suspicion. On the contrary, I was in such a fool's paradise that I believed my wife to be the chastest woman in all the city.

Time passed, gentlemen. One day, when I had come home unexpectedly from the country, after dinner, the child began crying and complaining. Actually it was the maid who was pinching him on purpose to make him behave so, because—as I found out later—this man was in the house.

Well, I told my wife to go and feed the child, to stop his crying. But at first she refused, pretending that she was glad to see me back after my long absence. At last I began to get annoyed, and I insisted on her going.

"Oh, yes!" she said. "To leave *you* alone with the maid up here! You mauled her about before, when you were drunk!"

I laughed. She got up, went out, closed the door—pretending that it was a joke—and locked it. As for me, I thought no harm of all this, and I had not the slightest suspicion. I went to sleep, glad to do so after my journey from the country.

Towards morning, she returned and unlocked the door.

I asked her why the doors had been creaking during the night. She explained that the lamp beside the baby had gone out, and that she had then gone to get a light from the neighbors.

I said no more. I thought it really was so. But it did seem to me, members of the jury, that she had done up her face with cosmetics, in spite of the fact that her brother had died only a month before. Still, even so, I said nothing about it. I just went off, without a word.

After this, members of the jury, an interval elapsed, during which my injuries had progressed, leaving me far behind. Then, one day, I was approached by an old hag. She had been sent by a woman—Eratosthenes' previous mistress, as I found out later. This woman, furious because he no longer came to see her as before, had been on the look-out until she had discovered the reason. The old crone, therefore, had come and was lying in wait for me near my house.

"Euphiletus," she said, "please don't think that my approaching you is in any way due to a wish to interfere. The fact is, the man who is wronging you and your wife is an enemy of ours. Now if you catch the woman who does your shopping and works for you, and put her through an examination, you will discover all. The culprit," she added, "is Eratosthenes from Oea. Your wife is not the only one he has seduced—there are plenty of others. It's his profession."

With these words, members of the jury, she went off.

At once I was overwhelmed. Everything rushed into my mind, and I was filled with suspicion. I reflected how I had been locked into the bedroom. I remembered how on that night the middle and outer doors had creaked, a thing that had never happened before; and how I had had the idea that my wife's face was rouged. All these things rushed into my mind, and I was filled with suspicion.

I went back home, and told the servant to come with me to market. I took her instead to the house of one of my friends; and there I informed her that I had discovered all that was going on in my house.

"As for you," I said, "two courses are open to you: either to be flogged and sent to the tread-mill, and never be released from a life of utter misery; or to confess the whole truth and suffer no punishment, but win pardon from me for your wrong-doing. Tell me no lies. Speak the whole truth."

At first she tried denial, and told me that I could do as I pleased—she knew nothing. But when I named Eratosthenes to her face, and said that he was the man who had been visiting my wife, she was dumbfounded, thinking that I had found out everything exactly. And then at last, falling at my feet and exacting a promise from me that no harm should be done to her, she denounced the villain. She described how he had first approached her after the funeral, and then how in the end she had passed the message on, and in course of time my wife had been over-persuaded. She explained the way in which he had contrived to get into the house, and how when I was in the country my wife had gone to a religious service with this man's mother, and everything else that had happened. She recounted it all exactly.

When she had told all, I said:

"See to it that nobody gets to know of this; otherwise the promise I made you will not hold good. And furthermore, I expect you to show me this actually happening. I have no use for words. I want the *fact* to be exhibited, if it really is so."

She agreed to do this.

Four or five days then elapsed, as I shall prove to you by important evidence. But before I do so, I wish to narrate the events of the last day.

I had a friend and relative named Sostratus. He was coming home from the country after sunset when I met him. I knew that as he had got back so late, he would not find any of his own people at home; so I asked him to dine with me. We went home to my place, and going upstairs to the upper storey, we had dinner there. When he felt restored, he went off; and I went to bed.

Then, members of the jury, Eratosthenes made his entry; and the maid wakened me and told me that he was in the house.

I told her to watch the door; and going downstairs, I slipped out noiselessly.

I went to the houses of one man after another. Some I found at home; others, I was told, were out of town. So collecting as many as I could of those who were there, I went back. We procured torches from the shop near by, and entered my house. The door had been left open by arrangement with the maid.

We forced the bedroom door. The first of us to enter saw him still lying beside my wife. Those who followed saw him standing naked on the bed.

I knocked him down, members of the jury, with one blow. I then twisted his hands behind his back and tied them. And then I asked him why he was committing this crime against me, of breaking into my house.

He answered that he admitted his guilt; but he begged and besought me not to kill him—to accept a money-payment instead.

But I replied:

"It is not I who shall be killing you, but the law of the State, which you, in transgressing, have valued less highly than your own pleasure. You have preferred to commit this great crime against my wife and my children, rather than to obey the law and be of decent behavior."

Thus, members of the jury, this man met the fate which the laws prescribe for wrong-doers of his kind.

Eratosthenes was not seized in the street and carried off, nor had he taken refuge at the altar, as the prosecution alleges. The facts do not admit of it: he was struck in the bedroom, he fell at once, and I bound his hands behind his back. There were so many present that he could not possibly escape through their midst, since he had neither steel or wood nor any other weapon with which he could have defended himself against all those who had entered the room.

No, members of the jury: you know as well as I do how wrong-doers will not admit that their adversaries are speaking the truth, and attempt by lies and trickery of other kinds to excite the anger of the hearers against those whose acts are in accordance with Justice.

(*To the Clerk of the Court*):

Read the law.

(*The Law of Solon is read, that an adulterer may be put to death by the man who catches him.*)

He made no denial, members of the jury. He admitted his guilt, and begged and implored that he should not be put to death, offering to pay compensation. But I would not accept his estimate. I preferred to accord a higher authority to the law of the State, and I took that satisfaction which you, because you thought it the most just, have decreed for those who commit such offences. Witnesses to the preceding, kindly step up.

(*The witnesses come to the front of the Court, and the Clerk reads their depositions. When the Clerk has finished reading, and the witnesses have agreed that the depositions are correct, the defendant again addresses the Clerk*):

Now please read this further law from the pillar of the Court of the Areopagus:

(*The Clerk reads another version of Solon's law, as recorded on the pillar of the Areopagus Court*)

You hear, members of the jury, how it is expressly decreed by the Court of the Areopagus itself, which both traditionally and in your own day has been granted the right to try cases of murder, that no person shall be found guilty of murder who catches an adulterer with his wife and inflicts this punishment. The Lawgiver was so strongly convinced of the justice of these provisions in the case of married women, that he applied them also to concubines, who are of less importance. Yet obviously, if he had known of any greater punishment than this for cases where married women are concerned, he would have provided it. But in fact, as it was impossible for him to invent any more severe penalty for corruption of wives, he decided to provide the same punishment as in the case of concubines.

(*To the Clerk of the Court*):

Please read me this Law also.

(*The Clerk reads out further clauses from Solon's laws on rape.*)

You hear, members of the jury, how the Lawgiver ordains that if anyone debauch by force a free man or boy, the fine shall be double that decreed in the case of a slave. If anyone debauch a woman—in which case it is *permitted* to kill him—he shall be liable to the same fine. Thus, members of the jury, the Lawgiver considered violators deserving of a lesser penalty than seducers: for the latter he provided the death-penalty; for the former, the doubled fine. His idea was that those who use force are loathed by the persons violated, whereas those who have got their way by persuasion corrupt women's minds, in such a way as to make other men's wives more attached to themselves than to their husbands, so that the whole house is in their power, and it is uncertain who is the children's father, the husband or the lover. . . .

Consider, members of the jury, their accusation that it was I who on that day told the maid to fetch the young man. In my opinion, gentlemen, I should have been justified in using any means to catch the seducer of my wife. If there had been only words spoken and no actual offence, I should have been doing wrong; but when by that time they had gone to all lengths and he had often gained entry into my house, I consider that I should have been within my rights whatever means I employ to catch him. But observe that this allegation of the prosecution is also false. You can easily convince yourselves by considering the following:

I have already told you how Sostratus, an intimate friend of mine, met me coming in from the country around sunset, and dined with me, and when he felt refreshed, went off. Now in the first place, gentlemen, ask yourselves whether, if on that night I had had designs on Eratosthenes, it would have been better for me that Sostratus should dine elsewhere, or that I should take a guest home with me to dinner. Surely in the latter circumstances Eratosthenes would have been less inclined to venture into the house. Further, does it seem to you probable that I would have let my guest go, and been left alone, without company? Would I not rather have urged him to stay, so that he could help me to punish the adulterer?

Again, gentlemen, does it not seem to you probable that I would have passed the word round among my friends during the daytime, and told them to assemble at the house of one of my friends who lived nearest, rather than have started to run round at night, as soon as I found out, without knowing whom I should find at home and whom away? Actually, I called for Harmodius and certain others who were out of town—I did not know it—and others, I found, were not at home, so I went along taking with me whomever I could. But if I had known beforehand, does it not seem to you probable that I would have arranged for servants and passed the word round to my friends, so that I myself could go in with the maximum of safety—for how did I know whether he too might not have had a dagger or something?—and also in order that I might exact the penalty in the presence of the greatest number of witnesses? But in fact, since I knew nothing of what was going to happen on that night, I took with me whomever I could get.

Witnesses to the preceding, please step up.

(*Further witnesses come forward, and confirm their evidence as read out by the Clerk.*)

You have heard the witnesses, members of the jury. Now consider the case further in your own minds, inquiring whether there had ever existed between Eratosthenes and myself any other enmity but this. You will find none. He never brought any malicious charge against me, nor tried to secure my banishment, nor prosecuted me in any private suit. Neither had he knowledge of any crime of which I feared the revelation, so that I desired to kill him; nor by carrying out this act did I hope to gain money. So far from ever having had any dispute with him, or drunken brawl, or any other quarrel, I had never even set eyes on the man before that night. What possible object could I have had, therefore, in running so great a risk, except that I had suffered the greatest of all injuries at his hands? Again, would I myself have called in witnesses to my crime, when it was possible for me, if I desired to murder him without justification, to have had no confidants?

It is my belief, members of the jury, that this punishment was inflicted not in my own interests, but in those of the whole community. Such villains, seeing the rewards which await their crimes, will be less ready to commit offenses against others if they see that you too hold the same opinion of them. Otherwise it would be far better to wipe out the existing laws and make different ones, which will penalize those who keep guard over their own wives, and grant full immunity to those who criminally pursue them. This would be a far more just procedure than to set a trap for citizens by means of the laws, which urge the man who catches an adulterer to do with him whatever he will, and yet allow the injured party to undergo a trial far more perilous than that which faces the law-breaker who seduces other men's wives. Of this, I am an example—I, who now stand in danger of losing life, property, everything, because I have obeyed the laws of the State.

ii. Antiphon, *Against a Step-mother, on a Charge of Poisoning*.

The prosecutor is the deceased's son by his first marriage; the defendant is the deceased's second wife, represented by her sons, the prosecutor's half-brothers. Ca. 420 B.C.

Members of the jury:

Young as I am, and still without experience of litigation, I am placed by this event in a position of terrible difficulty. Either I have to disobey the injunction laid on my by my father, that I should seek vengeance on his murderers; or if I do seek vengeance, I am driven into a feud with those with whom it is least desirable—my half-brothers and their mother. Events, and my half-brothers themselves, have driven me into bringing this suit against them. They are the very men who ought naturally to have come forward as avengers of the deceased, and allies of the avenger. But in fact, the precise opposite has come about: they have taken their stand here as my adversaries, on the side of murder as I and my indictment declare.

My plea to you, gentlemen, is this: if I prove that their mother did by intention and forethought cause the death of our father, and that she had been caught before, not once but several times, in the very act of plotting his murder, inflict punishment—avenge, in the first instance your laws, which you have received as an inheritance from heaven and your ancestors, and by which you must be guided when considering condemnation as judges in this Court; avenge, in the second instance him who is dead and gone, and with him me also, who, alone and deserted, am left to take his part! You, gentlemen, stand to me now in the place of my family, because those who should have been his avengers and my allies have come forward as the dead man's murderers and my opponents. To whom, then, can anyone turn to for help, or where can he go to seek sanctuary, except to you and to Justice? ...

There was in our house an upper room, which Philoneus used to occupy whenever he had business in town. This Philoneus was an honest, respectable man, a friend of my father's. He had a concubine, whom he was intending to dispose of to a brothel. My step-mother, having heard of this, made a friend of this woman; and when she got to know of the injury Philoneus was proposing to do her, she sent for her. When the woman came, my step-mother told her that she herself also was being wrongly treated, by my father; and that if the woman would do as she said, she was clever enough to restore the love of Philoneus for the concubine, and my father's love for herself. As she expressed it, hers was the creative part, the other woman's part was that of obeying orders. She asked her therefore if she was willing to act as her assistant; and the woman promised to do so—very readily, I imagine.

Later, it happened that Philoneus had to go down to the Piraeus in connection with a religious ceremony to Zeus, Guardian of Property; and at the same time my father was preparing for a voyage to Naxos. It seemed to Philoneus an excellent idea, therefore, that he should make the same trip serve a double purpose: that he should accompany my father, his friend, down to the harbor, and at the same time perform his religious duty and entertain him to a feast. Philoneus' concubine went with them, to help them with the sacrifice and the banquet.

When they arrived at the port, they of course performed the sacrifice. When the religious ceremony was over, the woman began to deliberate herself as to how and when she should administer the drug, whether before dinner or after dinner. The result of her deliberation was that she decided to do so after dinner, thus carrying out the instructions of this Clytaemnestra, my step-mother.

The whole story of the dinner would be too long for me to tell or you to hear; but I shall try to narrate the rest to you in the fewest possible words, that is, how the actual administration of the poison was accomplished. When they had finished dinner, they naturally—as one of them was sacrificing to Zeus and entertaining a guest, and the other was about to set off on a voyage and was dining with his friend—they naturally were proceeding to pour libations, and accompany them with an offering of incense. Philoneus' concubine, as she was serving them with the wine for the libation—a libation that was to accompany prayers destined, alas! gentlemen, not to be fulfilled—poured in the poison. And in the belief that she was doing something clever, she gave the bigger dose to Philoneus, thinking that perhaps the more she gave him, the more he would love her. She still did not know that she had been deceived by my step-mother, and did not find out until she was already involved in disaster. She poured in a smaller dose for my father. The two men poured out their libation; and then, taking in hand that which was their own destroyer, they drained their last draught.

Philoneus dropped dead instantly. My father was seized with

an illness from which he died in three weeks. For this, the woman who had acted under orders has paid the penalty for her offense, in which she was an innocent accomplice: she was handed over to the public executioner after being broken on the wheel. But the woman who was the real cause, who thought out and engineered the deed—she will pay the penalty now, if you and heaven so decree. . . .

Which is more just—that the murderer should pay the penalty, or not? Which is more just—to pity rather the dead man, or the woman who killed him? The dead man, I would say. That would be the far more just and more righteous course for you in the eyes of god and man. And so at this point I demand that as she destroyed him without pity and without mercy, so she too shall be destroyed by you and by Justice. She acted of her own free will and compassed his death with guile; he died by force, an unwilling victim. Can it be denied gentlemen, that he died by force—a man who was intending to set out on a voyage from this country, and who was dining with his friend? She it was who sent the poison, who gave the order that it should be given him to drink, and so killed my father. What claim has she to be pitied or to win consideration from you or anyone else? She did not see fit to have pity on her husband—no, but she wickedly and shamefully destroyed him.

Pity, as you know, is more properly bestowed in cases of involuntary suffering than of crime and offenses committed voluntarily and with malice aforethought. Even as she, fearing neither gods nor saints nor her fellow-men, destroyed the dead man, so let her in turn be destroyed by you and by Justice! Let her win neither consideration nor pity nor any sort of compunction from you, and thus meet with the punishment she has so justly earned!

I am amazed at my brother's hardihood, and puzzled as to his object, in declaring on oath, on his mother's behalf, that he "knows for certain" that she has not committed this crime. How can anyone "know for certain" about events at which he was not present? Naturally, people who are plotting the murder of their neighbors do not prepare their plans and make their preparations in the presence of witnesses. They do so with the greatest possible secrecy, so that no other human soul may know. But the victims of their machinations know nothing until they are caught in the grip of the menace; not till then do they recognize the destruction that is upon them. And then, if they are able—if they are not forestalled by death—they summon their friends and relatives, and give evidence and tell them the names of their murderers, and enjoin upon them to avenge the crime. Such was the injunction which my father laid on me when I was still a boy, when he was suffering from his last unhappy illness. . . .

I have now completed my account, and my effort on behalf of the dead man and the law. It rests with you to consider among yourselves what is to be done, and to pass a just verdict. It is my belief that the gods of the nether worlds have at heart the cause of those who are the victims of crime.

iii. Demosthenes, *Against Neaera* (excerpts)

This case, spitefully brought against the courtesan Neaera's pimp—lover Stephanus years after the facts described, when Neaera was in her seventies, concentrates not only on the legal issue of Neaera's citizenship, but on her past sexual activities.

She was one of seven little girls bought when small children by Nicaretê, a freedwoman who had been the slave of Charisius of Elis, and the wife of Charisius's cook Hippias. Nicaretê was a clever judge of beauty in little girls, and moreover she understood the art of rearing and training them skilfully, having made this her profession from which she drew her livelihood. She used to address them as daughters, so that she might exact the largest fee from those who wished to have dealings with them, on the ground that they were freeborn girls; but after she had reaped her profit from the youth of each of them, one by one, she then sold the whole lot of them together, seven in all: Anteia, Stratola, Aristocleia, Metaneira, Phila, Isthmias, and the defendant Neaera.

Now who were their respective purchasers, and how they were set free by those who bought them from Nicaretê, I will explain in the course of my speech, if you wish to hear, and if I have enough time. But the fact that the defendant Neaera did belong to Nicaretê and worked as a prostitute open to all comers—this is the point to which I wish to return.

Lysias the professor of rhetoric was the lover of Metaneira. He decided that in addition to the other expenses he had incurred for her, he would like to get her initiated. He thought that the rest of his expenditure went to her owner, but whatever he spent on her over the festival and initiation ceremony would be a present for the girl herself. He therefore asked Nicaretê to come to the Mysteries and bring Metaneira so that she could be initiated and he promised to instruct her himself in the Mysteries.

When they arrived, Lysias did not admit them to his house, out of respect for his own wife, who was the daughter of Brachyllus and his own niece, and for his mother, who was somewhat advanced in years and lived in the same house. Instead, he lodged them—that is, Metaneira and Nicaretê—with Philostratus of Celonus, who was still a bachelor and also a friend of his. The women were accompanied by the defendant Neaera, who was already working as a prostitute, though she was not yet of the proper age.

As witness to the truth of my statements, namely that she was the slave of Nicaretê and used to accompany her and was hired out to anyone willing to pay, I now call upon Philostratus himself.

(*Philostratus testifies.*) ...

On a later occasion, gentlemen, Simos the Thessalian brought Neaera here to the Great Panathenaic Festival. Nicaretê also accompanied them, and they put up at the house of Ctesippus son of Glauconidas. The defendant Neaera drank and dined with them in the presence of a large company, as a courtesan would do.

I now call witnesses to the truth of these statements. Please call Euphiletus son of Simon, and Aristomachus son of Critodemus.

(*They testify.*) ...

After that, she worked openly at Corinth as a prostitute, and became famous. Among her lovers were Xenoclides the poet and Hipparchus the actor, who had her on hire. For the truth of these statements, I am unable to put before you the deposition of Xenoclides, because he is debarred by law from giving evidence.... But I now call Hipparchus himself, and I shall compel him to give evidence or else take the oath disclaiming knowledge of the facts, according to the law; otherwise I will *subpoena* him.

(*He testifies.*) ...

After that, she acquired two lovers, Timanoridas of Corinth and Eucrates of Leucas. These men found Nicaretê's charges excessive, as she expected them to pay all the daily expenses of her household; so they paid down to Nicaretê 30 minas as the purchase-price of Neaera, and bought her outright from her mistress, according to the law of that city, to be their slave. They kept her and made use of her for as long as they wished. Then, being about to get married, they informed her that they did not wish to see the woman who had been their own mistress plying her trade in Corinth nor kept in a brothel: they would be glad to receive less money for her than they had paid, and to see her also reaping some benefit. They therefore offered to allow her, towards the price of her freedom, 1,000 drachmas, that is, 500 each; as for the 20 minas remaining, they told her to find this sum herself and repay it to them.

Neaera, on hearing these propositions from Timanoridas and Eucrates, sent messages to a number of her former lovers, asking them to come to Corinth. Among these was Phrynion, an Athenian from Paeania, the son of Demon, and the brother of Demochares, a man who was living a dissolute and extravagant life, as the older of you remember. When Phrynion arrived, she told him of the proposition made to her by Eucrates and Timanoridas, and handed him the money which she had collected from her other lovers as a contribution towards the purchase of her freedom, together with her own savings, asking him to make up the amount to the 20 minas, and pay it to Eucrates and Timanoridas, so that she should be free.

Phrynion was delighted to hear this proposition of hers. He took the money which had been contributed by her other lovers, made up the deficit himself, and paid the 20 minas to Eucrates and Timanoridas as the price of her freedom and on condition that she would not practice her profession in Corinth. As a proof of these statements, I will call the man who then witnessed the transaction. Please call Philagrus of the suburb of Melite.

(*He testifies.*)

When they arrived here at Athens, he kept her and lived with her in a most dissolute and reckless way. He took her out to dinner with him wherever he went, where there was drinking; and whenever he made an after-dinner excursion, she always went too. He made love to her openly, anywhere and everywhere he chose, to excite the jealousy of the onlookers at his privilege. Among the many houses to which he took her on an after-dinner call was that of Chabrias of the suburb Aexone, when the latter had won the victory at Delphi with a four-horse chariot team which he had bought from the sons of Mitys the Argive, and on his return from Delphi was celebrating victory down at Colias. On that occasion, many men made love to Neaera when she was drunk and Phrynion was asleep, including even some of

Chabrias' servants. In proof of this I shall produce before you the actual eyewitnesses.

Please call Chionides and Euthetion.

(*They testify.*)

However, finding herself treated with the most outrageous brutality by Phrynion, instead of being loved as she had expected, or having attention paid to her wishes, she packed up the goods in his house, including all the clothes and jewellery which he had provided for her personal adornment, and taking with her two servants, Thratta and Coccalina, ran away to Megara.

This happened when Asteius was Chief Magistrate at Athens[15] during your second war against Sparta. Neaera spent two years in Megara; but her profession did not produce sufficient income to run her house, as she was extravagant, and the Megarians are mean and stingy, and there was no great foreign colony there because it was war-time, and the Megarians favoured the Spartan side, but you were in command of the seas. She could not go back to Corinth because the terms of her release by Eucrates and Timanoridas were that she should not practice her profession there.

However, peace came [the next year]. It was then that our opponent Stephanus visited Megara. He put up at her house, as that of a prostitute, and became her lover. She told him her whole life-story and of her ill-treatment at the hands of Phrynion. She longed to live in Athens, but was afraid of Phrynion, because she had done him wrong and he was furious with her. She knew the violence and arrogance of his character. She therefore made the defendant Stephanus her protector, and while they were still in Megara, he talked encouragingly and filled her with hope, saying that Phrynion would be sorry for it if he laid hands on her, as he himself would take her as his wife, and would introduce the sons she already had to his clansmen as being his own, and would make citizens of them. No one on earth, he said, should do her any harm. And so he arrived here at Athens from Megara with her and her three children, Proxenus, Ariston and a daughter, who now bears the name of Phano. He took her and the children to the little house which he owned, alongside the Whispering Hermes, between the house of Dorotheus the Eleusinian and the house of Cleinomachus, which now Spintharus has bought from him for 7 minas. Thus, the place was the whole of Stephanus' property at that time—he had nothing else.

He had two reasons for bringing her here: first, that he would have a handsome mistress without expense; second, that her profession would provide him with the necessaries of life and keep the household, for he had no other source of income, except what he picked up by occasional blackmail.

When Phrynion heard that she was in Athens and living with the defendant, he took some young men with him and went to Stephanus' house to get her. Stephanus asserted her freedom, according to law, and Phrynion thereupon summoned her before the Polemarch, under surety.[16] In proof of this I will bring before you the Polemarch of that year....

Please call Aietes.

(*He testifies.*)

When she had thus been bailed out by Stephanus and was living with him, she carried on the same profession no less than before, but she exacted a larger fee from those who wished to consort with her, as having now a certain position to keep up and as being a married woman. Stephanus helped her by blackmail; if he caught any rich unknown stranger making love to her, he used to lock him up in the house as an adulterer caught with his wife, and extract a large sum of money from him— naturally, because neither Stephanus nor Neaera had anything, not even enough to meet their daily expenses, but their establishment was large. There were himself and herself to keep, and three small children—the ones she brought with her to him—and two maids and a man-servant; and above all, she had acquired the habit of good living, as formerly it had been others who had provided her with all necessaries....

To continue: Phrynion began his law-suit against Stephanus, on the grounds that Stephanus had robbed him of the defendant Neaera and made a free woman of her, and that Stephanus had received the goods of which Neaera had robbed him when she left. However, their friends brought them together and persuaded them to submit the dispute to arbitration. The arbitrator who sat on Phrynion's behalf was Satyrus of Alopece, the brother of Lacedaemonius, and on Stephanus' behalf, Saurias of Lampra; they chose as umpire Diogeiton of Acharnae. These three met in the temple, and after hearing the facts from both the litigants and also from the woman herself, they gave their judgment, which was accepted by the litigants: namely, that the woman should be free and her own mistress, but that the goods which Neaera had taken from Phrynion when she left should all be returned to Phrynion, except the clothes and jewellery and maid-servants which had been bought for Neaera herself; further, that she should spend the same number of days with each of them; but that if they agreed to any other arrangement, this same arrangement should hold good; that the woman's upkeep should be provided by the person with whom she was living at the time; and that for the future the litigants should be friends and should bear no malice. Such was the settlement brought about by the decision of arbitrators in the case of Phrynion and Stephanus, concerning the defendant Neaera. In proof of this, the Clerk will read you the deposition.

Please call Satyrus of Alopece, Saurias of Lampra, and Diogeiton of Acharnae.

(*They testify.*)

(*Terms of settlement.*)

The following were the terms of settlement between Phrynion and Stephanus: that each shall keep at his house and have the enjoyment of Neaera for an equal number of days per month, unless they come to some different agreement.

When the business was over, the friends of each party, those who had assisted them at the arbitration and the rest, did as I believe is usual in such cases, especially when a mistress is in dispute: they went to dine with each of them at the times when he had Neaera with him, and she dined and drank with them as mistresses do.....

Thus the young woman was openly adjudged to be an alien, although Stephanus had dared to pretend to have caught a man in adultery with her.

Yet the defendants Stephanus and Neaera had reached such a pitch of impudence that they were not content with merely declaring her to be a free-born Athenian woman. They noticed that Theogenes of Cothocidae had been chosen by the lot as King-Archon, a man of good family, but poor and without business experience; so Stephanus supported him at his examination, and helped him out with his expenses. When he entered upon office, Stephanus wormed his way in, and having bought from him the office of assessor, he gave him this woman, Neaera's daughter, as wife, guaranteeing her to be his own daughter: such was his contempt for you and for the laws! So this woman Phano performed for you the secret sacrifice for the safety of the State; she looked upon mysteries which she, as an alien, had to right to behold. This was the sort of woman who entered into the holy place where no other of all the great

Athenian people can enter only the wife of the King-Archon. She administered the oath to the reverend priestesses who officiate at the sacrifices; she went through the ceremony of the Bride of Dionysus, and carried out the ancestral religious duties of the State, fulfilling numerous sacred and mysterious functions. How can it be in accord with piety that things which the rest of the community are not allowed even to hear spoken of should actually be done by any woman chosen by chance, especially such a woman as this, and one who is guilty of such actions? . . .

(To the Clerk):

Now please take the law I have here, which deals with these matters, and read it.

(To the jury):

You will see from this that it was proper for her, as a woman of such a character and such activities, not only to keep away from all these rites, from seeing, from sacrificing, from performing any of the ceremonies laid down by ancestral usage for the safety of the State: she should have been debarred from all public occasions at Athens. The law decrees that where a woman is found with an adulterer, she is forbidden to attend any of the public sacrifices, even those which the laws permit an alien woman or slave to attend for the purpose of worship and prayer. The only class of woman forbidden by law to attend the public sacrifices is the woman caught in adultery; if she attends and breaks the law, the law allows any person who wishes to inflict upon her with impunity any punishment short of death, the right of punishment being legally granted to any chance person. The reason why the law permitted the infliction with impunity of any ill-treatment upon her except death, was to avoid any pollution or sacrilege in the temple; it holds out for women a threat terrifying enough to deter them from unrestraint or any sort of misbehavior, and compel them to carry out their duties at home, teaching them that if anyone misbehaves in this fashion, she will be banished not only from her husband's house but from the public places of worship. That this is so will be clear to you when you hear the law itself read out. . . .

Law on Adultery

If the husband catch the adulterer in the act, he (the husband) shall not be permitted to continue cohabitation with the wife. If he continues cohabitation, he shall be disfranchised. It shall not be lawful for the woman to be admitted to the public sacrifices, if she has been caught with an adulterer. If she gains

entrance, she shall be liable to suffer any ill-treatment whatsoever, short of death, and impunity. . . .

Each one of you must believe, therefore, that he is giving his
vote in defence of his wife, or his daughter, or his mother, or on
behalf of the State, the laws, and religion—to prevent respectable women from acquiring the same standing as the prostitute,
and to protect those who have been reared by their families in
every propriety and with every care, and given in marriage
according to law, from having no better position than this
woman, who with every sort of licentious behavior surrendered
herself dozens of times a day to dozens of men, whenever anyone
asked her. You must not think of me, the speaker, merely as
Apollodorus, nor of those who will speak on the side of the
defense as merely your fellow-citizens: you must regard this law-
suit as being fought by Neaera against the laws, over the actions
done by her. So that while you are considering the case for the
prosecution, you must listen to the laws themselves, by which
this City-State is governed and in accordance with which you
have sworn to give your verdict: you must ask what the laws
ordain, and how my opponents have transgressed them. But
while you are hearing the defense, bear in mind the accusation
put forward by the laws and the proof offered by the prosecution; take a look at the woman's appearance, and ask yourselves
one thing only: if she, Neaera, has done the things of which she
is accused.

E. MARRIAGE
PAPYRI

The papyrus, a plant which grew abundantly in the Nile, was used by the
Egyptians to produce a writing material which they exported throughout the
Mediterranean. While the damp weather of other countries caused the papyrus
sheets to disintegrate, Egypt's climate preserved them. As a result, the majority
of the hundreds of thousands of papyri which survive today come from Egypt,
and most were discovered in trash-piles and town dumps. Papyri written in
Greek, the language of Egypt after its occupation by Alexander the Great,
survive from the late fourth century B.C. to the end of the ancient world.

While many fragments have provided literary texts, we are concerned here
with the category known as "documentary papyri," which includes private letters
(often dictated to professional scribes by illiterate correspondents), public documents, and records of financial transactions, both public and private. Like
inscriptions, papyri can tell us about the ordinary people whom historians have
ignored, but they go further than the stone remains in giving us priceless, often
touching glimpses into the daily life of the lower classes.

i. Marriage Contract
Tebtunis papyrus 104; 92 B.C.

The year 22, Mecheir 11. Philiscus son of Apollonius, Persian of the Epigone, acknowledges to Apollonia also called Kellauthis, daughter of Heraclides, Persian, with her guardian her brother Apollonius, that he has received from her in copper money two talents and four thousand drachmas, which is the dowry agreed upon by him for her, Apollonia.... The keeper of the contract is Dionysius. [The foregoing is in the first hand; then in the second hand]

In the twenty-second year of the reign of Ptolemy also called Alexander, the god Philometor, in the priesthood of Alexander's priest and of the rest as written in Alexandria, in the month Xandikos 11, Mecheir 11, at Kerkeosiris of the division of Polemon of the Arsinoïte nome. Philiscus, son of Apollonius, Persian of the Epigone, acknowledges to Apollonia, also called Kellauthis, daughter of Heraclides, Persian, with her guardian her brother Apollonius, that he has received from her in copper money two talents and four thousand drachmas, the dowry agreed upon by him for her, Apollonia. Apollonia shall remain with Philiscus, obeying him as a wife should obey her husband, owning their property jointly with him. Philiscus, whether he is at home or away from home, shall furnish Apollonia with everything necessary and clothing and whatsoever is proper for a wedded wife, in proportion to their means. It shall not be lawful for Philiscus to bring home another wife in addition to Apollonia or to have a concubine or boy-lover, nor to beget children by another woman while Apollonia is alive nor to maintain another house of which Apollonia is not mistress, nor to eject or insult or illtreat her nor to alienate any of their property with injustice to Apollonia. If he be shown to be doing any of these things or do not furnish her with what is necessary or clothing or the rest as stipulated, Philiscus shall immediately pay back to Apollonia the dowry of the two talents and four thousand drachmas of copper. In the same way it shall not be lawful for Apollonia to spend night or day away from the house of Philiscus without Philiscus' knowledge, or to have intercourse with another man or to ruin the common household or to bring shame upon Philiscus in whatever causes a husband shame. If Apollonia voluntarily wishes to separate from Philiscus, Philiscus shall pay back to her the bare dowry within ten days from the day it is demanded. If he does not pay it back as stipulated he shall immediately forfeit the dowry he has received plus one half. The witnesses are Dionysius, son of Patron, Dionysius, son of Hermaïscus, Theon, son of Ptolemaeus, Didymus, son of Ptolemaeus, Dionysius, son of Dionysius, Heracles, son of Diocles, all six Macedonians of the Epigone. The keeper of the contract is Dionysius. [Then follows in a third hand].

I, Philiscus, son of Apollonius, Persian of the Epigone, acknowledge that I have received the dowry, the two talents and four thousand drachmas of copper, as written above, and I have deposited the agreement, which is valid, with Dionysius. Dionysius, son of Hermaïscus, the aforesaid, wrote for him since he is illiterate. [Then in the fourth hand]

I, Dionysius, have the contract which is valid. [Again, in the first hand]

Registered the year 22, Mecheir 11.

ii. Annulment of a Marriage Contract
Berlin papyrus 1104; Alexandria, first century B.C.

To Protarchus, from Dionysarion, daughter of Protarchus, with her brother Protarchus as guardian, and from Hermione daughter of Hermias, a citizen, on the authority of her brother, the son of Hermias. Dionysarion agrees that the contract is invalidated which the son of Hermione, Hermias, made with her, with Hermione serving as bondsman.... It is agreed, on behalf of her deceased husband, that Dionysarion take from Hermione's house by hand the dowry which she brought to Hermias, with Hermione serving as bondsman: a dowry of clothes, 240 silver pieces, earrings, and a ring.... The contract is invalidated on all grounds indicated by her: Dionysarion is not to return to Hermione, nor is any man acting on her behalf, not for any of the deceased Hermias' possessions nor concerning the dowry or support nor about any other written or unwritten agreement made in the past up to the present day. Since Dionysarion has become pregnant, she is not to return for childbirth, because she is more persuasive on that account; she is permitted to expose her baby and to join herself in marriage to another husband. She agrees that if she breaks this authorized agreement she is subject to damages and the established fine....

42

F. AGREEMENT TO TRANSFER A CONCUBINE
ELEPHANTINE PAPYRUS 3; 284/3 B.C.

Elaphion of Syria, with Pantarces as her guardian, herewith pays Antipatros of Arcadia a fee of 300 drachmas for having maintained her. Antipatros is hereby forbidden to approach her on the grounds that he is supporting her or that she has on any condition been enslaved to him or to anyone acting on his behalf. If he violates this agreement, access is forbidden to him and to his agent and Antipatros must pay a fine of 3000 drachmas to Elaphion or to the men currently maintaining her. This writ shall be in effect from the time Elaphion or someone acting on her behalf serves it on Antipatros, as Elaphion has written it. Witnesses; [signed] Pancrates of Arcadia, Caphisias of Phocis, Diphilus of Phocis, Epinicus of Chalcidia, Athenagoras of Alexandria, Xenocles of Rhodes.

A second papyrus (P. Eleph.4) records in identical language the payment of four hundred drachmas to Pantarces (her master in the preceding agreement), with Dion acting as her new guardian. Violation of the agreement is subject to a fine of ten thousand drachmas, and signatures of six witnesses are appended.

G. A. MOTHER'S LAST WILL AND TESTAMENT
SB X 10756 (EXCERPTS); OXYRHYNCHUS, 133 A.D.

This is the will of Taarpaesis, being of sound mind, also called Isidora, daughter of Apollonius (son of Apollonius) and of Tsenamounis from the city of Oxyrhynchus, with her half-brother Apollon, son of Apollonius and Diogenis from the same city as guardian, a public document...I Taarpaesis, also called Isidora, daughter of Apollonius, make my will as follows and leave after my death my children as executors, Ptolemaeus, Berenice, and Isidora (also called Apollonarion).

To Ptolemaeus: from my property in the city of Oxyrhynchus in the South Colonnade district, the house, atrium, courtyard, furnishings, entrances and exits; in the village of Phoboou, the walled lands in the sections from the west to the north, a fourth share of the garden, with the palm trees therein and plans and the well built of baked brick, with its furnishings and everything that belongs to it, and entrances and exits; and in the middle sections of that village my father's walled land, where there is a house and a hall, with entrances and exits, and near the same village [details of parcels of land, one of which she had inherited from her mother].

To Bernice and Isidora (also called Apollonarion), because of the agreement each of them has with her husband under the terms of which each keeps her own possessions; also under my will, share and share alike, from my property before Herais Tetos and other places in the city of Oxyrhynchus in the same South Colonnade district, and half share of the house, atrium, and furnishings, entrances and exits; and in the village of Phoboou in the shady section of my father's property a half share of the house and hall, with entrances and exits.

I leave to the son of my aforesaid first daughter Berenice, Eision son of Heraclides, one field, the property that I own near Ophis....

All other property that I leave, furniture, equipment, household goods, accounts receivable, etc., go to Psenesis [a close friend of the family] who is also called Eision Ptolemaeus, if he survives me; if he does not, then to my aforesaid son Ptolemaeus. This aforesaid Psenesis (also called Eision) will have from the time that I die as long as he lives the income from and habitation of all property remaining to me after taxes, and when Psenesis (also called Eision) dies my daughter Berenice will have the income after taxes and the assignment of the one field to her son Eision. If Ptolemaeus and Isidora die without issue, it is my wish that what is left of my possessions in Ptolemaeus' estate go to my two daughters Berenice and Isidora (also called Apollonarion) equally, and what is left in Isidora's (also called Apollonarion) estate go to Berenice, who should allow Psenesis (also called Eision) as long as he lives the income, habitation rights, and furnishings previously assigned to him. I am satisfied with the preceeding terms.

I am fifty-nine years of age, with a scar on the instep of my right foot, and my seal is Aphrodite's. I, Apollon, son of Apollonius and Diogenis, her half-brother, authorize my signature to the aforewritten.... I, Onnophrius son of Thonis, have written out the will on their behalf, since they do not know letters; I am about fifty-three years of age with a scar on my left foot. [Witnesses].

4. POLITICS

In antiquity the term "philosopher" described professors of general knowledge, both of how life was and of how life ought to be. Plato's constructions of theories of ideal behavior were later counterbalanced by his student Aristotle's systematic descriptions of observed existence.

A. WOMEN'S ROLE IN ATHENS

i. Aristotle, *Politics* (excerpts).

First then we may observe in living creatures both a despotical and a constitutional rule; for the soul rules the body with a despotical rule, whereas the intellect rules the appetites with a constitutional and royal rule. And it is clear that the rule of the soul over the body, and of the mind and the rational element over the passionate is natural and expedient; whereas the equality of the two or the rule of the inferior is always hurtful. The same holds good of animals as well as of men; for tame animals have a better nature than wild and all tame animals are better off when they are ruled by man; for then they are preserved. Again, the male is by nature superior, and the female inferior; and the one rules, and the other is ruled; this principle, of necessity, extends to all mankind....

Of household management we have seen that there are three parts—one is the rule of a master over slaves, which has been discussed already, another of a father, and the third of a husband. A husband and father rules over wife and children, both free, but the rule differs, the rule over his children being a royal, over his wife a constitutional rule. For although there may be exceptions to the order of nature, the male is by nature fitter for command than the female, just as the older and full-grown is superior to the younger and more immature. But in most constitutional states the citizens rule and are ruled by turns, for the idea of a constitutional state implies that the natures of the citizens are equal and the other is ruled we endeavor to create a difference of outward forms and names and titles of respect.... The relation of the male to the female is of this kind, but there the inequality is permanent. The rule of a father over his children is royal, for he receives both love and the respect due to age, exercising a kind of royal power. And therefore Homer has appropriately called Zeus 'father of gods and men,' because he is the king of them all. For a king is the natural superior of his subjects, but he should be of the same kin or kind with them, and such is the relation of elder and younger, of father and son....

The freeman rules over the slave after another manner from that in which the male rules over the female, or the man over the child; although the parts of the soul are present in all of them, they are present in different degrees. For the slave has no deliberative faculty at all; the woman has, but it is without authority, and the child has, but it is immature. So it must necessarily be with the moral virtues also; all may be supposed to partake of them, but only in such manner and degree as is required by each for the fulfilment of his duty. Hence the ruler ought to have moral virtue in perfection, for his duty is entirely that of a master artificer, and the master artificer is reason; the subjects, on the other hand, require only that measure of virtue which is proper to each of them. Clearly, then, moral virtue belongs to all of them; but the temperance of a man and of a woman, or the courage and justice of a man and of a woman, are not, as Socrates maintained, the same; the courage of a man is shown in commanding, of a woman in obeying.... All classes must be deemed to have their special attributes; as the poet says of women, "Silence is a woman's glory,"[17] but this is not equally the glory of man. The child is imperfect, and therefore obviously his virtue is not relative to himself alone, but to the perfect man and to his teacher, and in like manner the virtue of the slave is relative to a master....

Nor is there any way of preventing brothers and children and fathers and mothers from sometimes recognizing one another; for children are born like their parents, and they will necessarily be finding indications of their relationship to one another. Geographers declare such to be the fact; they say that in Upper Libya, where the women are common, nevertheless the children who are born are assigned to their respective fathers on the ground of their likeness. And some women, like the females of other animals—for example mares and cows—have a strong tendency to produce offspring resembling their parents, as was the case with the Pharsalian mare called Dicaea [the Just]....

The license of the Lacedaemonian women defeats the intention of the Spartan constitution, and is adverse to the good order of the state. For a husband and a wife, being each a part of every family, the state may be considered as about equally divided into men and women; and, therefore, in those states in which the condition of the woman is bad, half the city may be regarded as having no laws. And this is what has actually happened at Sparta; the legislator wanted to make the whole state hardy and temperate, and he has carried out his intention in the case of the men, but he has neglected the women, who live in every sort of intemperance and luxury. The consequence is that in such a state wealth is too highly valued, especially if the citizens fall under the dominion of their wives, after the manner of all warlike races, except the Celts and a few others who openly approve of male loves. The old mythologer would seem to have been right in uniting Ares and Aphrodite, for all warlike races are prone to the love either of men or of women. This was exemplified among the Spartans in the days of their greatness; many things were managed by their women. But what difference does it make whether women rule, or the rulers are ruled by women? The result is the same. Even in regard to courage, which is of no use in daily life, and is needed only in war, the influence of the Lacedaemonian women has been most mischievous. The evil showed itself in the Theban invasion [369 B.C.], when, unlike the women in other cities, they were utterly useless and caused more confusion than the enemy. This license of the Lacedaemonian women existed from the earliest times, and was only what might be expected. For, during the wars of the Lacedaemonians, first against the Argives, and afterwards against the Arcadians and Messenians, the men were long away from home, and, on the return of peace, they gave themselves into the Legislator's hand, already prepared by the discipline of a soldier's life (in which there are many elements of virtue), to receive his enactments. But, when Lycurgus, as tradition says, wanted to bring the women under his laws, they resisted, and he gave up the attempt. They, and not he, are to blame for what then happened, and this defect in the constitution is clearly to be attributed to them. We are not, however, considering what is or is not to be excused, but what is right or wrong, and the disorder of the women, as I have already said, not only of itself gives an air of indecorum to the state, but tends in a measure to foster avarice.

The mention of avarice naturally suggests a criticism on the inequality of property. While some of the Spartan citizens have quite small properties, others have very large ones; hence the land has passed into the hands of a few. And here is another fault in their laws; for, although the legislator rightly holds up to shame the sale or purchase of an inheritance, he allows any body who likes to give and bequeath it. Yet both practices lead to the same result. And nearly two-fifths of the whole country are held by women; this is owing to the number of heiresses and to the large dowries which are customary. It would surely have been better to have given no dowries at all, or, if any, but small or moderate ones. As the law now stands, a man may bestow his heiress on any one whom he pleases, and, if he die intestate, the privilege of giving her away descends to his heir. Hence, although the country is able to maintain 1500 cavalry and 30,000 hoplites, the whole number of Spartan citizens [at the time of the Theban invasion] fell below 1000. . . .

The good man, who is free and also a subject, will not have one virtue only, say justice—but he will have distinct kinds of virtue, the one qualifying him to rule, the other to obey, and differing as the temperance and courage of men and women differ. For a man would be thought a coward if he had no more courage than a courageous woman, and a woman would be thought loquacious if she imposed no more restraints on her conversation than the good man; and indeed their part in the management of the household is different, for the duty of the one is to acquire, and of the other to preserve. . . .

Again, the evil practices of the last and worst form of democracy are all found in tyrannies. Such are the power given to women in their families in the hope that they will inform against their husbands, and the license which is allowed to slaves in order that they may betray their masters; for slaves and women do not conspire against tyrants; and they are of course friendly to tyrannies and also to democracies, since under them they have a good time. For the people too would fain be a monarch. . . .

Since the time of generation is commonly limited within the age of seventy years in the case of a man, and of fifty in the case of a woman, the commencement of the union should conform to these periods. The union of male and female when too young is bad for the procreation of children; in all other animals the offspring of the young are small and ill-developed, and generally of the female sex, and therefore also in man, as is proved by the fact that in those critics in which men and women are accustomed to marry young, the people are small and weak.

ii. Plato, *The Laws* (selections)

Thanks to some providential necessity, Cleinias and Megillus, you have a splendid and — as I was saying — astonishing institution: communal meals for men. But it is entirely wrong of you to have omitted from your legal code any provision for your women, so that the practice of communal meals for them has never got under way. On the contrary, half the human race — the female sex, the half which in any case is inclined to be secretive and crafty, because of its weakness — has been left to its own devices because of the misguided indulgence of the legislator. Because you neglected this sex, you gradually lost control of a great many things which would be in a far better state today if they had been regulated by law. You see, leaving women to do what they like is not just to lose *half* the battle (as it may seem): a woman's natural potential for virtue is inferior to a man's, so she's proportionately a greater danger, perhaps even twice as great. So the happiness of the state will be better served if we reconsider the point and put things right, by providing that all our arrangements apply to men and women alike. But at present, unhappily, the human race has not progressed as far as that, and if you're wise you won't breathe a word about such a practice in other parts of the world where states do not recognize communal meals as a public institution at all. So when it comes to the point, how on earth are you going to avoid being laughed to scorn when you try to force women to take their food and drink in public? There's nothing the sex is likely to put up with more reluctantly: women have got used to a life of obscurity and retirement, and any attempt to force them into the open will provoke tremendous resistance from them, and they'll be more than a match for the legislator. Elsewhere, as I said, the very mention of the correct policy will be met with howls of protest. But perhaps this state will be different.

The Education of Females

Let me stress that this law of mine will apply just as much to girls as to boys. The girls must be trained in precisely the same way, and I'd like to make this proposal without any reservations whatever about horse-riding or athletics being suitable activities for males but not for females. You see, although I was already convinced by some ancient stories I have heard, I now know for sure that there are pretty well countless numbers of women, generally called Sarmatians, round the Black Sea, who not only ride horses but use the bow and other weapons. There, men and women have an equal duty to cultivate these skills, so cultivate them equally they do. And while we're on the subject, here's another thought for you. I maintain that if these results can be achieved, the state of affairs in our corner of Greece, where men and women do *not* have a common purpose and do *not* throw all their energies into the same activities, is absolutely stupid. Almost every state, under present conditions, is only half a state, and develops only half its potentialities, whereas with the same cost and effort, it could double its achievement. Yet what a staggering blunder for a legislator to make!

CLEINIAS: I dare say. But a lot of these proposals, sir, are incompatible with the average state's social structure. However, you were quite right when you said we should give the argument its head, and only make up our minds when it had run its course. You've made me reproach myself for having spoken. So carry on, and say what you like.

ATHENIAN: The point I'd like to make, Cleinias, is the same one as I made a moment ago, that there might have been something to be said against our proposal, if it had not been proved by the facts to be workable. But as things are, an opponent of this law must try other tactics. We are not going to withdraw our recommendation that so far as possible, in education and everything else, the female sex should be on the same footing as the male. Consequently, we should approach the problem rather like this. Look: if women are *not* to follow absolutely the same way of life as men, then surely we shall have to work out some other program for them?

CLEINIAS: Inevitably.

ATHENIAN: Well, then, if we deny women this position of equality we're now demanding for them, which of the systems actually in force today shall we adopt instead? What about the practice of the Thracians and many other peoples, who make their women work on the land and mind sheep and cattle, so that they turn into skivvies indistinguishable from slaves? Or what about the Athenians and all the other states in that part of the world? Well, here's how we Athenians deal with the problem: we "concentrate our resources," as the expression is, under one roof and let our women take charge of our stores and the spinning and wool-working in general. Or we could adopt the Spartan system, Megillus, which is a compromise. You make your girls take part in athletics and you give them a compulsory education in the arts; when they grow up, though dispensed from working wool, they have to "weave" themselves a pretty hard-working sort of life which is by no means despicable or useless: they have to be tolerably efficient at running the home and managing the house and bringing up children—but they *don't* undertake military service. This means that even if some extreme emergency ever led to a battle for their state and the lives of their children, they wouldn't have the expertise to use bows and arrows, like so many Amazons, nor could they join the men in deploying any other missile. They wouldn't be able to take up shield and spear and copy Athena, so as to terrify the enemy (if nothing more) by being seen in some kind of battle-array gallantly resisting the destruction threatening their native land. Living as they do, they'd never be anything like tough enough to imitate the Sarmatian women, who by comparison with such femininity would look like men. Anyone who wants to commend your Spartan legislators for this state of affairs, had better get on with it: I'm not going to change *my* mind. A legislator should go the whole way and not stick at half-measures; he mustn't just regulate the men and allow the women to live as they like and wallow in expensive luxury. That would be to give the state only half the loaf of prosperity instead of the whole of it.

How to Discourage Unnatural Sexual Intercourse

ATHENIAN: I want to put the law on this subject on a firm footing, and at the moment I'm thinking of a method which is, in a sense, simplicity itself. But from another point of view, nothing could be harder.

MEGILLUS: What are you getting at?

ATHENIAN: We're aware, of course, that even nowadays most men, in spite of their general disregard for the law, are very effectively prevented from having relations with people they find attractive. And they don't refrain reluctantly, either— they're more than happy to.

MEGILLUS: What circumstances have you in mind?

ATHENIAN: When it's one's brother or sister whom one finds attractive. And the same law, unwritten though it is, is extremely effective in stopping a man sleeping—secretly or otherwise—with his son or daughter, or making any kind of amorous approach to them. Most people feel not the faintest desire for such intercourse.

MEGILLUS: That's perfectly true.

ATHENIAN: So the desire for this sort of pleasure is stifled by a few words?

MEGILLUS: What words do you mean?

ATHENIAN: The doctrine that "these acts are absolutely

unholy, an abomination in the sight of the gods, and that nothing is more revolting." We refrain from them because we never hear them spoken of in any other way. From the day of our birth each of us encounters a complete unanimity of opinion wherever we go; we find it not only in comedies but often in the high seriousness of tragedy too, when we see a Thyestes on the stage, or an Oedipus or a Macareus, the clandestine lover of his sister. We watch these characters dying promptly by their own hand as a penalty for their crimes.

MEGILLUS: You're right in this, anyway, that when no one ventures to challenge the law, public opinion works wonders.

ATHENIAN: So we were justified in what we said just now. When the legislator wants to tame one of the desires that dominate mankind so cruelly, it's easy for him to see his method of attack. He must try to make everyone—slave and free, women and children, and the entire state without any exception—believe that this common opinion has the backing of religion. He couldn't put his law on a securer foundation than that.

MEGILLUS: Very true. But how on earth it will ever be possible to produce such spontaneous unanimity—

ATHENIAN: I'm glad you've taken me up on the point. This is just what I was getting at when I said I knew of a way to put into effect this law of ours which permits the sexual act only for its natural purpose, procreation, and forbids not only homosexual relations, in which the human race is deliberately murdered, but also the sowing of seeds on rocks and stones where it will never take root and mature into a new individual and we should also have to keep away from any female 'soil' in which we'd be sorry to have the seed develop. At present however, the law is effective only against intercourse between parent and child, but if it can be put on a permanent footing and made to apply effectively, as it deserves to, in other cases as well, it'll do a power of good. The first point in its favour is that it is a *natural* law. But it also tends to check the raging fury of the sexual instinct that so often leads to adultery; discourages excesses in food and drink, and inspires men with affection for their own wives. And there are a great many other advantages to be gained, if only one could get this law established.

B. WOMEN'S ROLE IN SPARTA

The Spartan way of life always intrigued other Greeks, who could never remain neutral on the subject. No other Greek city was like it. Sparta's social institutions and its famous discipline were designed for a single purpose: to protect the state by maintaining the best fighting force in the world. Women were trained to be fitting wives and mothers for these heroes. Their education included rigorous athletic training in which the spirit of competition was encouraged. Every effort was made to extirpate all traces of effeminacy: jewelry, cosmetics, perfumes, and colored clothing were all prohibited. Among Greek women, only Spartans did no wool work, the traditional female occupation.[18]

i. Plutarch, *Life of Lycurgus* 14-16 (excerpts)

For the good education of their youth (which, as I said before, Lycurgus[19] thought the most important and noblest work of a lawgiver), he went so far back as to take into consideration their very conception and birth, by regulating their marriages. For Aristotle is wrong is saying, that, after he had tried all ways to reduce the women to more modesty and sobriety, he was at last forced to leave them as they were, because that in the absence of their husbands, who spent the best part of their lives in the wars, their wives, whom they were obliged to leave absolute mistresses at home, took great liberties and assumed the superiority; and were treated with overmuch respect and called by the title of lady or queen. The truth is, he took in their case, also, all the care that was possible; he ordered the maidens to exercise themselves with wrestling, running, throwing the quoit, and casting the dart, to the end that the fruit they conceived might, in strong and healthy bodies, take firmer root and find better growth, and withal that they, with this greater vigor, might be the more able to undergo the pains of child-bearing. And to the end he might take away their overgreat tenderness and fear of exposure to the air, and all acquired womanishness, he ordered that the young women should go naked in the processions, as well as the young men, and dance, too, in that condition, at certain solemn feasts, singing certain songs, whilst the young men stood around, seeing and hearing them. On these occasions they now and then made, by jests, a befitting reflection upon those who had misbehaved themselves in the wars; and again sang encomiums upon those who had done any gallant action, and by these means inspired the younger sort with an emulation of their glory. Those that were thus commended went away proud, elated, and gratified with their honor among the maidens; and those who were rallied were as sensibly touched with it as if they had been formally reprimanded; and so much the more, because the kings and the elders, as well as the rest of the city, saw and heard all that passed. Nor was there anything shameful in this nakedness of the young women; modesty attended them, and all wantonness was excluded. It taught them simplicity and a care for good health, and gave them some taste of higher feelings, admitted as they thus were to the field of noble action and glory. Hence it was natural for them to think and speak as Gorgo, for example, the wife of Leonidas, is said to have done, when some foreign lady, as it would seem, told her that the women of Lacedaemon were the only women in the world who could rule men; "With good reason," she said, "for we are the only women who bring forth men."

These public processions of the maidens, and their appearing naked in their exercises and dancings, were incitements to marriage, operating upon the young with the rigor and certainty, as Plato says, of love, if not of mathematics.[20] ...

In their marriages, the husband carried off his bride by a sort of force; nor were their brides ever small and of tender years, but in their full bloom and ripeness. After this, she who superintended the wedding comes and clips the hair of the bride close round her head, dresses her up in man's clothes, and leaves her upon a mattress in the dark; afterwards comes the bridegroom, in his everyday clothes, sober and composed, as having supped at the common table, and, entering privately into the room where the bride lies, unties her virgin zone, and takes her to himself; and, after staying some time together, he returns composedly to his own apartment, to sleep as usual with the other young men. And so he continues to do, spending his days, and, indeed, his nights, with them, visiting his bride in fear and shame, and with circumspection, when he thought he should not be observed; she, also, on her part, using her wit to help and find favorable opportunities for their meeting, when company was out of the way. In this manner they lived a long time, insomuch that they sometimes had children by their wives before ever they saw their faces by daylight. Their interviews, being thus difficult and rare, served not only for continual exercise of their self-control, but brought them together with their bodies healthy and vigorous, and their affections fresh and lively, unsated and undulled by easy access and long continuance with each other; while their partings were always early enough to leave behind unextinguished in each of them some remaining fire of longing and mutual delight. After guarding marriage with this modesty and reserve, he was equally careful to banish empty and womanish jealousy. For this object, excluding all licentious disorders, he made it, nevertheless, honorable for men to give the use of their wives to those whom they should think fit, that so they might have children by them; ridiculing those in whose opinion such favors are so unfit for participation as to fight and shed blood and go to war about it. Lycurgus allowed a man who was advanced in years and had a young wife to recommend some virtuous and approved young man, that she might have a child by him, who might inherit the good qualities of the father, and be a son to himself. On the other side, an honest man who had love for a married woman upon account of her modesty and the well-favoredness of her children, might, without formality, beg her company of her husband, that he might raise, as it were, from this plot of good ground, worthy and well-allied children for himself.[21] And indeed, Lycurgus was of a persuasion that children were not so much the property of their parents as of the whole commonwealth, and, therefore, would not have his citizens begot by the first-comers, but by the best men that could be found; the laws of other nations seemed to him very absurd and inconsistent, where people would be so solicitious for their dogs and horses as to exert interest and to pay money to procure fine breeding, and yet kept their wives shut up, to be made mothers only by themselves, who might be foolish, infirm, or diseased; as if it were not apparent that children of a bad breed would prove their bad qualities first upon those who kept and were rearing them, and well-born children, in like manner, their good qualities. These regulations, founded on natural and social grounds, were certainly so far from that scandalous liberty which was afterwards charged upon their women, that they knew not what adultery meant....

Nor was it in the power of the father to dispose of the child as he thought fit; he was obliged to carry it before certain triers at a place called Lesche;[22] these were some of the elders of the tribe to which the child belonged; their business it was carefully to view the infant, and, if they found it stout and well made, they gave order for its rearing, and allotted it one of the nine thousand shares of land above mentioned for its maintenance, but, if they found it puny and ill-shaped, ordered it to be taken to what was called the Apothetae, a sort of chasm under Mt. Taygetus; as thinking it neither for the good of the child itself, nor for the public interest, that it should be brought up, if it did not, from the very outset, appear made to be healthy and vigorous. Upon the same account, the women did not bathe the new-born children with water, as is the custom in all other countries, but with wine, to prove the temper and complexion of their bodies; from a nation they had that epileptic and weakly children faint and waste away upon their being thus bathed, while, on the contrary, those of a strong and vigorous habit acquire firmness and get a temper by it, like steel. There was much care and art, too, used by the nurses; they had no swaddling bands; the children grew up free and unconstrained in limb and form, and not dainty and fanciful about their food; not afraid in the dark, or of being left alone; and without peevishness, or ill-humor, or crying. Upon this account Spartan nurses were often bought up, or hired by people of other countries; and it is recorded that she who suckled Alcibiades was a Spartan.

ii. Plutarch, *Sayings of Spartan Women* 240-242 (excerpts).

Being asked by a woman from Attica, "Why is it that you Spartan women are the only women that lord it over your men," [one woman] said, "Because we are the only women that are mothers of men."

As she was encouraging her husband Leonidas, when he was about to set out for Thermopylae, to show himself worthy of Sparta, she asked what she should do; and he said, "Marry a good man, and bear good children."

Another was burying her son, when a commonplace old woman came up to her and said, "Ah the bad luck of it, you poor woman." "No, by heaven," said she, "but good luck, for I bore him that he might die for Sparta, and this is the very thing that has come to pass for me."

When a woman from Ionia showed vast pride in a bit of her own weaving, which was very valuable, a Spartan woman pointed to her four sons, who were most well-behaved, and said, "Such should be the employments of the good and honorable woman, and it is over these that she should be elated and boastful."

A girl had secret relations with a man, and, after bringing on an abortion, she bore up so bravely, not uttering a single sound, that her delivery took place without the knowledge of her father and others who were near. For the confronting of her indecorum with decorum gained the victory over the poignant distress of her pains.

A Spartan woman who was being sold as a slave, when asked what she knew how to do, said, "To be faithful."

56

Another, taken captive, and asked a similar question, said, "To manage a house well."

Another, asked by a man if she would be good if he bought her, said, "Yes, and if you do not buy me."

Another who was being sold as a slave, when the crier inquired of her what she knew how to do, said, "To be free." And when the purchaser ordered her to do something not fitting for a free woman, she said, "You will be sorry that your meanness has cost you such a possession," and committed suicide.

iii. A Spartan Woman Athlete
AP XIII 16; early fourth century B.C.

My fathers and brothers were kings of Sparta. I, Cunisca, won a victory with my swift-running horses and set up this statue. I claim that I am the only woman from all Greece to have won this crown.

5. MEDICINE

Observable phenomena and deduction by analogy, not human dissection and clinical study, formed the premises on which ancient anatomical theories are based. Hence social norms, such as men's superiority over women, could provide acceptable "data" about human reproductive systems.

A. ANATOMY AND REPRODUCTION

i. Plato, *Timaeus* 91 (excerpts).

Those who on becoming men are timid, and pass through life unjustly, will according to assimilative reasoning be changed into women in their second generation. And at the same time through this cause the gods devised the love of copulation; composing an animal or animated substance, and placing one in us, but another in the female nature. But they produced each in the following manner. That procession of liquid aliment which passes through the lungs under the reins into the bladder, and which being compressed by the breath is emitted externally—

this the Gods receiving, they deduced it after the manner of a pipe into the concrete marrow, through the neck and spine of the back: and this is what we called seed in the former part of our discourse. But this, in consequence of being animated and receiving respiration, produces in the part where it respires a vital desire of effluxion; and thus perfects in us the love of begetting. On this account, that nature which subsists about the privy parts of men, becoming refractory and imperious, and as it were an animal unobedient to reason, endeavors through raging desire to possess absolute sway. In like manner the privities and matrix of women, forming an animal desirous of procreating children, when it remains without fruit beyond the flower of its age, or for a still more extended period, suffers the restraint with difficulty and indignation; and wandering every way through the body, obstructs the passage of the breath, does not permit respiration to take place, introduces other extreme difficulties, and causes all-various diseases; till the desire and love of the parts educe seed like fruit from a tree: but, when educed, they scatter it into the matrix as into a field. Hence women conceive animals invisible at first through their smallness, rude and unformed; when they become large, through dispersion of the seed, nourish them within, and, lastly, leading them into light perfect the generation of animals. In this manner, therefore, is the generation of women and every thing female performed.

ii. Aristotle on Anatomy, *On the Generation of Animals* 1, 4, 5

Explanation of the process of conception is deduced from external secretions: male semen has primary generative importance, female semen (i.e. menstrual fluid, which also sustains the developing embryo) purely nutritive value.

As far as animals are concerned, we must describe their generation just as we find the theme requires for each several kind as we go along, linking our account on to what has already been said. As we mentioned, we may safely set down as the chief principles of generation the male [factor] and the female [factor]; the male as possessing the principle of movement and of generation, the female as possessing that of matter. One is most likely to be convinced of this by considering how the semen is formed and whence it comes; for although the things that are formed in the course of Nature no doubt take their rise out of semen, we must not fail to notice how the semen itself is formed from the male and the female, since it is because this part is secreted from the male and the female, and because its secretion takes place in them and out of them, that the male and the female are the principles of generation. By a "male" animal we mean one which generates in another, by "female" one which generates in itself. This is why in cosmology too they speak of the nature of the earth as something female and call it "mother," while they give to the heaven and the sun and anything else of that kind the title of "generator," and "father."

Now male and female differ in respect of their *logos* in that the power or faculty possessed by the one differs from that possessed by the other; but they differ also to bodily sense, in respect of certain physical parts. They differ in their *logos*, because the male is that which has the power to generate in another (as was stated above), while the female is that which can generate in itself, i.e., it is that out of which the generated offspring, which is present in the generator, comes into being. . . . [23]

This much is evident: the menstrual fluid is a residue, and it is the analogous thing in females to the semen in males. Its behavior shows that this statement is correct. At the same time of life that semen begins to appear in males and is emitted, the menstrual discharge begins to flow in females, their voice changes and their breasts begin to become conspicuous; and similarly, in the decline of life the power to generate ceases in males and the menstrual discharge ceases in females. Here are still further indications that this secretion which females produce is a residue. Speaking generally, unless the menstrual discharge is suspended, women are not troubled by hemorrhoids or bleeding from the nose or any other such discharge, and if it happens that they are, then the evacuations fall off in quantity, which suggests that the substance secreted is being drawn off to the other discharges. Again, their blood vessels are not so prominent as those of males; and females are more neatly made and smoother than males, because the residue which goes to produce those characteristics in males is in females discharged together with the menstrual fluid. We are bound to hold, in addition, that for the same cause the bulk of the body in female Vivipara is smaller than that of the males, as of course it is only in Vivipara that the menstrual discharge flows externally, and most conspicuously of all in women, who discharge a greater amount than any other female animals. On this account it is always very noticeable that the female is pale, and the blood-vessels are not prominent, and there is an obvious deficiency in physique as compared with males.

Now it is impossible that any creature should produce two seminal secretions at once, and as the secretion in females which answers to semen in males is the menstrual fluid, it obviously follows that the female does not contribute any semen to generation; for if there were semen, there would be no menstrual fluid; but as menstrual fluid is in fact formed, therefore there is no semen. . . .

There are some who think that the female contributes semen during coition because women sometimes derive pleasure from it comparable to that of the male and also produce a fluid secretion. This fluid, however, is not seminal; it is peculiar to the part from which it comes in each several individual; there is a discharge from the uterus, which though it happens in some women does not in others. Speaking generally, this happens in fair-skinned women who are typically feminine, and not in dark women of a masculine appearance. Where it occurs, this discharge is sometimes on quite a different scale from the semen discharged by the male, and greatly exceeds it in bulk. Furthermore, differences of food cause a great difference in the amount of this discharge which is produced: e.g., some pungent foods cause a noticeable increase in the amount. . . .

Further, a boy actually resembles a woman in physique, and a woman is as it were an infertile male; the female, in fact, is female on account of inability of a sort, viz., it lacks the power to concoct semen out of the final state of the nourishment (this is either blood, or its counterpart in bloodless animals) because of the coldness of its nature. Thus, just as lack of concoction produces in the bowels diarrhea, so in the blood vessels it produces discharges of blood of various sorts, and especially the menstrual discharge (which has to be classed as a discharge of blood, though it is a natural discharge, and the rest are morbid ones).

Hence, plainly, it is reasonable to hold that generation takes place from this process; for, as we see, the menstrual fluid is semen, not indeed semen in a pure condition, but needing still to be acted upon. It is the same with fruit when it is forming. The nourishment is present right enough, even before it has been strained off, but it stands in need of being acted upon in order to purify it. That is why when the former is mixed with the semen, and when the latter is mixed with pure nourishment the one effects generation, and the other effects nutrition....

Now the opinion that the cause of male and female is heat and cold, and that the difference depends upon whether the secretion comes from the right side or from the left, has a modicum of reason in it, because the right side of the body is hotter than the left; hotter semen is semen which has been concocted; the fact that it has been concocted means that it has been set and compacted, and the more compacted semen is, the more fertile it is. All the same, to state the matter in this way is attempting to lay hold of the cause from too great a distance, and we ought to come as closely to grips as we possibly can with the primary causes.

We have dealt already elsewhere with the body as a whole and with its several parts, and have stated what each one is, and on account of what cause it is so. But that is not all, for (1) the male and the female are distinguished by a certain ability and inability. Male is that which is able to concoct, to cause to take shape, and to discharge, semen possessing the "principle" of the "form"; and by "principle" I do not mean that sort of principle out of which, as out of matter, offspring is formed belonging to the same kind as its parent, but I mean the *proximate motive principle*, whether it is able to act thus in itself or in something else. Female is that which receives the semen, but is unable to cause semen to take shape or to discharge it. And (2) all concoction works by means of heat. Assuming the truth of these two statements, it follows of necessity that (3) male animals are hotter than female ones, since it is on account of coldness and inability that the female is more abundant in blood in certain regions of the body. And this abundance of blood is a piece of evidence which goes to prove the opposite of the view held by some people, who suppose that the female must be hotter than the male, on account of the discharge of menstrual fluid.

When the "principle" is failing to gain the mastery and is unable to effect concoction owing to deficiency of heat, and does not succeed in reducing the material into its own proper form, but instead is worsted in the attempt, then of necessity the material must change over into its opposite condition. Now the opposite of the male is the female, and it is opposite in respect of that whereby one is male and the other female. And since it differs in the ability it possesses, so also it differs in the instrument which it possesses. Hence this is the condition into which the material changes over. And when one vital part changes, the whole make-up of the animal differs greatly in appearance and form. This may be observed in the case of eunuchs; the mutilation of just one part of them results in such a great alteration of their old semblance, and in close approximation to the appearance of the female. The reason for this is that some of the body's parts are "principles," and once a principle has been "moved" (i.e., changed), many of the parts which cohere with it must of necessity change as well. . . .

Also, the fact that the menstrual discharge in the natural course tends to take place when the moon is waning is due to the same cause. That time of month is colder and more fluid on account of the waning and failure of the moon (since the moon makes a summer and winter in the course of a month just as the sun does in the course of the whole year). . . .

So that if you reckon up (a) that the brain itself has very little heat, (b) that the skin surrounding it must of necessity have even less, and (c) that the hair, being the furthest off of the three, must have even less still, you will expect persons who are plentiful in semen to go bald at about this time of life.[24] And it is owing to the same cause that it is on the front part of the head only that human beings go bald, and that they are the only animals which do so at all; i.e., they go bald in front because the brain is there, and they alone do so, because they have by far the largest brain of all and the most fluid. Women do not go bald because their nature is similar to that of children: both are incapable of producing seminal secretion. Eunuchs, too, do not go bald, because of their transition into the female state, and the hair that comes at a later stage they fail to grow at all, or if they already have it, they lose it, except for the pubic hair: similarly, women do not have the later hair, though they do grow the pubic hair. This deformity constitutes a change from the male state to the female.

iii. Hippocrates, *On the Generating Seed and the Nature of the Child* 4-7, 13, 30.[25]

Doctors, who were throughout antiquity with very few exceptions male (see p. 172 below), concerned themselves only with *diseases*. The normal female functions of menstruation, childbirth, nursing, menopause, were dealt with by women—midwives and wet-nurses. Hence few records exist of normal procedures and reactions.

Now as regards women in copulation, I assert that when the genitals are rubbed and the womb agitated, there occurs in it a sort of tickling sensation, and the rest of the body derives pleasure and warmth from it. The woman has also a discharge that flows from the body sometimes into the womb so that the womb becomes moist, sometimes outside the womb too when the opening of the womb is wider than it ought to be. She feels pleasure from the beginning of intercourse all the time until the man lets her go; if she is hot for intercourse, she discharges before the man and no longer has the same enjoyment; if she is not in heat, her pleasure ceases with that of the man. The thing is this. Just as, if one pours into boiling water other cold water, the water stops boiling, in the same way the male semen when it is ejaculated into the womb extinguishes the heat and the pleasure of the woman. The pleasure and the heat first flare up when the semen is ejaculated into the womb, and then cease. Just as, if one pours wine on a flame, the flame first flares up and is for a moment increased by the poured wine, then ceases; in the same way the woman's heat flares up in response to the male semen and then ceases. In copulation, the woman has much less pleasure than the man, but she had it for a longer time than the man. The reason why the man has more pleasure is that the separation from the fluid occurs suddenly in him as a result of a more powerful perturbation than the woman's. Here is another trait in women. If they have relations with men, their health is better; worse, if they do not have them. For the womb becomes moist during intercourse and ceases to be dry; but if it is dryer than it ought to be, it contracts powerfully, and the powerful contraction causes bodily pain. At the same time, by heating the blood and making it more fluid, copulation provides easier passage for the menstrual discharge; moreover, if the menstrual discharge does not pass, women's bodies become unhealthy.…

If after intercourse, the woman is not going to conceive, the semen from both usually passes out at her will. If, on the other hand, she is going to conceive, the semen does not pass out but stays in the womb. For the womb after receiving it and closing keeps it inside, the orifice being clogged by the sticky fluid; and a mixture is effected of that which comes from the man and that which comes from the woman. If the woman has had experience with childbirth and observes when the semen does not pass out but remains, she will know on what day she conceived.

The following is furthermore to be noted. The seed of the woman is sometimes stronger, sometimes weaker; the same holds for the man. In the man there is female seed and male seed in the same way in the woman. The male seed is stronger than the female. For of necessity the male develops from the stronger seed. And here is another point. If the seed that comes from both is strong, a male is born, if weak, a female is born. Whichever prevails in quantity, that is what is born; for if the weak seed is much more abundant than the strong, the strong is overpowered and, being mixed with the weak, is diverted to female; if the strong is more abundant than the weak, and the weak is overpowered, this is diverted to male....

Now it is possible to conclude from what is seen to occur that both in the woman and in the man there is seed both of female and of male. For many women who had given birth to females with particular men have given birth to males when they passed to other men; and these same men with whom the women had been given birth to females, when they came to copulate with other women, begot male offspring, when they copulated with other women, produced female offspring. This account shows that both the man and the woman have both female seed and male. For in the case of men with whom they gave birth to female children, the stronger seed was overpowered since there was more of the weak, and females were born; in the case of men with whom they gave birth to males, the stronger predominated, and males were born. The same man does not always supply either strong seed or weak, but different sperm at different times. It is the same way with women. It is, therefore, not surprising that the same women and the same men produce both male and female offspring. The same thing is true of the generation of males and females in the case of livestock....

I myself have seen some semen which had stayed six days in the womb and which fell out; and it is from the qualities that it in my judgment exhibited at that time, that I now draw my remaining evidence. I shall explain how I came to see a six-day-old semen. A woman I knew owned a high-priced musical entertainer who kept company with men, and who had to avoid pregnancy so as not to be rated lower. That girl had heard what women say among themselves to the effect that, when a woman is going to conceive, the semen does not pass out but stays inside. Having heard this, she marked it and always kept watch. And when she noticed one time that the semen did not pass out, she told her mistress, and the report reached me. And I thereupon told her to jump in such a way that the heels touched the buttocks; she had now jumped seven times when the semen fell to the ground with a plop.[26] And when the woman saw this, she stared at it and exclaimed. I shall tell what it was like. It looked as if someone had removed the outer shell from a raw egg and through the inner membrane could be seen within it the inner liquid. Such was in brief its appearance. It was also red and roundish; within the membrane white thick fibers were visible, enclosed together with a thick and red, bloodlike fluid; around the membrane on the outside there were blood clots; in the middle of the membrane something thin was detached which seemed to me to be the navel, and I thought it provided a means of inbreathing and outbreathing for the semen at the start. From it extended the entire membrane enveloping the semen. That is what the six-day-old semen that I saw was like. A little later I will describe another test in addition to this one, that will enable anyone who seeks knowledge to see this for himself, as well as a proof that my whole discourse is correct, as far as that is possible for a mortal discussing such a matter. That completes my statement on this subject....

I shall now relate why pregnancy does not last more than ten months. The nourishment and the material for growth that descend from the mother are no longer sufficient for the child when ten months have passed and the embryo has grown. For it absorbs the sweetest part of the blood and also gets a little food from the milk. But whenever these sources become inadequate for it and the child is full-grown, it craves more nourishment than actually is available, and so strikes out and bursts the membranes. Now women in their first pregnancy are more affected than others by this condition, for in their case there is insufficient nourishment for the children to last for the ten months. There is insufficient food for the following reason. There are women in whom the monthly purge is adequate and others in whom it is too scanty. If this always happens, it is a natural and generic trait inherited from their mothers. But those who have a scanty menstrual discharge, they too supply too little nourishment for the children towards the end of the period when they are now full-grown, and so cause them to strike out and be in haste to come forth before the ten months; for blood comes from the mother in too small amount. Generally also the women who have a scanty menstrual discharge are more liable to have no milk; they are very dry and of compact flesh.

iv. Hippocrates, *Nature of Women* 98 (Contraception)

If a woman does not want to become pregnant, make as thick a mixture of beans and water as you can, make her drink it, and she will not become pregnant for a year.[27]

v. Hippocrates, *Diseases of Women* I, tr. A. Hanson, *Signs* 1 (1975). © by The University of Chicago Press.

Problems with the female organs effect the functioning of the entire organism. Cures are based on the premise that the sexual act and pregnancy (or simulation thereof, such as digital manipulation or the insertion of pessaries) can restore health.

1. The following concerns women's diseases. I say that a woman who has never given birth suffers more intensely and more readily from menstruation than a woman who has given birth to a child. For whenever a woman does give birth, her small vessels become more easy-flowing for menstruation [because the birth process stretches the vessels and so makes menstruation easier.]...

I say that a woman's flesh is more sponge-like and softer than a man's: since this is so, the woman's body draws moisture both with more speed and in greater quantity from the belly than does the body of a man....

And when the body of a woman — whose flesh is soft — happens to be full of blood and if that blood does not go off from her body, pain occurs, whenever her flesh is full and beomes heated. A woman has warmer blood and therefore she is warmer than a man. If the existing surplus of blood should go off, no pain results from the blood. Because a man has more solid flesh than a woman, he is never so totally overfilled with blood that pain results if some of his blood does not exit each month. He draws whatever quantity of blood is needed for his body's nourishment; since his body is not soft, it does not become overstrained nor is it heated up by fullness, as in the case of a woman. The fact that a man works harder than a woman contributes greatly to this; for hard work draws off some of the fluid.

2. Whenever in a woman who has never given birth the menses are suppressed and cannot find a way out, illness results. This happens if the mouth of the womb is closed or if some part of her vagina is prolapsed. For if one of these things happens,

the menses will not be able to find a way out until the womb returns to a healthy state. This disease occurs more frequently in women who have a womb narrow at the mouth or who have a cervix which lies far away from the vagina. For if either of these conditions exists and if the woman in question does not have intercourse and if her belly is more emptied than usual from some suffering, the womb is displaced.[28] The womb is not damp of its own accord (as, for example, in the case of a woman who does not have coitus) and there is empty space for the womb (as, for example, when the belly is more empty than usual) so that the womb is displaced when the woman is drier and more empty than normal.

There are also occasions when, after the womb is displaced, the mouth happens to be turned too far, such as in a case where the cervix lies far away from the vagina. But if her womb is damp from coitus and her belly is not empty, her womb is not easily displaced.

The following things also happen. For some women, when two months' menses are accumulated in quantity in the womb, they move off into the lungs whenever they are prevented from exiting. The woman suffers all the symptoms which have been mentioned in the discussion of phthisis and she cannot survive.

6. If a woman is healthy, her blood flows like that from a sacrificial animal and it speedily coagulates. Those women who habitually menstruate for longer than four days and whose menses flow in great abundance, are delicate and their embryos are delicate and waste away. But those women whose menstruation is less than three days or is meager, are robust, with a healthy complexion and a masculine appearance; yet they are not concerned about bearing children nor do they become pregnant.

7. If suffocation occurs suddenly, it will happen especially to women who do not have intercourse and to older women rather than to young ones, for their wombs are lighter. It usually occurs because of the following: when a woman is empty and works harder than in her previous experience, her womb, becoming heated from the hard work, turns because it is empty and light. There is, in fact, empty space for it to turn in because the belly is empty. Now when the womb turns, it hits the liver and they go together and strike against the abdomen—for the womb rushes and goes upward toward the moisture, because it has been dried out by hard work, and the liver is, after all, moist. When the womb hits the liver, it produces sudden suffocation as it occupies the breathing passage around the belly.

Sometimes, at the same time the womb begins to go toward the liver, phlegm flows down from the head to the abdomen (that is, when the woman is experiencing the suffocation) and sometimes, simultaneously with the flow of phlegm, the womb goes away from the liver to its normal place and the suffocation ceases. The womb goes back, then, when it has taken on moisture and has become heavy.... Sometimes, if a woman is empty and she overworks, her womb turns and falls toward the neck of her bladder and produces strangury—but no other malady seizes her. When such a woman is treated, she speedily becomes healthy; sometimes recovery is even spontaneous.

In some women the womb falls toward the lower back or toward the hips because of hard work or lack of food, and produces pain.

21. Now I shall discuss the diseases of pregnant women. Some women conceive a child easily, but are not able to carry it full term; the children are lost through miscarriage in the third or fourth month—even though the woman has suffered no physical injury nor eaten the wrong kind of food. In such women the cause of the circumstances mentioned is especially when the womb releases matter which would make the embryo grow. The woman's bowels become upset: weakness, high fever, and lack of appetite affect them during the time in which they are aborting their children. The following is also a cause, namely if the womb is smooth—either naturally or due to the presence of lacerations in the womb. Now if the womb is smooth, sometimes the membranes which envelop the child are detached from the womb when the child begins to move—because these membranes are less a part of the womb than they ought to be, due to the fact that the womb is smooth. Anyone would know all these details if he would carefully ask about them. Insofar as the smoothness of the womb is concerned, let another woman touch the womb when it is empty, for the smoothness is not immediately distinguishable. If the menses flow in these women, they come copiously. Occasionally some of these women carry their embryos to full term, and when such women are cared for, they have hope of a normal birth.

25. I say that if menses flow each month for a woman who is two or three months pregnant or more, she is necessarily thin and weak. Occasionally a fever grips her during the days until the menses flow. When the menstrual blood flows, she becomes pale, yet very little flows out. Her womb has come to gape open

more than it ought to and it releases matter which would make the embryo grow. Blood comes down from all the body when a woman is pregnant and gradually enters the womb, encircling that which is inside it; the blood makes it grow. But if the womb gapes open more than it should, it releases the blood each month just as it has been accustomed to do in the past, and that which is in the womb becomes thin and weak. When such a woman is cared for, the embryo also is better and the woman herself is healthy. If she is not cared for, she loses her child and, in addition, she runs the risk of having a long-lasting disease....

There are also many other dangers by which embryos are aborted: if, for example, a pregnant woman is sick and weak, and if she picks up a burden with all her bodily strength, or if she is beaten, or leaps into the air, or goes without food, or has a fainting spell, or takes too much or too little nourishment, or becomes frightened and scared, or shouts violently. Nurture is a cause of miscarriage, and so is a excessive drink. Wombs by themselves also have natural dispositions by which miscarriage can occur: wombs that are flatulent, for example, or tightly packed, loose, overly large, overly small, and other types which are similar.

If a pregnant woman feels distressed in her belly or in her lower back, one must fear lest the embryo bring on a miscarriage, since the membranes which surround it have been broken.

There are also women who lose their children if they eat or drink something pungent or something bitter contrary to their usual habits—if the child is in an early stage of its development. For whenever something happens to a child contrary to its usual habits, it will die when it is little, especially if the mother drinks or eats the kind of thing that strongly upsets her stomach when the child is in an early stage of development. For the womb perceives when a diarrhetic flux comes down from the belly.

33. If in the case of a pregnant woman the time for birth is already past, if labor pains are present, and if for a long time the woman has been unable to bring forth the child without injury to herself, usually the child is coming in lateral or breech position—yet it is better for it to come out head-first. The pain involved is of the following sort: as if, for example, someone would throw an olive pit into a small-mouthed oil flask, the pit is not naturally suited to be taken out when it is turned on its

side. In this way, then, the birth of the embryo laterally presented is also a very painful experience for the woman; it just doesn't go out. The pains are even more difficult if the embryo proceeds feet-first; many times the women die or the children or even both. A major cause of the embryo not going out easily is if it is dead, or paralysed, or if there are two of them.

62. All these diseases, then, happen more frequently to women who have not borne a child, yet they also happen to those who have. These diseases are dangerous, as has been said, and for the most part they are both acute and serious, and difficult to understand because of the fact that women are the ones who share these sicknesses. Sometimes women do not know what sickness they have, until they have experienced the diseases which come from menses and they become older. Then both necessity and time teach them the cause of their sicknesses. Sometimes diseases become incurable for women who do not learn why they are sick before the doctor has been correctly taught by the sick woman why she is sick. For women are ashamed to tell even of their inexperience and lack of knowlege. At the same time the doctors also make mistakes by not learning the apparent cause through accurate questioning, but they proceeed to heal as though they were dealing with men's diseases. I have already seen many women die from just this kind of suffering. But at the outset one must ask accurate questions about the cause. For the healing of the diseases of women differs greatly from the healing of men's diseases.

B. TYPES OF HYSTERIA ("WOMBINESS"): CAUSES AND CURES

i. Hysterical Suffocation
Hippocrates, *Diseases of Women* II. 126, 123

When the womb remains in the upper abdomen, the suffocation is similar to that caused by the purgative hellebore, with stiff breathing and sharp pains in the heart. Some women spit up acid saliva, and their mouths are full of fluid, and their legs become cold. In other cases, if the womb does not leave the upper abdomen directly, the women lose their voices, and their head and tongue are overcome by drowsiness. If you find such women unable to speak and with their teeth chattering, insert a pessary of wool, twisting it round the shaft of a feather in order to get it in as far as possible—dip it either in white Egyptian perfume or myrtle or bacchar or marjoram. Use a spatula to apply black medicine (the kind you use for the head) to her nostrils. If this is not available, wipe the inside of her nostrils with silphion, or insert a feather that you have dipped in vinegar, or induce sneezing. If her mouth is closed tight and she is unable to speak, make her drink castoreum in wine. Dip your finger in seal oil and wipe inside her nostrils. Insert a wool pessary, until the womb returns, and remove it when the symptoms disappear. But if, when you take the pessary out, the womb returns to the upper abdomen, insert the pessary as you did before, and apply beneath her nostrils fumigations of ground-up goat or deer horn, to which you have added hot ashes, so that they make as much smoke as possible, and have her inhale the vapor up through her nose as long as she can stand it. It is best to use a fumigation of seal oil: put the coals in a pot and wrap the woman up—except for her head. So that as much vapor as possible is emitted, drip a little fat on it, and have her inhale the vapor. She should keep her mouth shut. This is the procedure if the womb has fallen upward out of place.

*

When the womb moves toward her head and suffocation occurs in that region, the woman's head becomes heavy, though there are different symptoms in some cases. One symptom: the woman says the veins in her nose hurt her and beneath her eyes, and she becomes sleepy, and when this condition is alleviated, she foams at the mouth.

You should wash her thoroughly with hot water, and if she does not respond, with cold, from her head on down, using cool water in which you have previously boiled laurel and myrtle. Rub her head with rose perfume, and use sweet scented fumigations beneath her vagina, but foul-scented ones at her nose. She should eat cabbage, and drink cabbage juice.

ii. Dislocated Womb
Hippocrates, *Nature of Women 8 and 3*

If her womb moves toward her hips, her periods stop coming, and pain develops in her lower stomach and abdomen. If you touch her with your finger, you will see the mouth of the womb turned toward her hip.[29]

When this condition occurs, wash the woman with warm

water, make her eat as much garlic as she can, and have her drink undiluted sheep's milk after her meals. Then fumigate her and give her a laxative. After the laxative has taken effect, fumigate the womb once again, using a preparation of fennel and absinthe mixed together. Right after the fumigation, pull the mouth of the womb with your finger. Then insert a pessary made with squills; leave it in for a while, and then insert a pessary made with opium poppies. If you think the condition has been corrected, insert a pessary of bitter almond oil, and on the next day, a pessary of rose perfume. She should stop inserting pessaries on the first day of her period, and start again the day after it stops. The blood during the period provides a normal interruption. If there is no flow, she should drink four cantharid beetles with their legs, wings and head removed, four dark peony seeds, cuttlefish eggs, and a little parsley seed in wine. If she has pain and irregular flow, she should sit in warm water, and drink honey mixed with water. If she is not cured by the first procedure, she should drink it again, until her period comes. When it comes, she should abstain from food and have intercourse with her husband. During her period she should eat mercury plant, and boiled squid, and keep to soft foods. If she becomes pregnant she will be cured of this disease.

*

When her womb moves towards her liver, she suddenly loses her voice and her teeth chatter and her coloring turns dark. This condition can occur suddenly, while she is in good health. The problem particularly affects old maids and widows—young women who have been widowed after having had children.

When this condition occurs, push your hand down below her liver, and tie a bandage below her ribs. Open her mouth and pour in very sweet-scented wine; put applications on her nostrils and burn foulscented vapors below her womb.

iii. Dropsy in the Womb
Hippocrates, *Nature of Women* 2.

When there is a dropsy in her womb, her monthly periods become smaller and weaker, and then stop suddenly, and her stomach bloats up, and her breasts dry out, and everything else suffers, and she seems to be pregnant—this is how you know she has dropsy. A further indication is the condition of the mouth of the womb: when she touches it, it seems withered. Fever and swelling attack her. As time goes on, pain develops in her lower stomach and loins and abdomen. This disease is usually brought on by miscarriage, but there are other causes.

When swelling in the womb occurs, one should wash the woman with warm water and apply warm poultices where she has pain. One should make her drink a laxative. After the laxative, put her in a vapor bath made with cow dung, then insert a pessary made with cantharid beetle, and after three days, a pessary made of bile. Leave this in for one day, and then after three days give her a vinegar douche. Then if her stomach becomes soft and her fever goes away, and her period comes, have her sleep with her husband. If not, follow the previous procedure over again, until her period comes, and have her use some suppositories. In the days between suppositories have her drink samphire bark and dark peony berries, and eat as much mercury plant as possible, and garlic both raw and cooked. Have her eat soft foods such as squid and other soft animals. If she gives birth, she will be cured.

C. CASE HISTORIES

V.

i. Hippocrates, Epidemics V. 12 and 25

In Pheres a woman for a long time had headaches and no one could help her at all, not even when she had her head drained. It was easier for her when her period passed easily. When she had a headache, scented pessaries in her womb were helpful, and she was drained [of the fluid in her head] somewhat. But when she became pregnant, her headaches disappeared.

In Larissa a servant in Dyseris' household, when she was young, suffered severe labor pains whenever she had intercourse—otherwise she had no pains. She had never been pregnant. When she was sixty, she felt labor pains in the middle of the day, as severe as if in childbirth. Before that she had eaten a large number of leeks. When a pain came that was more severe than any she had had before, she stood up and felt something rough in the mouth of her womb. Then, after she had fainted, another woman inserted her hand and squeezed out a rough stone, like the whorl of a spindle. And the woman recovered immediately and stayed well thereafter.

ii. Peek 1237, Egypt, second/first century B.C.

A child Dosithea, daughter of—. Look at these letters on the polished rock. Thallus' son Chaeremon married me in his great house. I die in pain, escaping the pangs of childbirth, fifteen years old, from a disease which my brother died of before, and I succumbed after. I lie here in Schedes. This is my tomb.

iii. IG XII 5, 310 (in part); second century B.C.

Nicander was my father, my country was Paros, and my name Socratea. My husband Parmenion buried me when I died, granting me that favor so that my seemly life might be remembered even among those to come. The Erinys of bearing a child (which none can guard against) destroyed my pleasant life through a hemorrhage. Nor by my travail could I bring the baby into the light, but he lies here among the dead in my own womb.

6. DAILY LIFE

A. AN ENCOUNTER IN A MEADOW

The male narrator of the poem propositions a young woman, but promises to avoid penetration.

Archilochus; Cologne papyrus inv. no. 7511.

"...totally keeping yourself, and I'd hold out to do the same;
but if you are pressed, if your heart drives hard,
  here in our household there is—and wants so much to marry
now—a lovely, tender girl: you won't, I think,
  find any fault in her looks. Make her, not me, your very own."
So much she said. I answered point for point:
"Daughter of Amphimedo, that woman excellent and wise
whom now the moldering earth keeps down below,
  many delights are derived from Aphrodite for young men
besides the main one. One of those will do;
  while as for this, in good time, whenever you have grapes
grown ripe, both you and I, god willing, will decide.
  I'm going to do as you say: you think I'm pressing very hard;
but here beneath the rim and shading gates

don't make a thing of it, dear, since I will keep my course to
grassy gardens—that for now. Neobule, no!

Somebody else marry her! *Aiai*! She's more than overripe: her
girlhood flower has withered and dropped off,

also the grace that was there. Her fill she never ever got; the
woman's crazed; she long since showed her prime.

Out to the crows! Keep her off! May never he who rules the
gods decree that I, for keeping one like her,

stand as a neighborhood butt. Instead I much prefer you, for
you are neither faithless nor two-faced.

She, though, is only too keen, makes many men her very own.
I fear I'd get a misfit—premature—

pressing on quickly with her: just like the hasty bitch, blind
pups." So much I said, but then I took the girl

into the flowers in bloom and laid her down, protecting her
with my soft cloak, her neck held in my arms.

Though out of fear like a fawn she hindered, I encouraged her
and her breasts with my hands I gently grasped.

She, then and there, herself showed young flesh—the onset of
her prime—and, all her lovely body fondling, I

also let go with my force, just touching, though, her tawny
down.

B. ON TRAINING A WIFE.

Xenophon *Oeconomicus* 7-10.
VII

Seeing him then one day sitting in the colonnade of Zeus the
Deliverer, I went over to him, and as he seemed to be at leisure,
I sat down with him and spoke. "Why are you sitting like this,
Ischomachos, you who are so unaccustomed to leisure? For I
mostly see you either doing something or at least hardly at
leisure in the market place."

"Nor would you see me now, Socrates," said Ischomachos, "if I
hadn't made an appointment to meet some foreigners here."

"When you aren't doing this sort of thing," I said, "by the
gods, how do you spend your time and what do you do?" ...

"As to what you asked me, Socrates," he said, "I never spend
time indoors. Indeed," he said, "my wife is quite able by herself
to manage the things within the house."

"It would please me very much, Ischomachos," I said, "if I

might also inquire about this—whether you yourself educated your wife to be the way she ought to be, or whether, when you took her from her mother and father, she already knew how to manage the things that are appropriate to her."

"How, Socrates," he said, "could she have known anything when I took her, since she came to me when she was not yet fifteen, and had lived previously under diligent supervision in order that she might see and hear as little as possible and ask the fewest possible questions? Doesn't it seem to you that one should be content if she came knowing only how to take the wool and make clothes, and had seen how the spinning work is distributed among the female attendants? For as to matters of the stomach, Socrates," he said, "she came to me very finely educated; and to me, at any rate, that seems to be an education of the greatest importance both for a man and a woman."

"And in other respects, Ischomachos," I said, "did you yourself educate your wife to be capable of concerning herself with what's appropriate to her?"

"By Zeus," said Ischomachos, "not until I had sacrificed and prayed that I might succeed in teaching, and she in learning, what is best for both of us."

"Didn't your wife sacrifice with you and pray for these same things?" I said.

"Certainly," said Ischomachos; "she promised before the gods that she would become what she ought to be, and made it evident that she would not neglect the things she was being taught."

"By the gods, Ischomachos," I said, "relate to me what you first began teaching her. I'd listen to you relating these things with more pleasure than if you were telling me about the finest contest in wrestling or horsemanship."

And Ischomachos replied: "Well, Socrates," he said, "when she had gotten accustomed to me and had been domesticated to the extent that we could have discussions, I questioned her somewhat as follows. 'Tell me, woman, have you thought yet why it was that I took you and your parents gave you to me? That it was not for want of someone else to spend the night with —this is obvious, I know, to you too. Rather, when I considered for myself, and your parents for you, whom we might take as the best partner for the household and children, I chose you, and your parents, as it appears, from among the possibilities chose me. Should a god grant us children, we will then consider, with respect to them, how we may best educate them; for this too is a good common to us—to obtain the best allies and the best supporters in old age; but for the present this household is what is common to us. As to myself, everything of mine I declare to be in common, and as for you, everything you've brought you have deposited in common. It's not necessary to calculate which of us has contributed the greater number of things, but it is necessary to know this well, that whichever of us is the better partner will be the one to contribute the things of greater worth.' To this, Socrates, my wife replied: 'What can I do to help you?' she said. 'What is my capacity? But everything depends on you: my work, my mother told me, is to be moderate.' 'By Zeus, woman,' I said, 'my father told me the same thing. But it's for moderate people—for man and woman alike— not only to keep their substance in the best condition but also to add as much as possible to it by fine and just means.' 'Then what do you see,' said my wife, 'that I might do to help in increasing the household?' 'By Zeus,' I said, 'just try to do in the best manner possible what the gods have brought you forth to be capable of and what the law praises.' 'And what are these things?' she said. 'I suppose they are things of no little worth,' I said, 'unless, of course, the leading bee in the hive also has charge of works of little worth. For it seems to me, woman, that the gods have used great consideration in joining together the pair called male and female so that it may be of the greatest benefit to itself in its community. First, that the races of living things may not be extinguished, the pair is brought together for the production of children; then, from this pairing it is given to human beings at least to possess supporters in old age; but then the way of life of human beings is not, as is that of cattle, in the open air, but evidently needs shelter. Still, if human beings are going to have something to bring into the dwellings, someone is needed to work in the open air. For plowing the fallow, sowing, planting, and herding are all works of the open air, and from them the necessary things are gotten. But when these things have been brought into the dwelling, someone is needed to keep them secure and to do the works that need shelter. The rearing of newborn children also needs shelter; shelter is needed for the making of bread from the crop, and similarly for the working of clothes from wool. Since, then, work and diligence are needed both for the indoor and for the outdoor things, it seems to me that the god directly prepared the woman's nature for indoor works and indoor concerns. For he equipped the man, in body and in soul, with a greater capacity to endure cold and heat, journeys and expeditions, and so has ordered him to the outdoor works; but in bringing forth, for the woman, a body that is less capable in these respects, the god has, it seems to me, ordered her to the indoor works. But knowing that he had implanted in the woman, and ordered her to, the nourishment of newborn children, he also gave her a greater affection for the newborn infants than he gave to the man. Since he had also ordered the woman to the guarding of the things brought in, the god, under- standing that a fearful soul is not worse at guarding, also gave the woman a greater share of fear than the man. And knowing too that the one who had the outdoor works would need to defend himself should someone act unjustly, to him he gave a greater share of boldness. But because it's necessary for both to give and to take, he endowed both with memory and diligence in like degree, so that you can't distinguish whether the male or the female kind has the greater share of these things. As for self-control in the necessary things, he endowed both with this too in like degree; and the god allowed the one who proved the better, whether the man or the woman, to derive more from this good. Since, then, the nature of each has not been brought forth to be naturally apt for all of the same things, each has need of the other, and their pairing is more beneficial to each, for where one falls short the other is capable. Now, O woman, as we know what has been ordered to each of us by the god, we must, separately, do what's appropriate to each. The law too praises these things in pairing man and woman; and as the god made them partners in children, so too does the law appoint them partners. And the law shows that what the god has brought forth each to be capable of is fine as well. It is a finer thing for the woman to stay indoors than to spend time in the open, while it is more disgraceful for the man to stay indoors than to con- cern himself with outdoor things. But when someone acts in a way contrary to what the god has brought forth, perhaps in causing some disorder he is noticed by the gods and pays the penalty for neglecting his own works or for doing the woman's works. And it seems to me,' I said, 'that the leader of the bees also toils in this way to accomplish the works that the god has ordered her to do.' 'In what way,' she said, 'are the works of the leader of the bees similar to the works I must do?' 'In that she remains in the hive,' I said, 'and doesn't let the bees be inactive but sends them to the work whenever some are needed to work outside; she knows what each of them brings in, receives it, and keeps it secure until it is needed for use. When the season for using it comes around, she distributes to each what is just. She also has charge of the weaving of the cells inside, to see that they are finely and quickly woven, and when the offspring are born, she is concerned with their nourishment; and once the young are fully grown and able to work, she sends them out as a colony, with one of them as leader.' 'Will it be necessary, then,' said my wife, 'for me to do these things as well?' 'It will be necessary,' I said, 'for you to remain indoors and to send out those of the servants whose work is outside; as for those whose work is to be done inside, these are to be in your charge; you must receive what is brought in and distribute what needs to be expended, and as for what needs to be set aside, you must use forethought and guard against expending in a month what was intended to last a year. When wool is brought to you, it must be your concern that clothes be made for whoever needs them. And it must be your concern that the dry grain be fine and fit for eating. There is one thing, however,' I said, 'among the concerns appropriate to you, that will perhaps seem less agreeable: whenever any of the servants become ill, it must be your concern that all be attended.' 'By Zeus,' said my wife, 'that will be most agreeable, at least if those who have been well tended are going to be grateful and feel more good will than before.' I admired her reply," said Ischomachos, "and spoke: 'Isn't it through this kind of forethought that the leader of the hive so disposes the other bees to her that when she leaves the hive, not one of the bees supposes they must let her go, but rather they all follow?' My wife replied: 'I wonder whether the works of the leader are not rather yours than mine. For my guarding and distribution of the indoor things would look somewhat ridiculous, I suppose, if it weren't your concern to bring in something from outside.' 'On the other hand,' I said, 'it would look ridiculous for me to bring anything in if there weren't someone to keep secure what had been brought in. Don't you see,' I said, 'how those who are said to draw water with a leaking jar are to be pitied, since they seem to toil in vain?' 'By Zeus,' said my wife, 'they are miserable indeed, if this is what they do.' 'Other private concerns will prove pleasant for you, woman,' I said, 'as when you take someone who knows nothing of spinning and make her knowledgeable, so that she is worth twice as much to you; or when you take someone who knows nothing of housekeeping or waiting and make her a knowledgeable, trusted, and skilled waiting maid, worth any sum; or when you're allowed to treat well those who are both moderate and beneficial to your household, and to punish anyone who looks to be wicked. But the most pleasant thing of all: if you look to be better than I and make me your servant, you will have no need to fear that with advancing age you will be honored any less in the household, and you may trust that as you grow older, the better a partner you prove to be for me, and for the children the better a guardian of the household, by so much more will you be honored in the household. For the fine and good things increase for human beings, not by ripening like fair fruits, but through the exercise of the virtues in life.' I seem to remember saying such things to her, Socrates, at the time of our first discussion."

"Did you notice, Ischomachos," I said, "that she was stirred to diligence by these things?"

"Yes, by Zeus," said Ischomachos. "I know she once became very upset, and blushed deeply, when she was unable to give me one of the things I had brought in when I asked for it. Seeing she was irritated, I spoke. 'Don't be discouraged, woman,' I said, 'because you can't give me what I happen to ask for. It is indeed clear poverty not to have a thing to use when it's needed; at the same time our present want—to look for something and be unable to find it—is certainly a less painful thing than not to look for it at all, knowing it's not there. But you aren't at fault in this, rather I am, since I handed over these things to you without giving orders as to where each kind of thing should be put, so that you would know where to put them and where to find them again. There is nothing, woman, so useful or fine for human beings as order....

"'That an ordered arrangement of implements is a good, then, and that it is easy to find in the house an advantageous place for each kind of thing, has been established. But how fine it looks, too, when shoes of any kind are set out in a regular manner; it is fine to see clothes of any kind when they are sorted, as also bedcovers, bronze kettles, the things pertaining to the table, and—what of all things would be most ridiculed, not indeed by the solemn man but by the wit—even pots have a graceful look when distinctly arranged. Indeed, all other things look somehow finer when they are kept in order. Each kind of thing looks like a chorus of implements, and even the space between them looks fine, as everything has been kept out of it—just as a circular chorus is not only itself a fine sight, but even the space within it looks pure and fine. If I am speaking the truth, woman,' I said, 'it will be possible for us to try these things without suffering much loss or going to much trouble. Nor should we be discouraged, woman, by the difficulty of finding someone who can learn the places and remember to replace each kind of thing. For we know very well that the whole city has ten thousand times what we have, yet when you tell any one of the servants to buy something for you in the market place, he is never at a loss—every one of them evidently knows where he has to go for each kind of thing. The cause of this is nothing other than that everything is kept ordered in its place. But if someone goes looking for another human being—who may at the same time be looking for him—he very frequently gives up before finding him. And the cause of this is nothing other than that there is no ordered place for their meeting.' As regards the order of implements and their use, I seem to remember discussing with her things of this sort."

"What then, Ischomachos?" I said. "Did your wife seem to listen at all to what you were trying so seriously to teach her?"

"What else did she do if not promise to be diligent, manifest her very great pleasure, as though she had found some easy means out of a difficulty, and ask me to order things separately as quickly as possible in the way I had stated?"

"How, then, Ischomachos," I said, "did you separately order them for her?"

"What else seemed best to me if not to show her first the capacity of the house? For it is not adorned with decorations, Socrates; the rooms were planned and built simply with a view to their being the most advantageous receptacles for the things that would be in them, so that each calls for what is suitable to it. The bedroom, being in an interior part of the house, invites the most valuable bedcovers and implements; the dry parts of the dwelling, the grain; the cool places, the wine; and the well-lighted places, the works and implements that need light. And I displayed to her the areas for the daily use of human beings, furnished so as to be cool in summer and warm in winter. And I displayed to her the house as a whole, and how it lies open to the south—obviously, so as to be well exposed to the sun in winter and well shaded in summer. Then I pointed out to her the women's apartments, separated from the men's by a bolted door, so that nothing may be taken out that shouldn't be and so that the servants may not produce offspring without our knowledge. For the useful ones, for the most part, feel even more good will once they have had children, but when wicked ones are paired together, they become only more resourceful in their bad behavior. When we had gone through these things," he said, "we then proceeded to separate our belongings according to tribes. We began first by collecting whatever we use for sacrifices. After this we distinguished the woman's ornaments for festivals, the man's dress for festivals and war, bedcovers for the women's apartments, bedcovers for the men's apartments, shoes for women, shoes for men. Another tribe consisted of arms, another of instruments for spinning, another of instruments for bread-making, another of instruments for cooking, another of the things for bathing, another of the things for kneading bread, another of the things for the table; and all these things were further divided according to whether they were used every day or only for festivals. We also set apart the expenses for each month from the amount that had been calculated and reserved for the whole year; for in this way we could better see how things would come out at the end. And when we had sorted our belongings according to tribes, we took each kind of thing to its appropriate place. After this, as to the implements the servants use from day to day—those for the making of bread, for cooking, for spinning, and others of this sort—we pointed out to those who would be using them where each must go, handed them over, and gave orders that they be kept secure. Those we use for festivals, for entertaining foreigners, or only from time to time we handed over to the housekeeper, and after pointing out to her their places and counting and making lists of the various kinds of things, we told her to give each what he needed of them, to remember what she had given someone, and when she had got it back, to return it to the place she had taken it from. We chose as housekeeper the one who upon examination seemed to us the most self-controlled as regards food, wine, sleep, and intercourse with men, and who, in addition, seemed to have a good memory and the forethought to avoid punishment for negligence and to consider how, by gratifying us in some way, she might be honored by us in return. We taught her also to feel good will toward us, sharing our delights when we were delighted in some way, and when there was something painful, inviting her aid. We further educated her to be eager to increase the household, making her thoroughly acquainted with it and giving her a share in its prosperity. And we inspired justice in her, honoring the just more than the unjust and displaying to her that they live richer and freer lives than the unjust. We then installed her in the place. But in addition to all these things, Socrates," he said, "I told my wife that there would be no benefit in any of this unless she herself was diligent in seeing that the order is preserved in each thing. I taught her that in the cities subject to good laws the citizens do not think it enough merely to have fine laws, but in addition choose guardians of the laws to examine them, to praise the one who acts lawfully, and to punish the one who acts contrary to the laws. Then I suggested that my wife consider herself a guardian of the laws regarding the things in the house; that she inspect the implements whenever it seems best to her, just as a garrison commander inspects his guards; that she test the fitness of each thing, just as the council tests the fitness of horses and horsemen; and that, like a queen, she praise and honor the deserving, to the limit of her capacity, and rebuke and punish the one who needs such things. In addition, I taught her that she could not be justly annoyed if I gave her many more orders in regard to our possessions than I gave to the servants, displaying to her that the servants share in their master's wealth only to the extent that they carry it, attend to it, or guard it, and that no one of them is allowed to use it unless the lord gives it to him, whereas everything is the master's to use as he wishes. To the one deriving the greatest benefit from its preservation and the greatest harm from its destruction belongs the greatest concern for a thing—this I declared to her."

"What then?" I said. "After your wife had heard these things, Ischomachos, did she at all obey you?"

"What else did she do," he said, "if not tell me I didn't understand her correctly if I supposed that in teaching her to be concerned with our substance I had ordered her to do something hard. For as she told me, it would have been much harder if I had ordered her to neglect her own things than if she were required to concern herself with the goods of the household. For just as it seems natural for a sensible woman to be concerned for her offspring rather than to neglect them, so, she said, it's more pleasant for a sensible woman to be concerned for those of the possessions that delight her because they are her own than to neglect them."

On hearing that his wife had replied to him in this way, I spoke. "By Hera, Ischomachos, you display your wife's manly understanding."

"There are other instances of her high-mindedness that I am willing to relate to you," said Ischomachos, "instances of her obeying me quickly in some matter after hearing it only once."

"In what sort of thing?" I said. "Speak; for to me it is much more pleasant to learn of the virtue of a living woman than to have had Zeuxis display for me the fine likeness of a woman he had painted."

"And yet once, Socrates," he said, "I saw she had applied a good deal of white lead to her face, that she might seem to be fairer than she was, and some dye, so that she would look more flushed than was the truth, and she also wore high shoes, that she might seem taller than she naturally was. 'Tell me, woman,' I said, 'would you judge me more worthy to be loved as a partner in wealth if I showed you our substance itself, didn't boast of having more substance than is really mine, and didn't hide any part of our substance, or if instead I tried to deceive you by saying I have more substance than is really mine and by displaying to you counterfeit money, necklaces of gilt wood, and purple robes that lose their color, and asserting they are genuine?' She broke in straightway. 'Hush,' she said; 'don't you become like that; if you did, I could never love you from my soul.' 'Haven't we also come together, woman,' I said, 'as partners in one another's bodies?' 'Human beings say so, at least,' she said. 'Would I then seem more worthy to be loved,' I said, 'as a partner in the body, if I tried to offer you my body after concerning myself that it be healthy and strong, so that I would really be well complexioned, or if instead I smeared myself with vermilion, applied flesh color beneath the eyes, and then displayed myself to you and embraced you, all the while deceiving you and offering you vermilion to see and touch instead of my own skin?' 'I wouldn't touch vermilion with as much pleasure as I would you,' she said, 'or see flesh color with as much pleasure as your own, or see painted eyes with as much pleasure as your healthy ones.' 'You must believe, woman, that I too am not more pleased by the color of white lead or dye than by your color, but just as the gods have made horses most pleasant to horses, oxen to oxen, and sheep to sheep, so human beings suppose the pure body of a human being is most pleasant. Such deceits may in some way deceive outsiders and go undetected, but when those

84

who are always together try to deceive one another they are
necessarily found out. For either they are found out when they
rise from their beds and before they have prepared themselves,
or they are detected by their sweat or exposed by tears, or they
are genuinely revealed in bathing.'"

"By the gods," I said, "what did she reply to this?"

"What else," he said, "was her reply, if not that she never did
anything of the sort again and tried always to display herself
suitably and in a pure state. At the same time she asked me if I
could not advise her how she might really come to sight as fine
and not merely seem to be. I advised her, Socrates," he said,
"not always to sit about like a slave but to try, with the gods'
help, to stand at the loom like a mistress, to teach others what
she knew better than they, and to learn what she did not know
as well; and also to examine the breadmaker, to watch over the
housekeeper in her distribution of things, and to go about and
investigate whether each kind of thing is in the place it should
be. In this way, it seemed to me, she could both attend to her
concerns and have the opportunity to walk about. And I said it
would be good exercise to moisten and knead the bread and to
shake out and fold the clothes and bedcovers. I said that if she
exercised in this way, she would take more pleasure in eating,
would become healthier, and so would come to sight as better
complexioned in truth. And a wife's looks, when in contrast to a
waiting maid she is purer and more suitably dressed, become
attractive, especially when she gratifies her husband willingly
instead of serving him under compulsion. On the other hand,
women who always sit about in pretentious solemnity lend themselves to comparison with those who use adornments and deceit.
And now, Socrates," he said, "know well, my wife still arranges
her life as I taught her then and as I tell you now."

C. ON CHASTITY

Thesleff pp. 151-54.

Treatise attributed to members of the Pythagorean community in Italy, third-
second centuries, B.C.[30]

In general a woman must be good and orderly—and this no
one can become without virtue.... A woman's greatest virtue is

chastity. Because of this quality she is able to honor and to cherish her own particular husband.

Now some people think that it is not appropriate for a woman to be a philosopher, just as a woman should not be a cavalry officer or a politician.... I agree that *men* should be generals and city officials and politicians, and *women* should keep house and stay inside and receive and take care of their husbands. But I believe that courage, justice, and intelligence are qualities that men and women have in common.... Courage and intelligence are more appropriately male qualities because of the strength of men's bodies and the power of their minds. Chastity is more appropriately female.

Accordingly a woman must learn about chastity and realize what she must do quantitatively and qualitatively to be able to obtain this womanly virtue. I believe that there are five qualifications (1) the sanctity of her marriage bed (2) the cleanliness of her body (3) the manner in which she chooses to leave her house (4) her refusal to participate in secret cults or Cybeline rituals (5) her readiness and moderation in sacrificing to the gods.

Of these the most important quality for chastity is to be pure in respect to her marriage bed, and for her not to have affairs with men from other households. If she breaks the law in this way she wrongs the gods of her family and provides her family and home not with its own offspring but with bastards. She wrongs the gods of her own being, the gods to whom she swore by her own male ancestors and by her relatives to join in the sharing of life and the begetting of children according to law. She wrongs her own fatherland, because she does not abide by its established rules.... She should also consider the following: that there is no means of atoning for this sin; no way she can approach the shrines or the altars of the gods as a pure woman, beloved of god.... The greatest glory a free-born woman can have—her foremost honor—is the witness her own children will give to her chastity towards her husband, the stamp of likeness they bear to the father whose seed produced them....[31]

As far as cleanliness of the body is concerned, the same arguments apply. She should be dressed in white, natural, plain. Her clothes should not be transparent or ornate. She should not put on silken material, but moderate, white-colored clothes. In this way she will avoid being overly dressed or luxurious or made-up, and not give other women cause to be uncomfortably envious.

She should not wear gold or emeralds at all—materialism and extravagance are characteristic of prostitutes.[32] She should not apply imported or artificial coloring to her face—with her own natural coloring, by washing only with water, she can ornament herself with modesty.

Women of importance leave the house to sacrifice to the leading divinity of the community on behalf of themselves and their husbands and their households. They do not leave home at night nor in the evening, and they make their departures from the market-place openly, to attend a religious festival or to make some purchase, accompanied by a single female servant or at most leading two servants by the hand.[33]

They offer prayers at sacrifice to the gods also, to the best of their abilities. They keep away from secret cults and Cybeline orgies in their homes. For public law prevents women from participating in these rites, particularly because these rites encourage drunkenness and ecstasy.[34] The mistress of the house and head of the household should be chaste and untouched in all respects.

D. CONVERSATIONS

i. Herodas, *Mimes* 6.

A poem representing a discussion between two middle-class women about the virtues of a particular dildo, referred to here not by its generic name *olisbos* ("slipper"), but euphemistically as a "pacifier" (*baubon*, from *baubao*, "sleep"), made by a shoemaker named *Kerdon*, "Greedy." The male poet manages to imply that the two famous women poets Nossis and Erinna are collaborators in this dirty little pastime.

KORITTO: Metro, sit down. (To her slave) Get up and give the lady your chair—I have to *tell* her to do everything—you couldn't do anything on your own, could you? Bah, she's a stone, sitting in the house, not a slave. But when I measure out your barley ration you count the crumbs, and if even a little bit falls off the top you complain for the entire day—the walls fall in with your shouting. Oh, now you're polishing and making it shine, you pirate, just when we need it. Offer a prayer to my friend, since without her here you'd have had a taste of my hands.

METRO: Dear Koritto, our necks are worn out by the same

yoke: I bark like a dog yelling at these unmentionable creatures day and night. But the reason I've come to your house—get the hell out of the way, you smart-asses, all ears and tongues, and days-off the rest of the time—please, don't hold back, dear Koritto, who was the man that made the red Pacifier for you?

KORITTO: Metro—you haven't seen it, have you?

METRO: Nossis got it from Erinna a couple of days ago. Mm, a nice gift.

KORITTO: Nossis? Where'd she get it?

METRO: Will you tell on me if I tell you?

KORITTO: By your sweet eyes, dear Metro, nothing you say will be heard escaping from Koritto's mouth.

METRO: Bitas' wife Euboule gave it to her and told her no one should find out about it.

KORITTO: *Women.* That woman will wear me out. She begged me and I took pity on her and gave it to her, Metro, before I could even get to use it myself. And she snatches it away like some hidden treasure and gives it to people who shouldn't get it. A fond farewell to friends like that. She can look for somebody else instead of me. I'm not pleased that she lent my things to Nossis (if I'm complaining more than is right, forgive me, Nemesis). Out of the one thousand I own, I won't give her one, not even if it's a rotten one.

METRO: No, Korrito, don't let anger flare in your nostrils, when you hear of some silly story. It's a respectable woman's duty to put up with anything. I'm the one who's responsible for telling you all about this, and I ought to have my tongue cut out. But remember what I particularly wanted to find out from you? Who made it for you? If you love me, tell me. Why are you looking at me and laughing? Is this the first time you've ever seen me, Metro? Why is it such a thrill for you? Please, Koritto, don't hold back, and tell me who made it.

KORITTO: Oh, why plead with me? Kerdon made it.

METRO: Who? tell me! Kerdon? There are two Kerdons. One has grey eyes, Myrtaline's neighbor (Kylaethis' friend). But he couldn't sew a plectrum to a lyre. The other one lives near Hermodorus' tenement houses, as you go out from Main Street. He was somebody once, but now he's gotten old. The old lady, Kylaethis, used to use him. (Piously) Her friends and family remember her in death.

KORITTO: As you say, Metro, it isn't either of *them.* He is—I don't know, either from Chios or Erythrae, bald, a little man.

You'd say he was Prexinus—they're as alike as fig and fig, except when he talks, then you know it's Kerdon and not Prexinus. He works at home and sells undercover—every door these days fears the tax collectors. But his workmanship—what workmanship. You'd think Athena's hands, not Kerdon's went into it. I—he came bringing *two* of them, Metro. When I saw them, my eyes swam at the sight—men don't have such firm pricks! Not only that, but it's *smoothness* is sleep, and its straps are like wool, not leather. You couldn't find a kinder women's shoemaker.

METRO: Why did you let the other one go?

KORITTO: Metro, why didn't I buy it? What sort of charm didn't I use to besiege him? I kissed him, and rubbed his bald head, and gave him something sweet to drink, and called him "Daddy"—the only thing I didn't give him to use was my body.

METRO: Well, you should have given him that if he'd asked for it.

KORITTO: Yes, I would have. But it's not a good idea to talk about what's not becoming a lady. Bitas' wife Euboule came in in the middle of it. She has worn down my millstone night and day and turned it into trash, just so she wouldn't need to spend four obols to have her own sharpened.

METRO: How did he manage to come to your house, all this long way, dear Koritto, don't hold back from me.

KORITTO: Artemeis sent him, the wife of Kandas the tanner—she pointed my house out.

METRO: Artemeis always finds out about new discoveries—she can outdrink [...] But since you couldn't rescue the two of them you ought to have found out who ordered the other one.

KORITTO: I begged him, but he swore that he wouldn't tell me.

METRO: What you're telling me means that I must take a trip. I'm going now, to Artemeis' house, so I can find out who this Kerdon is. Stay well, Koritto dear. (Ambiguously) *Someone* is hungry, and it's time for me [...]

KORITTO: Close the door. You—count the hens, give them some darnel seed. You can be sure bird-snatchers will steal them, unless you hold them in your lap.

ii. Theocritus, *Idylls* 15 (excerpt).

Gorgo, a housewife, visits her friend Praxinoa on the day of the festival of Adonis in Alexandria.

GORGO: Is Praxinoa in?

PRAXINOA: Gorgo dear — how long it's been — yes, I'm in. I'm amazed that you've come at last. See that she has a chair, Eunoa; put a cushion on it.

GORGO: I'm so incompetent. I barely got here in one piece, Praxinoa, there was such a crowd, so many chariots, so many boots, men everywhere wearing cloaks. And the road is endless. Every time you move further away.

PRAXINOA: It's that crazy man. He brings me here to the ends of the earth, and gets me a hovel, not a house, so that we can't be neighbors, out of spite, plain envy; he never changes.

GORGO: Don't talk about your husband that way, dear, when the little boy is around. You see, Praxinoa, how he's looking at you. Dont' worry, Zopyrion, sweet baby—she isn't talking about Daddy.

PRAXINOA: The child understands, by Persephone.

GORGO: Nice daddy.

PRAXINOA: Daddy (that man) the other day — just the other day I said to him: "Daddy, go buy some soap and rouge at the booth," and he came back with *salt*, the big ox.

GORGO: Mine's like that too. He's a spendthrift, Diocleidas. For seven drachmas he bought dog skins, pluckings of old wallets — five fleeces, yesterday, all of it dirt, work and more work. But come on, get your dress and your cloak. Let's go to the house of the king, rich Ptolemy, to see Adonis. I hear the queen has done a beautiful job of decorating it.

PRAXINOA: In fine homes everything's fine.

GORGO: When you've seen it, what won't you be able to say to someone who hasn't. It must be time to go.

PRAXINOA: Every day is a holiday if you don't work. Eunoa — you lazy — pick up that spinning and put it back in the center again. Weasels like to sleep on soft beds. Move, bring me some water, right now. She was supposed to bring water; she brought soap. Give it to me anyway. Not so much, you pirate. Pour on the water. Stupid, why are you getting my cloak wet? Now stop. In the way that it pleases the gods, I am washed. Where is the key to the big chest? Then bring it.

GORGO: Praxinoa, that pleated dress suits you. Tell me—how much did the cloth cost off of the loom?

PRAXINOA: Don't remind me, Gorgo. More than two minas of pure silver. I put my heart into the handwork.

GORGO: Well, it lives up to your expectations. You can say that.

PRAXINOA: Bring me my cloak and my hat. Put them on right. I'm not taking you, baby. Mormo the bogy; horse will bite you. Cry as much as you like, I won't let you be lame. Let's go. Phrygia, take the baby and play with him, call the dog inside, and lock the front door.

E. LETTERS

i. Thesleff, pp. 123-124

A letter on how to hire a wet-nurse, with a characteristically Pythagorean emphasis on measure and balance in all things.

Myia to Phyllis, greetings. Here is my advice to you now that you have become a mother. Choose a proper and clean wet-nurse, a modest woman who is inclined neither to drowsiness nor to drunkenness. Such a woman can make the best judgments about how to care for children appropriately, since she has milk to nourish them and will not easily be persuaded to sleep with men. The contribution of the nurse in the process of her nursing to the child's life is great, initial and prefatory to his whole life, since she will do everything well, at the proper time. The nurse will give him the nipple and breast not at his whim, but after due consideration. In this way she will encourage the baby's health. She will not succumb to sleep when she is tired, but when the newborn wants to rest. She will not offer the child temporary satisfaction.

The wet-nurse should not be temperamental or talkative or uncontrolled in her appetite for food, but orderly and temperate —this is possible for both Greeks and foreigners. It is best, if she puts the baby down to sleep when it is filled with milk. Such rest is sweet for little ones and such feeding most effective. If other food is given, it should be as simple as possible. One should stay away from wine completely if one wants the child to be strong, or mix it sparingly with its evening meal of milk. She should not give him continual baths; it is better to have occasional temperate ones. Along the same lines, the atmosphere around the baby should have an even balance of hot and cold, and his housing should be neither too airy nor too close. Moreover, his water should not be too hard nor too soft, nor his bed too rough—rather, it should fall comfortably on his skin. In each of these areas Nature desires what is rightfully hers, not luxuries.

This much then I think it is useful to write at present—my hopes based on Nursing according to Plan. As god assists in the child's development, we shall be able to enjoy in the future appropriate memories.

ii. Oxyrhynchus papyrus 744; 1 B.C.

Hilarion to Alis his sister,[35] heartiest greetings, and to my dear Berous and Apollonarion. Know that we are still even now in Alexandria. Do not worry if when all the others return I remain in Alexandria. I beg and beseech of you to take care of the little child, and as soon as we receive wages I will send them to you. If— good luck to you!—you bear offspring, if it is a male, let it live; if it is a female, expose it. You told Aphrodisias, "Do not forget me." How can I forget you? I beg you therefore not to worry.

The 29th year of Caesar, Pauni 23.

F. A BENEFACTRESS

Pleket 5; Priene, first century B.C.

Friend of Apollonius, wife of Thessalus son of Polydeuces; she was awarded a wreath, first woman to put running water in her household and to set up aqueducts in the city.

7. RELIGION

The politically oppressed often turn to ecstasy as a temporary means of possessing the power they otherwise lack: orgiastic ritual, secret cults, trances, and magic provided such outlets, especially for women, who could not justify meeting together for any other purpose.[36]

A. DIONYSUS

i. Plutarch, *Greek Questions* 38

The story is that the daughters of Minyas, Leucippe and Arsionoe and Alcathoe, went crazy.[37] They developed a craving for human meat and drew lots to choose among their children.

Leucippe won and offered up her son Hippasos to be torn to pieces. Their husbands were called "Psoloeis" (i.e., "sooty") because in their pain and grief they were shabbily dressed. The daughters of Minyas were called Oleiae (i.e., "destroyers") because they were destructive.

Today the people of Orchomenus still call women in this family by that name. Every year at the festival of Agrionia the Oleiae flee and are pursued by the priest of Dionysus, sword in hand. If he captures one of the women he is permitted to kill her, and in my day the priest Zoilus did kill one. But the killing did the people of Orchomenus no good. Zoilus became sick as a result of a small wound he had, which became gangrenous, and eventually died. The people of Orchomenus were beset by suits for damages and adverse judgments. They took the priesthood away from Zoilus' family, and picked as new priest the best man in the city.

ii. Equipment for Women's Orgiastic Rites
Hibeh papyrus 54; Ankyron (Egypt), ca. 245 B.C.

Demophon to Ptolemaeus, greetings. Send us at your earliest opportunity the flutist Petoun with the Phrygian flutes, plus the other flutes. If it's necessary to pay him, do so, and we will reimburse you. Also send us Zenobius with the soft drum, cymbals, and castanets. The women need them for their festival. Be sure he is wearing his most elegant clothing. Get the special goat from Aristion and send it to us. . . . Send us also as many cheeses as you can, a new jug, and vegetables of all kinds, and meat if you have it. Your health! Throw in some policemen at the same time to accompany the boat.

B. DEMETER

i. Homeric Hymn to Demeter (verses 370-495)

When he said this, wise Persephone was filled with joy and hastily sprang up for gladness. But he on his part secretly gave her sweet pomegranate seed to eat, taking care for himself that she might not remain continually with grave, dark-robed Demeter. Then Aidoneus the Ruler of Many openly got ready his deathless horses beneath the golden chariot. And she mounted on the chariot, and the strong Slayer of Argus took reins and whip in his dear hands and drove forth from the hall, the horses speeding readily. Swiftly they traversed their long course, and neither the sea nor river-waters nor grassy glens nor mountain-peaks checked the career of the immortal horses, but they clave the deep air above them as they went. And Hermes brought them to the place where rich-crowned Demeter was staying and checked them before her fragrant temple.

And when Demeter saw them, she rushed forth as does a Maenad down some thick-wooded mountain, while Persephone on the other side, when she saw her mother's sweet eyes, left the chariot and horses, and leaped down to run to her, and falling upon her neck, embraced her. But while Demeter was still holding her dear child in her arms, her heart suddenly misgave her for some snare, so that she feared greatly and ceased fondling her daughter and asked of her at once: "My child, tell me, surely you have not tasted any food while you were below? Speak out and hide nothing, but let us both know. For if you have not, you shall come back from loathly Hades and live with me and your father, the dark-clouded Son of Cronus and be honored by all the deathless gods; but if you have tasted food, you must go back again beneath the secret places of the earth, there to dwell a third part of the seasons every year: yet for the two parts you shall be with me and the other deathless gods. But when the earth shall bloom with the fragrant flowers of spring in every kind, then from the realm of darkness and gloom thou shalt come up once more to be a wonder for gods and mortal men. And now tell me how he rapt you away to the realm of darkness and gloom, and by what trick did the strong Host of Many beguile you?"

Then beautiful Persephone answered her thus: "Mother, I will tell you all without error. When luck-bringing Hermes came, swift messenger from my father the Son of Cronus and the other Sons of Heaven, bidding me come back from Erebus that you might see me with your eyes and so cease from your anger and fearful wrath against the gods, I sprang up at once for joy; but he secretly put in my mouth sweet food, a pomegranate seed, and forced me to taste against my will. Also I will tell how he rapt me away by the deep plan of my father the Son of Cronus and carried me off beneath the depths of the earth, and will relate the whole matter as you ask. All we were playing in a lovely meadow, Leucippe and Phaeno and Electra and Ianthe,

Melita also and Iache with Rhodea and Callirhoe and Melobosis and Tyche and Ocyrhoe, fair as a flower, Chryseis, Ianeira, Acaste and Admete and Rhodope and Pluto and charming Calypso; Styx too was there and Urania and lovely Galaxaura with Pallas who rouses battles and Artemis delighting in arrows: we were playing and gathering sweet flowers in our hands, soft crocuses mingled with irises and hyacinths, and rose-blooms and lilies, marvellous to see, and the narcissus which the wide earth caused to grow yellow as a crocus. That I plucked in my joy; but the earth parted beneath, and there the strong lord, the Host of Many, sprang forth and in his golden chariot he bore me away, all unwilling, beneath the earth: then I cried with a shrill cry. All this is true, sore though it grieves me to tell the tale."

So did they then, with hearts at one, greatly cheer each the other's soul and spirit with many an embrace: their hearts had relief from their griefs while each took and gave back joyousness.

Then bright-coiffed Hecate came near to them, and often did she embrace the daughter of holy Demeter: and from that time the lady Hecate was minister and companion to Persephone.

And all-seeing Zeus sent a messenger to them, rich-haired Rhea, to bring dark-cloaked Demeter to join the families of the gods: and he promised to give her what rights she should choose among the deathless gods and agreed that her daughter should go down for the third part of the circling year to darkness and gloom, but for the two parts should live with her mother and the other deathless gods. Thus he commanded. And the goddess did not disobey the message of Zeus; swiftly she rushed down from the peaks of Olympus and came to the plain of Rharus, rich, fertile corn-land once, but then in nowise fruitful, for it lay idle and utterly leafless, because the white grain was hidden by design of trim-ankled Demeter. But afterwards, as springtime waxed, it was soon to be waving with long ears of corn, and its rich furrows to be loaded with grain upon the ground, while others would already be bound in sheaves. There first she landed from the fruitless upper air: and glad were the goddesses to see each other and cheered in heart. Then bright-coiffed Rhea said to Demeter:

"Come, my daughter; for far-seeing Zeus the loud-thunderer calls you to join the families of the gods, and has promised to give you what rights you please among the deathless gods, and has agreed that for a third part of the circling year your daughter shall go down to darkness and gloom, but for the two parts shall be with you and the other deathless gods: so has he declared it shall be and has bowed his head in token. But come, my child, obey, and be not too angry unrelentingly with the dark-clouded Son of Cronus; but rather increase forthwith for men the fruit that gives them life."

So spake Rhea. And rich-crowned Demeter did not refuse but straightway made fruit to spring up from the rich lands, so that the whole wide earth was laden with leaves and flowers. Then she went, and to the kings who deal justice, Triptolemus and Diocles, the horse-driver, and to doughty Eumolpus and Celcus, leader of the people, she showed the conduct of her rites and taught them all her mysteries, to Triptolemus and Polyxeinus and Diocles also,—awful mysteries which no one may in any way transgress or pry into or utter, for deep awe of the gods checks the voice. Happy is he among men upon earth who has seen these mysteries; but he who is uninitiate and who has no part in them, never has lot of like good things once he is dead, down in the darkness and gloom.

But when the bright goddess had taught them all, they went to Olympus to the gathering of the other gods. And there they dwell beside Zeus who delights in thunder, awful and reverend goddesses. Right blessed is he among men on earth whom they freely love: soon they do send Plutus as guest to his great house, Plutus who gives wealth to mortal men.

And now, queen of the land of sweet Eleusis and sea-girt Paros and rocky Antron, lady, giver of good gifts, bringer of seasons, queen Deo, be gracious, you and your daughter all beauteous Persephone, and for my song grant me heart-cheering substance. And now I will remember you and another song also.[38]

ii. Callimachus, *Hymns* 6 (excerpt).

Sing, ye maidens, and ye mothers, say with them: "Demeter, greatly hail! Lady of much bounty, of many measures of corn." And as the four white-haired horses convey the Basket, so unto us will the great goddess of wide dominion come bringing white spring and white harvest and winter and autumn, and keep us to another year. And as unsandalled and with hair unbound we walk the city, so shall we have foot and head unharmed for ever. And as the van-bearers bear vans full of gold, so may we get gold unstinted. Far as the City Chambers let the uninitiated

follow, but the initiated even unto the very shrine of the goddess—as many as are under sixty years. But those that are heavy
and she that stretches her hand to Eileithyia [goddess of child-
birth] and she that is in pain—sufficient it is that they go so far
as their knees are able. And to them Deo [i.e., Demeter] shall
give all things to overflowing, even as if they came unto her
temple.

Hail, goddess, and save this people in harmony and in prosperity, and in the fields bring us all pleasant things! Feed our kine,
bring us flocks, bring us the corn-ear, bring us harvest! and
nurse peace, that he who sows may also reap. Be gracious, O
thrice-prayed for, great Queen of goddesses!

C. ASCLEPIUS

Cures of sterility and pregnancy in the cult of Asclepius

√Incubation was a "treatment" associated with the god Asclepius. The patient
would sleep within a temple precinct, see the god in a dream, and be miracu-
lously cured. The following case histories were inscribed on the shrine of Asclepius at Epidaurus.

IG IV² 121-122

Cleo was pregnant for five years. After she had been pregnant
for five years she came as a suppliant to the god and slept in the
adytum. As soon as she left it and was outside the sanctuary,
she gave birth to a son, and he, immediately after birth, washed
himself at the fountain and walked about with his mother. After
obtaining these results she had the following inscribed on her
votive tablet: "Wondrous the greatness, not of this tablet but of
the god, seeing that Cleo bore for five years the weight in her
womb until she slept in the shrine and he made her sound."

A three-year pregnancy. Ithmonice of Pellene came to the
sanctuary for offspring. After going to sleep here she saw a
vision. She dreamt she asked of the god that she conceive a
daughter and Asclepius said she would become pregnant and if
she asked for something else he would bring that about too, but
she said she didn't need anything more. She became pregnant
and carried in her womb for three years, until she approached
the god as a suppliant regarding the birth. She went to sleep
here and saw (another) vision. She dreamt the god asked her
whether she had not obtained all that she had asked for, since

she was now pregnant; she hadn't said a word about birth even though he had asked her if she needed anything else she should say so and he would do that too; since she had now come to him as a suppliant for that, he said he would accomplish that too for her. After that she quickly left the adytum, and when she was outside the sanctuary she gave birth to a daughter.

Arata, a Spartan woman, a case of dropsy. She remained in Sparta and her mother slept here for her and had a dream. She dreamt the god cut off her daughter's head and hung her body with the neck down; then after a copious effusion he took down the body and put the head back on the neck. After having this dream she want back to Sparta and found that her daughter had had the same dream and was now well.

Aristagora of Troezen. Suffering from a tapeworm in her belly, she slept in the precinct of Asclepius in Troezen and had a dream. She dreamt that when the god was not there but away in Epidaurus his sons cut off her head and, finding themselves unable to put it back again, sent someone to ask Asclepius to come; meanwhile daylight overtakes them and the priest sees the head severed from the body; with the coming of night Aristagora saw a vision; she dreamt the god arrived from Epidaurus and put her head back on her neck, then cut open her belly, removed the tapeworm and stitched her up again. After that she was well.

Sostrata, of Pherae, had a false pregnancy. In fear and trembling she came in a litter to the sanctuary and slept here. But she had no clear dream and started for home again. Then, near Curni she dreamt that a man, comely in appearance, fell in with her and her companions; when he learned about their bad luck he bade them set down the litter on which they were carrying Sostrata; then he cut open her belly, removed an enormous quantity of worms—two full basins; then he stitched up her belly and made the woman well; then Asclepius revealed his presence and bade her send thank-offerings for the cure to Epidaurus.

Andromache, an Epeirote, for offspring. In her sleep here she had a dream: she dreamt that a blooming young boy uncovered her and then the god touched her with his hand. After that Andromache bore a son to Arybbas.

A woman of Troezen, for offspring. In her sleep here she had a dream: she dreamt the god said she would give birth and asked if she wanted a boy or a girl and she said a boy. Within a year a son was born to her.

Agameda of Ceus. She came for offspring and in her sleep here had a dream: she dreamt in her sleep that a snake lay on her belly. Thereafter she gave birth to five children.

Nicasiboula, a Messenian, for offspring. In her sleep here she had a dream: she dreamt the god approached her carrying a snake, and she had intercourse with it. Within a year she gave birth to twin sons.

D. SERAPIS

The cult of the Egyptian god Serapis grew out of the worship, at Memphis, of Apis, the sacred bull. Beginning under the first Ptolemy and continuing through the Roman Empire, Serapis came to combine features of Egyptian, Greek, and Roman gods, namely, Osiris, Zeus-Jupiter, Hades-Pluto, Asclepius, Helios, and Dionysus. Incubation was associated with his cult as well as with that of Asclepius.

UPZ 19 (Memphis, 163/162 B.C.)

To King Ptolemy and Queen Cleopatra the sister, gods Philometores, greeting. We, Thaues and Taous are twins, who minister in the great Serapeum at Memphis. On a former occasion when you were in residence at Memphis and had gone up to the temple to sacrifice, we petitioned you, and gave in a petition, bringing before you our plea that we are not receiving the contribution of necessaries which it is fitting should be given to us both from the Serapeum and the Asclepeum. And having failed to receive them up to the present time in full, we have been compelled, under pressure of necessity, wasting away as we are through starvation, to petition you again, and in a few words to set before you the selfishness of those who are injuring us. For although you already from former times have proclaimed a contribution for the Serapeum and Asclepeum, and in consequence of this the twins who were there before us daily received what they required, to us also when we first went up to the temple straightway for a few days the impression was conveyed as if everything fitting would be done for us in good order, but for the remainder of the time this was not carried out. Wherefore we both sent repeatedly to the supervisors persons to petition on our behalf, and laid information on these matters before you, on the occasion of your visits to Memphis. And when those who had been appointed to the administration in the Serapeum and Asclepeum had insolently maltreated us, and were removing the privileges conferred on you by us, and were paying no regard to religious scruple, and when we were being crushed by our wants, we often made representations even to Achomarres the supervisor of the temple to give us (our rights). And we approached the son of Psintaes the supervisor of the sacrifices, when he went up to the temple the day before yesterday, and gave him detailed information. And having called Achomarres to him, he strictly commanded him to give what was owing to us. And he, being by nature the most unfeeling of all mankind, promised us that he would perform what he had been directed to do, but no sooner had the son of Psintaes departed from Memphis than he took no further account of the matter. And not only this man, but also others connected with the Serapeum, and others connected with the Asclepeum in the administration, from whom it is usual for us to receive what we need, are defrauding, whose names and obligations, because they are numerous, we have decided not to record.

We beg you therefore, having as our one hope the assistance that lies in your power, to send away our petition to Dionysius Privy Councillor and strategus, that he may write to Apollonius the supervisor to compel them to render to us (what is owing), when he has received from us the written list of the necessaries owing to us and what further debts are due us along with the periods for which they have been owing and the persons who owe them, so that, when we have everything in order, we may be much better able to perform our regular duties to Serapis and to Isis, both for your own sakes and for the sake of your children. May it be given you to hold fast all the territory you desire. Farewell.

E. WITCHCRAFT

i. Apollonius of Rhodes, *Argonautica* III. 838-867.

Medea concocts a drug to protect Jason.

She had twelve maids, young as herself and all unmarried, who slept in the ante-chamber of her own sweet-scented room. She called them now and told them to yoke the mules to her carriage at once, as she wished to drive to the splendid Temple of Hecate; and while they were getting the carriage ready she took a magic ointment from her box. This salve was named after

Prometheus. A man had only to smear it on his body, after propitiating the only-begotten Maiden with a midnight offering, to become invulnerable by sword or fire and for that day to surpass himself in strength and daring. It first appeared in a plant that sprang from the blood-like ichor of Prometheus in his torment, which the flesh-eating eagle had dropped on the spurs of Caucasus. The flowers, which grew on twin stalks a cubit high, were of the color of Corycian saffron, while the root looked like flesh that has just been cut, and the juice like the dark sap of a mountain oak. To make the ointment, Medea, clothed in black, in the gloom of night, had drawn off this juice in a Caspian shell after bathing in seven perennial streams and calling seven times on Brimo, nurse of youth, Brimo, night-wanderer of the underworld, Queen of the dead. The dark earth shook and rumbled underneath the Titan root when it was cut, and Prometheus himself groaned in the anguish of his soul.

Such was the salve that Medea chose.

ii. A Love Potion

Theocritus, *Idylls* 2 (excerpt).

A courtesan's attempt to win back a handsome lover.

Where are my bay-leaves? Go get them, Thestylis. And where are my drugs? Put a wreath of crimson wool round the bowl, so I can bind my dear lover, who is cruel to me. It's now the twelfth day that the beast hasn't come here, and he doesn't know if I'm dead or alive; cruel man, he hasn't knocked on my door. I'm sure that Love has gone off and taken his fickle heart elsewhere, and so has Aphrodite. I'll go to Timagetus' wrestling-ring tomorrow, so I can see him, and I'll complain about what he has done to me.

But today I will bind him with what I burn here. Now, Moon, shine brightly, and I will sing to you softly, goddess, and to Hecate underground, before whom even dogs tremble as she comes from the graves of the dead and their black blood. Hail, Hecate unapproachable, and guide me until I am finished; make these drugs of mine in no way inferior to Circe's or Medea's or blonde Perimede's. *Magic wheel, draw my lover to my house.*

First barley melts on the fire. Sprinkle them on, Thestylis. Fool, where have your wits flown to? You curse, do you also think of me as a plaything? Sprinkle it on and say as follows: "I sprinkle the bones of Delphis." *Magic wheel, draw my lover to my house.*

Delphis has hurt me. So I burn this bay upon Delphis. As they catch fire, crackle loudly and are consumed in an instant and I can't see even their ashes, so may Delphis' flesh be consumed in flames. *Magic wheel, draw my lower to my house.*

Now I'll burn the bran. Artemis, you can move the power of Death and anything else that is immovable—Thestylis, dogs all round the city are barking; the goddess is at the crossroads. As quick as you can, clash the cymbals. *Magic wheel, draw my lover to my house.*

As I melt this wax with the goddess's assistance, so may Delphis from Mydus melt with desire. As this bronze wheel of Aphrodite's spins, so may Delphis spin in front of my door. *Magic wheel, draw my lover to my house.*

I shall pour three libations and say three times as follows, "O goddess: whether a woman lies beside him or whether a man does, let him forget that person as fast as they say Theseus once forgot fair-haired Ariadne." *Magic wheel, draw my lover to my house.*

Coltsfoot is an herb that grows in Arcadia, and for it all the mares and colts run mad through the mountains, swift mares. May I see Delphis like that; may he rush to this house like a madman, from the glistening wrestling-ring. *Magic wheel, draw my lover to my house.*

Delphis lost this, the fringe of his cloak. I now shred it and throw it in the wild fire. *Ai ai*, painful Desire, why have you drunk the black blood from my flesh, all of it, like a marsh leech stuck to me?

I'll grind up a lizard and bring it tomorrow for him to drink. Now, Thestylis, take these flowers and knead them over his threshold, while it's still night, and say in a whisper, "I knead the bones of Delphis." *Magic wheel, draw my lover to my house.*

II. The Roman World

Seated Dancer. A silver statuette, inlaid with gold. The girl sitting on a hassock, is putting on her slipper. About A.D. 350 to 400. (Museum of Fine Arts, Boston)

8. WOMEN'S LIVES—AS SEEN BY WOMEN

Though other Roman women are known to have written poetry—Melinno (second century A.D.) composed sapphic stanzas (in Greek) in praise of Rome, Sulpicia is the only Roman woman of whose work we possess more than fragments. She was the ward of M. Valerius Messala Corvinus, writer, politician, and patron of the arts during the Augustan age. Among his circle was the poet Albius Tibullus, who seems to have befriended the young Sulpicia. The identity of her love, whom she calls "Cerinthus," is unknown. The poems are preserved in book III of Tibullus' works.

14

I hate my birthday, but it's coming soon. I hate the country too,
but I'll have to go there, sad as it makes me. And—
without Cerinthus!
What could be nicer than staying here in town?
Is a farmhouse any fit place for a girl?
Or a freezing cold river in Arretium—
in the sticks!
Now, Messala, you've been worrying about me too much.
Relax!
Journeys, you know, can come at quite the wrong time.
You can take me away; I will leave my heart and soul behind,
though you won't let me use my own better judgment.

15

Did you know that that loathesome trip no longer troubles your
sweetie's heart? Now I can spend my birthday here—in Rome!
Let's everybody celebrate my birthday.
This year, it's a birthday surprise for *you.*

17

Cerinthus, don't you care about your sweetie?
I'm so weak, and the fever is tormenting me.
Oh, I wouldn't even *think* about getting well,
if I didn't know that's what you wanted.
What good would getting well do me, if you could watch me
suffer without suffering some yourself?

18

Light of my life! May you never feel the fire for me
that (I think) you felt a few days ago,
if I am ever so stupid again.
I've not lived long, but I'm still sorrier for this than for

anything I've ever done.
The only reason I ran out on you last night was—
to hide the fire I felt myself.

9. WOMEN'S LIVES—AS SEEN BY MEN

A. EPITAPHS

While most Roman epitaphs are short and simple, containing only a dedication
to the gods of the underworld and the name and age of the deceased, some
contain a eulogy and brief biography. In some texts the survivor who dedicated
the tomb speaks directly to the soul of the deceased or to the passer-by. Many
inscriptions give the impression that the soul is living inside the tomb and
wishes to maintain a friendly relationship with the living. As cemeteries were
most frequently situated along the main roads to and from towns, strangers
constantly passed the tombs during the course of their daily business. For this
reason, benches and gardens were often provided in tomb plots, where the
passer-by might stop and rest and feel grateful to the dead. He was expected to
show proper respect for the tomb, legally a sanctified place, and was sometimes
cursed or fined if he did not.

i. *ILLRP* 973; second century B.C.

Friend, I have not much to say; stop and read it. This tomb,
which is not fair, is for a fair woman. Her parents gave her the
name Claudia. She loved her husband in her heart. She bore two
sons, one of whom she left on earth, the other beneath it. She
was pleasant to talk with, and she walked with grace. She kept
the house and worked in wool. That is all. You may go.

ii. *ILS* 5213; first century B.C.

(The grave) of Eucharis, freedwoman of Licinia, an unmarried girl who was educated and learned in every skill. She lived
fourteen years.
Ah, as you look with wandering eye at the house of death, stay
your foot and read what is inscribed here. This is what a
father's love gave his daughter, where the remains of her body
lie gathered. "Just as my life with its young skills and growing

years brought me fame, the sad hour of death rushed on me and forbade me to draw another breath in life. I was educated and taught as if by the Muses' hands. I adorned the nobility's festivals with my dancing, and first appeared before the common people in a Greek play.

"But now here in this tomb my enemies the Fates have placed my body's ashes. The patrons of learning—devotion, passion, praise, honor, fall silent before my burnt corpse and are made silent by my death.

"His child, I left lamentation to my father, though born after him, I preceded him in the day of my death. Now I observe my fourteenth birthday here among the shadows in Death's ageless home.

"I beg you when you leave, ask that the earth lie light upon me."

iii. *ILLRP* 971; first century B.C.

Posilla Senenia, daughter of Quartus, and Quarta Senenia, freedwoman of Gaius.

Stranger, stop and, while you are here, read what is written: that a mother was not permitted to enjoy her only daughter, whose life, I believe, was envied by some god.

Since her mother was not allowed to adorn her while she was alive, she does so just the same after death; at the end of her time, (her mother) with this monument honors her whom she loved.

iv. *ILLRP* 793; first century B.C.

A man and a woman, hands joined, are shown in relief on this tombstone.

(*On the left*)
Lucius Aurelius Hermia, freedman of Lucius, a butcher from the Viminal Hill.

My wife, who died before me, chaste in body, my one and only, a loving woman who possessed my heart, she lived as a faithful wife to a faithful husband with affection equal to my own, since she never let avarice keep her from her duty. Aurelia Philmatio, freedwoman of Lucius.
(*On the right*)
Aurelia Philmatio, freedwoman of Lucius.

When I was alive I was called Aurelia Philematium. I was

106

chaste and modest; I did not know the crowd; I was faithful to my husband. He whom, alas, I have lost was my fellow-freedman and was truly more than a father to me. When I was seven years old, he took me to his bosom; now at forty, I am possessed by violent death. He, through my diligent performance of duty, flourished at all [times . . .]. [The rest is lost.]

v. ILLRP 977; first century B.C.

Publius Larcius Nicia, freedman of Publius; Saufeia Thalea, freedwoman of Aulus; Lucius Larcius Rufus, son of Publius; Publius Larcius Brocchus, son of Publius; Larcia Horaea, freedwoman of Publius (and Saufeia).[39]

I was respected by good people and was envied by no woman of character. I was obedient to my old master and mistress, and to this man, my husband, I was dutiful. They honored me with my freedom, he with a (matron's) robe. I kept the house for twenty years, beginning as as little girl. My last day made its judgment; death snatched away my soul but did not take my life's honor.

Lucius Eprius Chilo, messenger of the tribune of the people, Epria Cri [. . .] [The rest is lost.]

vi. Amer. Journal of Archaeology 77 (1973) 165; first century A.D.

Trebia Saturnina, daughter of Gaius, lived for thirteen years. The torch of the unlucky girl had hoped for another use;[40] its job is different now. Alas for the ones she left on earth! Ready for the bridal bed, just the age for marriage, lamented she abandoned her betrothed and his parents.

B. EULOGIES FROM INSCRIPTIONS

i. CIL VI. 1527 = ILS 8393 (abridged); Rome, 9 or 10 B.C.

Funerary eulogy for Turia (identity uncertain), written by her husband, whom she saved from proscription in 42 B.C.

Before the day fixed for our marriage, you were suddenly left an orphan, by the murder of your parents in the solitude of the country. . . .

Through your efforts chiefly, their death did not remain unavenged. For I had departed for Macedonia and C. Cluvius, your sister's husband, into the province of Africa.

So active were you in the performance of this pious duty, in searching out and insistently demanding the punishment [of the guilty] that, had we ourselves been present, we could not have done more. You share the credit for this with that pious woman, your sister.

While you were busy with these matters, to shield your honor, immediately after the punishment of the assassins, you retired from your father's house to the home of your mother's sister, where you awaited my return. . . .

In our day, marriages of such long duration, not dissolved by divorce, but terminated by death alone, are indeed rare. For our union was prolonged in unclouded happiness for forty-one years. Would that it had been my lot to put an end to this our good fortune and that I as the older—which was more just—had yielded to fate.

Why recall your inestimable qualities, your modesty, deference, affability, your amiable disposition, your faithful attendance to the household duties, your enlightened religion, your unassuming elegance, the modest simplicity and refinement of your manners? Need I speak of your attachment to your kindred, your affection for your family,—when you respected my mother as you did your own parents and cared for her tomb as you did for that of your own mother and father,—you who share countless other virtues with Roman ladies most jealous of their fair name? These qualities which I claim for you are your own, equalled or excelled by but few; for the experience of men teaches us how rare they are.

With common prudence we have preserved all the patrimony which you received from your parents. Entrusting it all to me, you were not troubled with the care of increasing it; thus did we share the task of administering it, that I undertook to protect your fortune, and you to guard mine. On this point, I pass by many things in silence, for fear of attributing to myself a portion of your own deserts. Suffice it for me to indicate your sentiments.

You gave proof of your generosity not only towards several of your kin, but especially in your filial devotion. . . . You brought up in your own home, in the enjoyment of mutual benefits, some young girls of your kinship. And that these might attain to a station in life worthy of our family, you provided them with dowries. C. Cluvius and myself, by common accord, executed your intentions, and, approving of your generosity, in order that your patrimony might suffer no diminution, offered our own family possessions instead and gave up our personal property to provide the dowries, settled upon by you. This I relate, not to sing my own praises, but to show the unanimity of our counsels, that we held ourselves in honor bound to execute those obligations, incurred by you out of the fullness of your heart.

I owe you no less a debt than to Caesar Augustus himself, for this my return from exile to my native land. For unless you had prepared the way for my safety, even Caesar's promises of assistance had been of no avail. So I owe no less a debt to your loyal devotion than to the clemency of Caesar.

Why shall I now conjure up the memory of our domestic counsels and plans stored away in the hidden recesses of the heart? That, aroused by the sudden arrival of messages from you to a realization of the present and imminent perils, I was saved by your counsel? That you suffered me not to be recklessly carried away by a foolish rashness, or that, when bent on more temperate plans, you provided for me a safe retreat, having as sharers in your plans for my safety, when an exile—fraught with danger as they were for you all—your sister and her husband, C. Cluvius. But I should not finish, were I to attempt to touch on all these matters. Suffice it for me, and for your memory, that the retreat provided by you insured my safety.

I should confess, however, that on this occasion I suffered one of the bitterest experiences of my life, in the fate that befell you, much against my will. When the favor and permission of Caesar Augustus, then absent [from Rome], had restored me to my country, still a useful citizen perhaps, M. Lepidus, his colleague, then present in the city, interposed objections. Then prostrating yourself at his feet, he not only did not raise you up, but, dragged along and abused as though a common slave, your body all covered with bruises, yet with unflinching steadfastness of purpose, you recalled to him Caesar's edict [of pardon] and the letter of felicitation on my return, that accompanied it. Braving his taunts and suffering the most brutal treatment, you denounced these cruelties publicly so that he [Lepidus] was branded as the author of all my perils and misfortunes. And his punishment was not long delayed.

Could such courage remain without effect? Your unexampled patience furnished the occasion for Caesar's clemency, and, by guarding my life, he branded the infamous and savage cruelty [of the tyrant Lepidus]. ...

When all the world was again at peace and the Republic re-established, peaceful and happy days followed. We longed for children, which an envious fate denied us. Had Fortune smiled on us in this, what had been lacking to complete our happiness? But an adverse destiny put an end to our hopes. ... Disconsolate to see me without children ... you wished to put an end to my chagrin by proposing to me a divorce, offering to yield the place to another spouse more fertile, with the only intention of searching for and providing for me a spouse worthy of our mutual affection, whose children you assured me you would have treated as your own. ... Nothing would have been changed, only you would have rendered to me henceforth the services of a devoted sister or mother-in-law.

I will admit that I was so irritated and shocked by such a proposition that I had difficulty in restraining my anger and remaining master of myself. You spoke of divorce before the decree of fate had forced us to separate, and I could not comprehend how you could conceive of any reason why you, still living, should not be my wife, you who during my exile had always remained most faithful and loyal. ...

Would that our time of life had permitted our union to have endured until I, the older, had passed away which was more just —and that you might perform for me the last sad rites and that I might have departed, leaving you behind, with a daughter to replace me at your side.

By fate's decree your course was run before mine. You left me the grief, the heart-ache, the longing for you, the sad fate to live alone. ...

The conclusion of this discourse will be that you have deserved all, and that I remain with the chagrin of not being able to give you all. Your wishes have always been my supreme law; and whatever it will be permitted me to accord them still, in this I shall not fail.

May the gods, the Manes, assure and protect your repose!

ii. CIL VI. 10230 = ILS 8394.

Funeral eulogy for Murdia, spoken by her son by his first marriage. Rome, around the time of Augustus (27 B.C.-14 A.D.).

110

[The first part of the inscription is lost.]

She made all her sons equal heirs, after she gave a bequest to her daughter. Her love as a mother is formed from affection for her children and her fairness to each. She willed her husband [the speaker's stepfather] a fixed sum, so that his dower right would be increased by the honor of her discretion.

When she made her will she called my father's memory into consultation, and kept the agreement she made with him in her planning, nor did she resort to the sort of mentality that would prefer me to my stepbrothers and cause injury to them. But rather, with my father's generosity in mind, she gave me my due —all that in her husband's judgment she had received from my father's estate, and she gave orders to restore to my ownership what had been entrusted to her.

In such action she determined to maintain the marriages given to her by her parents to worthy men, with obedience and propriety, and as a bride to become more beloved because of her merits, to be thought dearer because of her honor, to be considered more glorious because of her discretion, and after her death to be praised in the judgment of her fellow citizens, since the division of her estate indicated her grateful and honorable intentions towards her husbands, her fairness to her children, and, in truth, her justice.

For these reasons praise for all good women is simple and similar, since their native goodness and the trust they have maintained do not require a diversity of words. Sufficient is the fact that they have all done the same good deeds with the fine reputation they deserve, and since it is hard to find new forms of praise for a woman, since their lives fluctuate with less diversity, by necessity we cherish the values they hold in common, so that nothing may be lost from fair precepts and harm what remains.

Still, my dearest mother deserved greater praise than all others, since in modesty, propriety, chastity, obedience, woolworking, industry, and honor she was on an equal level with other good women, nor did dangerous times deflect her in any respect from virtue, work, and wisdom. Certainly she was zealous.... [The rest is lost.]

iii. Pleket 10; Thasos, first century A.D.

Pythion son of Hicesius set up this common memorial to himself and to his wife Epicydilla daughter of Epicydes. He was married at eighteen and she at fifteen, and for fifty years of life together they shared agreement unbroken, and were fathers of fathers (*sic*), twice archons of their city, happy among the living and blessed among the dead. If anyone places another body here, he must pay to the city 12,000 minae.

iv. Peek 1243; Memphis (Egypt), second/third centuries A.D.

A good plant from a holy root—citizens, weep for me. I was pleasing to all, blameless in my mother's eyes, faultless in my father's. I lived five years.

v. Pleket 20; Pergamum, second century A.D.

Farewell, lady Panthia, from your husband. After your departure, I keep up my lasting grief for your cruel death. Hera, goddess of marriage, never saw such a wife: your beauty, your wisdom, your chastity. You bore me children completely like myself; you cared for your bridegroom and your children; you guided straight the rudder of life in our home and raised high our common fame in healing—though you were a woman you were not behind me in skill. In recognition of this your bridegroom Glycon built this tomb for you. I also buried here the body of [my father] immortal Philadelphus, and I myself will lie here when I die, so that for eternity I might share my bed with you alone, and so settle in ground that we share.

vi. *CIL* VI. 37965; Rome, third century A.D. (?)

Scholars have found this unusual inscription difficult to classify. It may have been intended as a serious encomium, but parts of it, at least, may have been meant deliberately to be amusing.

To the gods of the dead, (the tomb) of Aulus' freedwoman, Allia Potestas.

Here lies a woman from Perugia. None was more precious than she in the world. One so diligent as she has never been seen before. Great as you were you are now held in a small urn. Cruel arbiter of fate, and harsh Persephone, why do you deprive us of good, and why does evil triumph, everyone asks. I am tired of answering. They give me their tears, tokens of their good will.

She was courageous, chaste, resolute, honest, a trustworthy guardian. Clean at home, sufficiently clean when she went out, famous among the populace. She alone could confront whatever happened. She would speak briefly and so was never reproached. She was first to rise from her bed, and last to return to her bed to rest after she had put each thing in its place. Her yarn never left her hands without good reason. She took first place in obedience and healthy habits. But she was not pleased that she never seemed free to herself.

Her skin was white, she had beautiful eyes, and her hair was gold. An ivory glow always shone from her face—no mortal (so they say) ever possessed a face like it. The curve of her breasts was small on her snow-white bosom. And her legs? Atalanta's figure is comic beside hers.

She never stayed worried for long; on her generous body she carried her fair limbs lightly; she sought out every hair. Perhaps you may be angry that she must remain with the cruel dead.

Nothing satisfied her, unless she did it herself with her own hands. There was never a topic which she thought she knew well enough. And she was well known for never conceding a point.

While she was still living two of her young lovers set up this monument, that they might by this action seem to be like Pylades and Orestes—one house would hold them both and one spirit.[41] But now that she is dead, they will separate, and each grow old by himself. A woman could join such men together, but now the times have injured them—look at Troy, to see what a woman once did. I pray that it be right to use such grand comparisons for this lesser event.

These verses for you your patron—whose tears never end—writes in tribute. You are lost, but never will be taken from his heart. These are the gifts he believes the lost will enjoy. After you no woman can seem good. A man who has lived without you has seen his own death while alive. He carries your name in gold back and forth on his arm, where he can keep it, possessing Potestas.[42] As long as these published words of ours survive, so long will you live in these little verses of mine.

In your place I have only your image as solace; this we cherish with reverence and lavish with flowers. When I come with you, it follows in attendance. But still—in my sorrow—on which of you am I bestowing these rites? If this statue were living, which I believe in so deeply, with this one possession I could be happy, perhaps, now that you are gone. But—woe is me—you have won the contest—my fate and yours are the same.

The man who tries to harm this tomb, dares to harm the gods: this tomb, distinguished by its inscription, believe me, has divinity.

vii. Pleket 7 (excerpt); Corinth, ca. 43 A.D.

The deme of Patareis has decreed: Whereas Junia Theodora, a Roman resident in Corinth, a woman held in highest honor ... who copiously supplied from her own means many of our citizens with generosity, and received them in her home and in particular never ceased acting on behalf of our citizens in regard to any favor asked—the majority of citizens have gathered in assembly to offer testimony on her behalf. Our people in gratitude agreed to vote: to commend Junia and to offer testimony of her generosity to our native city and of her good will, to testify that she increased her good will toward the city, because she knew that our people also would not cease in their good will and gratitude to her and would do everything for the excellence and the glory that she deserved. For this reason (with good fortune), it was decreed to commend her for all that she had done.

viii. Pleket 9; Delphi, ca. 45 A.D.

Hermesianax, son of Dionysius. Caesareus of Tralles (also from Corinth), for his daughters, who themselves have the same citizenships.

1) Tryphosa, at the Pythian Games with Antigonus and Cleomachis as judges, and at the Isthmian Games, with Juventius and Proclus as judges, each time placed first in the girls' single-course race.

2) Hedea, at the Isthmian Games with Cornelius Pulcher as judge, won the race in armor, with her chariot; at the Nemean Games she won the single-course race with Antigonus as judge and also in Sicyon with Menoites as judge. She also won the children's lyre contest at the Augustan Games in Athens with Nusius son of Philinus as judge. She was first in her age group ... citizen ... a girl.

3) Dionysia won at... with Antigonus as judge, the single-course race at the Asclepian Games at the sanctuary of Epidaurus with Nicoteles as judge.

To Pythian Apollo.

ix. Pleket 30; Apollonia in Mysia, second/third century A.D.

For Magnilla the philosopher, daughter of a philosopher, wife of Menius the philosopher.

x. Pleket 31; Paros, ca. 300 A.D.

To the most renowned and in all respects excellent Aurelia Leite, daughter of Theodotus, wife of the foremost man in the city, Marcus Aurelius Faustus, high priest for life of the cult of Diocletian and his co-rulers, priest of Demeter and gymnasiarch. She was gymnasiarch when the city of Paros, a city more glorious than many other great cities had possessed and no longer had use (after a span of many long years) for a dilapidated gymnasium. The city received from her more honor than it gave, for which the city on many occasions voted its gratitude. The city has set up a marble statue of her: she loved wisdom, her husband, her children, her native city. This woman, with her wisdom, best of mothers, his wife Leite, renowned Faustus glorifies.

C. EULOGIES IN LITERATURE

i. Seneca, *On Consolation* 16

L. Annaeus Seneca, Stoic philosopher, politician, and tutor to the young Nero, spent eight years (41-49 A.D.) in Corsica, exiled because the empress Messallina had accused him (falsely, no doubt) of adultery with Julia Livilla, Caligula's sister. During this period he wrote the essay, *To Helvia on Consolation*, to comfort his mother, Helvia.

It is not for you to avail yourself of the excuse of being a woman, who, in a way, has been granted the right to inordinate, yet not unlimited, tears. And so our ancestors, seeking to compromise with the stubbornness of a woman's grief by a public ordinance, granted the space of ten months as the limit of mourning for a husband. They did not forbid their mourning, but limited it; for when you lose one who is most dear, to be illed with endless sorrow is foolish fondness, and to feel none is nhuman hardness. The best course is the mean between affec- ion and reason—both to have a sense of loss and to crush it. There is no need for you to regard certain women, whose sorrow ance assumed ended only with their death—some you know, who, having put on mourning for sons they had lost, never laid the garb aside. From you life, that was sterner from the start, requires more; the excuse of being a woman can be of no avail o one who has always lacked all the weaknesses of a woman.

Unchastity, the greatest evil of our time, has never classed you with the great majority of women; jewels have not moved you, nor pearls; to your eyes the glitter of riches has not seemed he greatest boon of the human race; you, who were soundly rained in an old-fashioned and strict household, have not been perverted by the imitation of worse women that leads even the virtuous into pitfalls; you have never blushed for the number of your children, as if it taunted you with your years, never have you, in the manner of other women whose only recommendation ies in their beauty, tried to conceal your pregnancy as if an unseemly burden, nor have you ever crushed the hope of chil- dren that were being nurtured in your body; you have not defiled your face with paints and cosmetics; never have you fancied the kind of dress that exposed no greater nakedness by being removed. In you has been seen that peerless ornament, hat fairest beauty on which time lays no hand, the chiefest glory which is modesty. You cannot, therefore, allege your wom- anhood as an excuse for persistent grief, for your very virtues set you apart; you must be as far removed from woman's tears as from her vices. But even women will not allow you to pine away from your wound, but will bid you finish quickly with necessary sorrow, and then rise with lighter heart—I mean, if you are willing to turn your gaze upon the women whose con- spicuous bravery has placed them in the rank of mighty heroes.

Cornelia bore twelve children, but Fortune had reduced their number to two; if you wished to count Cornelia's losses, she had lost ten, if to appraise them, she had lost the two Gracchi.[43] Nevertheless, when her friends were weeping around her and cursing her fate, she forbade them to make any indictment against Fortune, since it was Fortune who had allowed the Grac- chi to be her sons. Such a woman had right to be the mother of him who exclaimed in the public assembly: "Do you dare to revile the mother who gave birth to me?" But to me his moth- er's utterance seems more spirited by far; the son set great value on the birthday of the Gracchi, but the mother on their funerals as well.

Rutilia followed her son Cotta[44] into exile, and was so wrapped up in her love for him that she preferred exile to losing him; and only her son's return brought her back to her native land. But when, after he had been restored and now had risen to honor in the state, he died, she let him go just as bravely as she had clung to him; and after her son was buried no one saw her shed any tears. When he was exiled, she showed courage, when she lost him, wisdom; for in the one case she did not desist from her devotion, and in the other did not persist in useless and foolish sorrow. In the number of such women as these I wish you to be counted. In your effort to restrain and suppress your sorrow your best course will be to follow the example of those women whose life you have always copied.

ii. Pliny the Younger, *Letters*.

III. 16. On Arria.

I think I have remarked that the more famous words and deeds of men and women are not necessarily their greatest. I was strengthened in this opinion by a conversation I had yesterday with Fannia, granddaughter of the famous Arria who sustained and encouraged her husband by her example at the time of his death. She told me several things about her grandmother which were quite as heroic though less well known, and I think they will make the same impression on you as you read them as they did on me during their telling.

Arria's husband, Caecina Paetus, was ill, so was their son, and it was thought that neither could recover. The son died, a most beautiful boy with an unassuming manner no less remarkable, and dear to his parents for reasons beyond the fact that he was their son. Arria made all the preparations for his funeral and took her place at the ceremony without her husband knowing; in fact whenever she entered his room she pretended that their son was alive and even rather better, and when Paetus kept asking how the boy was, she would answer that he had had a good sleep and was willing to take some food. Then when the tears she had held back for so long could no longer be kept from breaking out, she left the room; not till then did she give way to her grief. Her weeping over, she dried her eyes, composed her ace, and returned as if she had left the loss of her child outside the room. It was a glorious deed, I know, to draw a sword, plunge it into her breast, pull it out, and hand it to her husband with the immortal, almost divine words: "It does not hurt, Paetus."[45] But on that well-known occasion she had fame and immortality before her eyes. It was surely even more heroic when she had no hope of any such reward, to stifle her tears, hide her grief, and continue to act the mother after she had lost her son.

At the time of the revolt against Claudius raised by Scribonianus in Illyricum [42 A.D.], Paetus had joined his party, and after Scribonianus' death was being brought as a prisoner to Rome. He was about to board ship when Arria begged the soldiers to take her with him. "This is a senator of consular rank," she insisted, "and of course you will allow him a few slaves to serve his meals, dress him and put on his shoes; all of which I can do for him myself." Her request was refused. She then hired a small fishing smack, and the great ship sailed with her following in her tiny boat.

Again, when she came before Claudius and found the wife of Scribonianus volunteering to give evidence of the revolt, "Am I to listen to you," she cried, "who could go on living after Scribonianus died in your arms?" This proves that her determination to die a glorious death was not a sudden impulse. Indeed, when her son-in-law Thrasea was trying to persuade her not to carry out her resolve, in the course of his argument he asked her whether if he ever had to die she would wish her daughter to die with him.[46] "If she lives as long and happily with you," she said, "as I have with Paetus—yes." This answer increased the anxiety felt for her by her family and she was watched even more carefully. Perceiving this, "It is no good," she said. "You can make me choose a painful death, but you cannot make it impossible." With these words she leaped out of her chair and dashed her head against the wall opposite, so that she fell senseless from the violent blow. When she came round, "I told you," she said, "that I should find a hard way to die if you denied me an easy one."

Surely you think these words greater than the well-known "It does not hurt, Paetus" which was their culmination? And yet this is widely famous, while the earlier sayings are not known at all. Hence the inference with which I began this letter, that the words and deeds which win fame are not always the greatest.[47]

VII. 19. On Fannia

I am very worried about Fannia's illness. She contracted it while nursing Junia, one of the Vestal Virgins, a duty she undertook voluntarily at first (Junia being a relative of hers) and then by order of the priests. (For when sickness compels the Virgins to leave the hall of Vesta, they are always committed to the care of some married woman.) This service Fannia was faithfully performing when she fell a victim to her present illness. Her fever never leaves her, her cough grows worse, and she is painfully thin and weak. There remain only the courage and the spirit worthy of her husband Helvidius and her father Thrasea.[48] In every other way she is failing, and my anxiety on her behalf is coupled with grief, grief that so great a woman will be lost to the sight of her country when her like may not be seen again: such are her purity and integrity, her nobility and loyal heart. Twice she followed her husband into exile, and a third time was banished herself on his account.[49] For when Senecio was on trial for having written a life of Helvidius, and said in his defense that he had done so at Fannia's request, Mettius Carus then demanded in a threatening tone if this was true. She replied that it was. Had she lent Senecio her husband's diaries? "Yes." Did her mother know of this?[50] "No." Not a word in fact did she utter through fear of danger. Moreover, although the Senate was driven through fear of the times to order the destruction of the books in question, she managed to save them when her possessions were confiscated, and took them with her into the exile they had caused.

At the same time she has such friendliness and charm, the rare gift, in fact, of being able to inspire affection as well as respect. Will there be anyone now whom we can hold up as a model to our wives, from whose courage even our own sex can take example, and whom we can admire as much as the heroines of history while she is still in our midst? To me it seems as though her whole house is shaken to its very foundations and is tottering to its fall, even though she may leave descendants; for how can their deeds and merits be sufficient to assure that the last of her line has not perished in her?

A further and more personal pain and grief for me is my feeling that I am losing her mother again—to whom I can pay no higher tribute than by calling her the famous mother of a great woman. The mother was restored to us in her daughter, but soon will be taken away with her, leaving me the pain of a re-opened wound to bear as well as this fresh blow. I honored and loved them both—I cannot say which the more, nor did they wish a distinction to be drawn. My services were at their command alike in prosperity and adversity; I was their comfort in exile and their champion after their return. I could never make them an adequate return, and so I am all the more anxious for Fannia's life to be spared to give me time to pay my debt. These are my troubles at the time of writing to you; but, if one of the gods will turn them to joy, I shall make no complaint about my present fears.

IV. 21. On the Helvidiae.

This premature death of Helvidius' daughters is tragic[51]—both sisters giving birth to girls and dying in labor. I am deeply distressed, and not unduly, for these were noble young women in the flower of their youth and I must mourn to see them the victims of their motherhood. I grieve too for the plight of their infants left motherless at birth, and for their excellent husbands, and I grieve no less on my own account; for my love for their father has remained constant since his death, as my defense of him and my published speeches bear witness. Now only one of his three children survives, left as the sole prop and stay of a family which not so long ago had many members to support it. But if Fortune will keep him at least safe and sound, and make him as fine a man as his father and his grandfather, I can take comfort in my sorrow. I am all the more anxious for his safety and character now that he is the last of his line. You know my nervous apprehensions for anyone I love, so you must not be surprised at my fears being worst where my hopes are highest.

V. 16. On Minicia Marcella

I am writing to you in great distress: our friend Fundanus has lost his younger daughter.[52] I never saw a girl so gay and lovable, so deserving of a longer life or even a life to last for ever. She had not yet reached the age of fourteen, and yet she combined the wisdom of age and dignity of womanhood with the sweetness and modesty of youth and innocence. She would cling to her father's neck, and embrace us, his friends, with modest affection; she loved her nurses, her attendants and her teachers, each one for the service given her; she applied herself intelligently to her books and was moderate and restrained in her play. She bore her last illness with patient resignation and, indeed, with courage; she obeyed her doctor's orders, cheered her sister and father, and by sheer force of will carried on after her physical strength had failed her. This will power remained with her to the end, and neither the length of her illness nor fear of death could break it. So she has left us all the more sad reasons for lamenting our loss. Hers is a truly tragic and untimely end — death itself was not so cruel as the moment of its coming. She was already engaged to marry a distinguished young man, the day for the wedding was fixed, and we had received our invitations. Such joy, and now such sorrow! No words can express my grief when I heard Fundanus giving his own orders (for one heart-rending detail leads to another) for the money he had intended for clothing, pearls and jewels to be spent on incense, ointment and spices (for the funeral). He is indeed a cultivated man and a philosopher who has devoted himself from youth to higher thought and the arts, but at the moment he rejects everything he has so often heard and professed himself: he has cast off all his other virtues and is wholly absorbed by his love for his child. You will forgive and even admire him if you think of what he has lost—a daughter who resembled him in character no less than in face and expression, and was her father's living image in every way.

If then you write anything to him in his very natural sorrow, be careful not to offer any crude form of consolation which might suggest reproof; be gentle and sympathetic. Passage of time will make him readier to accept this; a raw wound shrinks from a healing hand but later permits and even seeks help, and so the mind rejects and repels any consolation in its first pangs of grief, then feels the need of comfort and is calmed if this is kindly offered.

iii. Valerius Maximus, *Memorable Deeds and Sayings* VI. 7.1-3.

Loyalty to her husband was, in the opinion of Roman men, the highest virtue a woman could attain. The following three examples can join Arria and Fannia in the pantheon of saintly wives.

Tertia Aemilia, wife of Scipio Africanus and mother of Cornelia (the Gracchi's mother), was a woman of such kindness and
patience that, although she knew that her husband was carrying
on with a little serving girl, she looked the other way, lest a
woman prosecute her great husband, Africanus, a conqueror of
the world, for a dalliance. So little was she interested in revenge
that, after Scipio's death, she freed the girl and gave her in
marriage to one of her own freedmen [191 B.C.].

[Some scholars have suggested that this is the woman honored
in the inscription on p. 106.] When Quintus Lucretius [Vespillo]
was proscribed by the triumvirs, his wife Thuria hid him in her
bedroom above the rafters. A single maidservant knew the
secret. At great risk to herself, she kept him safe from imminent death. So rare was her loyalty that, while the other men
who had been proscribed found themselves in foreign, hostile
places amongst the worst tortures of body and soul and were
barely managing to escape, Lucretius was safe in the bedroom in
the arms of his wife [42 B.C.].

Sulpicia, despite the very close watch her mother Julia was
keeping on her so she would not follow her husband to Sicily
(he was Lentulus Cruscellio, proscribed by the triumvirs),
nevertheless put on slave's clothing and, taking two maids and
the same number of manservants, fled secretly and went to him.
She was not afraid to risk proscription herself, and her fidelity
to her proscribed spouse was firm [42 B.C.].

iv. Dio Cassius, *History of Rome* LXXVIII-LXXIX (excerpts)

Julia Domna, born in Syria, was the wife of the emperor Septimius Severus and
mother of Caracalla (Antoninus). She was known for her love of learning and
her wit. After her husband's death, she supported her younger son, Geta, in his
unsuccessful claim to the throne against Caracalla.

Antoninus [i.e., Caracalla] wished to murder his brother at
the Saturnalia, but was unable to do so; for his evil purpose had
already become too manifest to remain concealed, and so there
now ensued many sharp encounters between the two, each of
whom felt that the other was plotting against him, and many
defensive measures were taken on both sides. Since many soldiers and athletes, therefore, were guarding Geta, both abroad
and at home, day and night alike, Antoninus induced his mother
to summon them both, unattended, to her apartment, with a

view to reconciling them. Thus Geta was persuaded, and went in with him; but when they were inside, some centurions, previously instructed by Antoninus, rushed in in a body and struck down Geta, who at sight of them had run to his mother, hung about her neck and clung to her bosom and breasts, lamenting and crying: "Mother that didst bear me, mother that didst bear me, help! I am being murdered." And so she, tricked in this way, saw her son perishing in most impious fashion in her arms, and received him at his death into the very womb, as it were, whence he had been born; for she was all covered with his blood, so that she took no note of the wound she had received on her hand. But she was not permitted to mourn or weep for her son, though he had met so miserable an end before his time (he was only twenty-two years and nine months old), but, on the contrary, she was compelled to rejoice and laugh as though at some great good fortune; so closely were all her words, gestures, and changes of color observed. Thus she alone, the Augusta, wife of the emperor and mother of the emperors, was not permitted to shed tears even in private over so great a sorrow. . . .

Neither in these matters nor in any others did [Antoninus] heed his mother, who gave him much excellent advice. And yet he had appointed her to receive petitions and to have charge of his correspondence in both languages, except in very important cases, and used to include her name, in terms of high praise, together with his own and that of the legions, in his letters to the senate, stating that she was well. Need I add that she held public receptions for all the most prominent men, precisely as did the emperor? But, while she devoted herself more and more to the study of philosophy with these men, he kept declaring that he needed nothing beyond the necessaries of life and plumed himself over his pretended ability to live on the cheapest kind of fare; yet there was nothing on land or sea or in the air that we did not regularly supply to him both by private gifts and by public grants. . . .

Now Julia, the mother of Tarautas, chanced to be in Antioch, and at the first information of her son's [Caracalla's] death she was so affected that she dealt herself a violent blow and tried to starve herself to death. Thus she mourned, now that he was dead, the very man whom she had hated while he lived; yet it was not because she wished that he were alive, but because she was vexed at having to return to private life. This led her to indulge in much bitter abuse of [his successor] Macrinus. Then, as no change was made in her royal retinue or in the guard of Pretorians in attendance upon her, and the new emperor sent her a kindly message, although he had heard what she had said, she took courage, put aside her desire for death, and without writing him any reply, began intriguing with the soldiers she had about her, who [were mutinous] to begin with, [were very fond of] her, and were [angry] with Macrinus, and [consequently] held her son in [pleasant]er remembrance; for she hoped to become sole ruler and make herself the equal of Semiramis and Nitocris, inasmuch as she came in a sense from the same part [of the world] as they....

She heard, moreover, what was said in Rome about her son, she no longer cared to live, but hastened her death by refusing food, though one might say that she was already in a dying condition by reason of the cancer of the breast that she had had for a very long time; it had, however, been quiescent until, on the occasion referred to, she had inflamed it by the blow with which she had smitten her breast on hearing of her son's death.

And so this woman, sprung from the people and raised to a high station, who had lived during her husband's reign in great unhappiness because of Plautianus,[53] who had beheld her younger son slain in her own bosom and had always from first to last borne ill will toward her elder son while he lived, and finally had received such tidings of his assassination, fell from power during her lifetime and thereupon destroyed herself.

D. CENSURE

i. Cicero, *In Defense of Caelius* (excerpts).[54]

Our whole concern in this case, jurors, is with Clodia,[55] a woman not only noble but also notorious. Of her I will say no more than is necessary to refute the charges. And you too, Gnaeus Domitius,[56] sensible man that you are, you understand that our whole business here is with her and her only. If she does not admit that she obliged Caelius with the loan of the gold, if she does not accuse him of preparing poison for her, then my behavior is ungentlemanly in dragging in a matron's name otherwise than the respect due to ladies requires. But if on the contrary aside from that woman their case against Caelius is deprived of all strength and foundation, what else can I do as an advocate but repel those who press the assault? Which I would do all the more vehemently if I did not have cause for ill-feeling toward that woman's lover—I am sorry; I meant to say "brother." I am always making that slip. But now I will handle her with moderation, and proceed no further than my honor and the case itself demand. I have never thought it right to take up arms against a lady, especially against one whose arms are so open to all.

First I would like to ask her: "Shall I deal with you severely and strictly and as they would have done in the good old days? Or would you prefer something more indulgent, bland, sophisticated?" If in that austere mode and manner, I shall have to call up someone from the dead, one of those old gentlemen bearded not with the modern style of fringe that so titillates her, but with one of those bristly bushes we see on antique statues and portrait-busts. And he will scold the woman and speak for me and keep her from getting angry with me as she might otherwise do. So let us call up some ancestor of hers, preferably old blind Appius Claudius himself.[57] He will be the least likely to be grieved, since he won't have to look at her. Doubtless if he rose among us he would say something about like this:

"Woman, what business did you have with Caelius, a man scarce out of his teens, a man not your husband? Why were you so friendly with him as to lend him gold? Or how did you grow so unfriendly as to fear his poison? Did you never hear that your father, uncle, grandfather, great-grandfather, great-great-grand-father, and great-great-great-grandfather were consuls? Did you forget that only recently you were the wife of Quintus Metellus, a gentleman of the highest type, a distinguished patriot who had only to show his face to eclipse almost all other citizens in character, reputation, dignity? Born of a high-ranking family, married into a prominent family, how did it happen that you admitted Caelius to such familiarity? Was he a relative or friend of your husband? Not at all. What was it then but hot and headstrong passion? If the portraits of us male ancestors meant nothing to you, how could my granddaughter, Quinta Claudia, have failed to inspire you to emulate her domestic virtue and womanly glory? Or that Vestal Virgin of our name who kept her arms around her father throughout his triumph and foiled the tribune's attempt to drag him from his chariot? Why choose to imitate your brother's vices in preference to the good qualities of your father and grandfather and of men and women of our line on back to myself? Did I break the agreement with King Pyrrhus that you might every day enter into disgusting agreements with your paramours? Did I bring in the Appian Aqueduct that you might put its waters to your dirty uses? Did I build the Appian Way that you might ride up and down with other women's husbands?"

But perhaps it was a mistake for me to introduce such an august personage, gentlemen. He might suddenly turn on Caelius and make him feel the weight of his censorial powers. Though I will see to this later; I am convinced I can justify Marcus Caelius' behavior to the most captious of critics. But as for you, woman — I am not speaking to you now through the mouth of another — if you have in mind to make good what you are doing, saying, pretending, plotting, and alleging, you had better do some explaining as well, and account for this extraordinarily intimate association. The prosecutors have been lavish with their tales of affairs, amours, adulteries, Baiae,[58] beach-picnics, banquets, drinking-bouts, songfests, musical ensembles, and yachting-parties. And they indicate that they are describing all this with your full permission. Since for some rash, mad purpose you have been willing to have all these stories come out at a trial in the forum, you must either tone down their effect by showing they are groundless, or else admit that no one need believe your charges and your testimony.

But if you would rather I dealt with you more suavely, I will take this tack: I will whisk that old fellow off the scene, unfeeling rustic that he is, and will bring on someone of your own day, your younger brother, say, the most sophisticated of all that crew. He loves you dearly. When he was a young sprout he used to sleep with big sister because, I am told, he was subject to mysterious nervousness and fanciful fears at night. Suppose we let him talk to you: "Why are you making such a fuss, sister? Why are you behaving like an insane woman?

    Why, with shout and speech inflate
    A little thing into a great?[59]

You saw a young man living nearby. He had a fresh complexion. He was tall. He was handsome. His eyes were attractive. You were much taken with all this. You wanted to see him more often. You met sometimes on the same suburban estates. A woman of means, you thought to bind the young man with fetters of gold, still dependent on a tightfisted father. But you can't. He kicks, he spits, he bucks. He doesn't set much value on your presents. Well, go somewhere else. You have gardens on the Tiber. You deliberately chose them for their location, since they are at the very place where all the young men go in swimming. You can pick your bargains there any day. Why do you bother with this fellow who spurns you?"

[Caelius] will have no trouble defending all his conduct. I am not saying anything against that woman now; but if there were someone — not the same as her, you understand— some woman who made herself cheap and easy to approach, who always had some man or other hanging about openly acknowledged as her current interest, in whose gardens and home and place at Baiae anybody and everybody could arrange assignations with her permission, who even boarded young men and made up deficiencies in their allowances out of her own purse, if this person, being widowed, lived loosely, being forward, lived wantonly, being right, lived extravagantly, being prurient, lived like a harlot, am I to think a man an adulterer if he does not address her exactly like a lady?

ii. Plutarch, *Life of Mark Antony* 25-29

"For Rome, who had never condescended to fear any nation or people, did in her time fear two human beings; one was Hannibal, and the other was a woman."[60]

[Caesar and Pompey were acquainted with Cleopatra when she was] a girl, young and ignorant of the world, but she was to meet Antony in the time of life [age 29] when women's beauty is most splendid and their intellects are in full maturity. She made great preparation for her journey, of money, gifts, and ornaments of value, such as so wealthy a kingdom might afford, but she brought with her her surest hopes in her own magic arts and charms.

She received several letters, both from Antony and from his friends, to summon her, but she took no account of these orders[61] and at last, as if in mockery of them, she came sailing up the river Cydnus, in a barge with gilded stern and outspread sails of purple, while oars of silver beat time to the music of flutes and fifes and harps. She herself lay all along under a canopy of cloth of gold, dressed as Venus in a picture, and beautiful young boys, like painted Cupids, stood on each side to fan her. Her maids were dressed like sea nymphs and graces, some steering at the rudder, some working at the ropes. The perfumes diffused themselves from the vessel to the shore, which was covered with multitudes, part following the galley up the river on either bank, part running out of the city to see the sight. The market-place was quite emptied, and Antony at last was left alone sitting upon the tribunal; while the word went through all the multitude that Venus was come to feast with Bacchus, for the common good of Asia. . . .

The next day Antony invited her to supper, and was very desirous to outdo her as well in magnificence as contrivance; but he found he was altogether beaten in both, and was so well convinced of it that he was himself the first to jest and mock at his poverty of wit and his rustic awkwardness. She, perceiving that his raillery was broad and gross and savored more of the soldier than the courtier, rejoined in the same taste and fell into it at once, without any sort of reluctance or reserve. For her actual beauty, it is said, was not in itself so remarkable that none could be compared with her, or that no one could see her without being struck by it, but the contact of her presence, if you lived with her, was irresistible; the attraction of her person, joining with the charm of her conversation, and the character that attended all she said or did, was something bewitching. It was a pleasure merely to hear the sound of her voice, with which, like an instrument of many strings, she could pass from one language to another; so that there were few of the barbarian nations that she answered by an interpreter; to most of them she spoke herself, as to the Ethiopians, Troglodytes, Hebrews, Arabians, Syrians, Medes, Parthians, and many others, whose language she had learnt; which was all the more surprising because most of the kings, her predecessors, scarcely gave themselves the trouble to acquire the Egyptian tongue, and several of them quite abandoned the Macedonian.

Antony was so captivated by her that, while Fulvia his wife maintained his quarrels in Rome against Caesar by actual force of arms, and the Parthian troops were assembled in Mesopotamia and ready to enter Syria, he could yet suffer himself to be carried away by her to Alexandria, there to keep holiday, like a boy, in play and diversion, squandering and fooling away in enjoyments that most costly (as Antiphon says) of all valuables, time. . . .

Plato admits four sorts of flattery, but she had a thousand. Were Antony serious or disposed to mirth, she had at any moment some new delight or charm to meet his wishes; at every turn she was upon him, and let him escape her neither by day nor by night. She played at dice with him, drank with him, hunted with him; and when he exercised in arms, she was there to see. At night she would go rambling with him to disturb and torment people at their doors and windows, dressed like a serv-ant-woman, for Antony also went in servant's disguise, and from these expeditions he often came home very scurvily answered and sometimes even beaten severely, though most people guessed who it was. However, the Alexandrians in general liked it all well enough, and joined good-humoredly and kindly in his frolic and play, saying they were much obliged to Antony for acting his tragic parts at Rome and keeping his comedy for them. It would be trifling without end to be particular in his follies, but his fishing must not be forgotten. He went out one day to angle with Cleopatra, and, being so unfortunate as to catch nothing in the presence of his mistress, he gave secret orders to the fishermen to dive under water, and put fishes that had been already taken upon his hooks; and these he drew so fast that the Egyptian[62] perceived it. But, feigning great admi-ration, she told everybody how dexterous Antony was, and invited them next day to come and see him again. So, when a number of them had come on board the fishing-boats, as soon as he had let down his hook, one of her servants was beforehand with his divers, and fixed upon his hook a salted fish from Pontus. Antony, feeling his line give, drew up the prey, and when, as may be imagined, great laughter ensued, "Leave," said Cleopatra, "the fishing-rod general, to us poor sovereigns of Pharos and Canopus; your game is cities, provinces, and king-doms."

iii. Juvenal, *Satires* 6 (excerpts)

Ancient biographers, characteristically confusing poet and poetry, regarded this famous satire as factual evidence that Juvenal hated women. Stories of the same type were attributed to Lucretius (the first-century B.C. poet), because of his caustic statements about marriage in book 4 of his *De Rerum Natura*.

Eppia, though the wife of a senator, went off with a gladiator to Pharos and the Nile on the notorious walls of Alexandria (though even Egypt condemns Rome's disgusting morals). For-getting her home, her husband, and her sister, she showed no concern whatever for her homeland (she *was* shameless) and her children in tears, and (you'll be dumbfounded by this) she left the theater and Paris the actor behind. Even though when she was a baby she was pillowed in great luxury, in the down of her father's mansion, in a cradle of the finest workmanship, she didn't worry about the dangers of sea travel (she had long since stopped worrying about her reputation, the loss of which among rich ladies' soft cushions does not matter much). Therefore with heart undaunted she braved the waves of the Adriatic and the wide-resounding Ionian Sea (to get to Egypt she had to change seas frequently).

You see, if there's a good reason for undertaking a dangerous voyage, then women are fearful; their cowardly breasts are chilled with icy dread; they cannot stand on their trembling feet. But they show courageous spirit in affairs they're determined to enter illictly. If it's their *husband* who wants them to go, then it's a problem to get on board ship. They can't stand the bilgewater; the skies spin around them. The woman who goes off with her *lover* of course has no qualms. She eats dinner with the sailors, walks the quarter-deck, and enjoys hauling rough ropes. Meanwhile the first woman gets sick all over her husband.

And yet what was the glamor that set her on fire, what was the prime manhood that captured Eppia's heart. What was it she saw in him, that would compensate for her being called *Gladia-trix*? Note that her lover, dear Sergius, had now started shaving his neck, and was hoping to be released from duty because of a bad wound on his arm. Moreover, his face was deformed in a number of ways: he had a mark where his helmet rubbed him, and a big wart between his nostrils, and a smelly discharge always dripping from his eye. But he was a *gladiator*. That made him look as beautiful as Apollo's friend Hyacinth. This is what she preferred to her children and her homeland, her sister and her husband. It's the *sword* they're in love with: this same Sergius, once released from service, would begin to seem like her husband Veiento.

Do you care about a private citizen's house, about Eppia's doings? Turn your eyes to the gods' rivals. Hear what the Emperor Claudius had to put up with. As soon as his wife thought that he was asleep, this imperial whore[63] put on the hood she wore at night, determined to prefer a cheap pad to the royal bed, and left the house with one female slave only. No, hiding her black hair in a yellow wig she entered the brothel, warm with its old patchwork quilts and her empty cell, her very own. Then she took her stand, naked, her nipples gilded, assuming the name of Lycisca, and displayed the stomach you came from, noble Brittanicus. She obligingly received customers and asked for her money, and lay there through the night taking in the thrusts of all comers. Then when the pimp sent the girls home, at last she went away sadly, and (it was all she could do) was the last to close up her cell — she was still burning, her vagina stiff and erected; tired by men, but not yet satisfied, she left, her face dirty and bruised, grimy with lampsmoke, she brought back to her pillow the smell of the brothel.

Isn't there anyone then in such large herds of women that's worth marrying? Let her be beautiful, graceful, rich, fertile, let her place on her porticoes her ancestors' statues; let her be more virginal than the Sabine women (the ones that with their dishevelled hair brought the war with Rome to an end); let her be a phoenix on earth, something like a black swan—but who could stand a wife who has every virtue? I'd rather have (much rather) a gal from Venusia than you, Cornelia, mother of the Gracchi, if along with your great excellence you bring a snob's brow and count your family's triumphs as part of your dowry.[64]

All chance of domestic harmony is lost while your wife's mother is living. She gets her to rejoice in despoiling her husband, stripping him naked. She gets her to write back politely and with sophistication when her seducer sends letters. She tricks your spies or bribes them. Then when your daughter is feeling perfectly well she calls in the doctor Archigenes and says that the blankets are too heavy. Meanwhile, her lover, in hiding shut off from her, impatient at the delay, waits in silence and stretches his foreskin. Maybe you think that her mother will teach her virtuous ways—ones different from her own? It's much more productive for a dirty old lady to bring up a dirty little girl.

There's hardly a case in court where the litigation wasn't begun by a female. If Manilia can't be defendant, she'll be the plaintiff.[65] They'll draw up indictments without assistance, and are ready to tell Celsus the lawyer how to begin his speech and what arguments he should use.

Who doesn't know about the Tyrian wrappers and the ointment for women's athletics? Who hasn't seen the wounds in the dummy, which she drills with continual stabbings and hits with her shield and works through the whole course of exercise—a matron, the sort you'd expect to blow the trumpet at the Floralia[66]—unless in her heart she is plotting something deeper still, and seriously training for the actual games? How can a woman who wears a helmet be chaste? She's denying her sex, and likes a man's strength. But she wouldn't want to turn into a man, since we men get so little pleasure.

Yet what a show there would be, if there were an auction of your wife's stuff—her belt and gauntlets and helmet and half-armor for her left leg. Or she can try the other style of battle— lucky you, when she sells her greaves. Yet these same girls sweat even in muslin, even the thinnest little netting burns their delicacies. Look at the noise she makes when she drives home the blows her trainer showed her, at the weight of her helmet, how solidly she sits on her haunches (like the binding around a thick tree), and laugh when she puts her armor aside to pick up her chamber-pot.

You ask where these monsters come from, the source that they spring from? Poverty made Latin women chaste in the old days, hard work and a short time to sleep and hands calloused and hardened with woolworking, and Hannibal close to the city,[67] and their husbands standing guard at the Colline Gate— that kept their humble homes from being corrupted by vice. But now we are suffering from the evils of a long peace. Luxury, more ruthless than war, broods over Rome and takes revenge for the world she has conquered. No cause for guilt or deed of lust is missing, now that Roman poverty has vanished. Money, nurse of promiscuity, first brought in foreigners' ways, and effete riches weakened the sinews of succeeding generations. What does Venus care when she's drunk? She can't tell head from tail when she eats big oysters at midnight, and when her perfume foams with undiluted wine, when she drinks her conch-shell cup dry, and when in her dizziness the roof turns round and the table rises up to meet two sets of lights.

An even worse pain is the female who, as soon as she sits down to dinner, praises Vergil and excuses Dido's suicide:[68] matches and compares poets, weighing Vergil on one side of the scale and Homer in the other. Schoolmasters yield; professors are vanquished; everyone in the party is silenced. No one can speak, not a lawyer, not an auctioneer, not even another woman. Such an avalanche of words falls, that you'd say it's like pans and bells being beaten. Now no one needs trumpets or bronzes: this woman by herself can come help the Moon when she's suffering from an eclipse.[69] As a philosopher she sets definitions on moral behavior. Since she wants to seem so learned and eloquent she ought to shorten her tunic up to her knees[70] and bring a pig to Sylvanus [forbidden to women] and go to the penny bath with the philosophers. Don't let the woman who shares your marriage bed adhere to a set style of speaking or hurl in well-rounded sentences the enthymeme shorn of its premise. Don't let her know all the histories. Let there be something in books she does not understand. I hate the woman who is continually poring over and studying Palaemon's[71] treatise, who never breaks the rules or principles of grammar, and who quotes verses I never heard of, ancient stuff that men ought not to worry about. Let her correct her girlfriend's verses—she ought to allow her husband to commit a solecism.

Pauper women endure the trials of childbirth and endure the burdens of nursing, when fortune demands it. But virtually no gilded bed is laid out for childbirth—so great is her skill, so easily can she produce drugs that make her sterile or induce her to kill *human beings* in her womb. You fool, enjoy it, and give her the potion to drink, whatever it's going to be, because, if she wants to get bloated and to trouble her womb with a live baby's kicking, you might end up being the father of an Ethiopian— soon a wrong-colored heir will complete your accounts, a person whom it's bad luck to see first thing in the morning.

10. LAW

A. THE LAWS OF ROMULUS

Although the history of Rome's regal period is based mostly on legend, and was so in antiquity, tradition was strong, and many of Rome's laws and customs, committed to writing much later, have their roots in the distant past. The following are attributed to Romulus, the founder, who is traditionally said to have reigned from 753 to 716 B.C.

Romulus compelled the citizens...to rear every male child and the first-born of the females, and he forbade them to put to death any child under three years of age, unless it was a cripple or a monster from birth. He did not prevent the parents from exposing such children, provided that they had displayed them first to their five nearest neighbors and had secured their approval. For those who disobeyed the law he prescribed the confiscation of half of their property as well as other penalties.

By the enactment of a single ... law ... Romulus brought the women to great prudence and orderly conduct. ... The law was as follows: A woman united with her husband by a sacred marriage[72] shall share in all his possessions and in his sacred rites.

The cognates sitting in judgment with the husband ... were given power to pass sentence in cases of adultery and ... if any wife was found drinking wine Romulus allowed the death penalty for both crimes.

He also made certain laws, one of which is severe, namely, that which does not permit a wife to divorce her husband, but gives him power to divorce her for the use of drugs or magic on account of children[73] or for counterfeiting the keys or for adultery. The law ordered that if he should divorce her for any other cause part of his estate should go to the wife and that part should be dedicated to Ceres. Anyone who sold his wife was sacrificed to the gods of the underworld.

It is strange, ... when he established no penalty against patricides, that he called all homicide patricide.

If a daughter-in-law strikes her father-in-law she shall be dedicated as a sacrifice to his ancestral deities.

B. THE TWELVE TABLES (excerpts)

FIRA, p. 23 (traditional date 450 B.C.)

These laws, the basis of Roman civil law, have their origins in what the Romans called *mos maiorum*, the tradition of their ancestors. The codification and publication of the ancestral laws on twelve bronze tablets in the Roman Forum represented a victory for the plebeian class, which hitherto had been subject to prejudiced legal interpretations by the patricians. Though some of the laws became outdated, the code was never abolished.

Table IV. Paternal Power

A notably deformed child shall be killed immediately.

To repudiate his wife her husband shall order her ... to have her own property for herself, shall take the keys, shall expel her.[74]

A child born within ten months of the father's death shall enter into the inheritance ...

Table V. Inheritance and Guardianship

... Women, even though they are of full age, because of their levity of mind shall be under guardianship... except Vestal Virgins, who... shall be free from guardianship.[75]

The conveyable possessions of a woman who is under guardianship of male agnates[76] shall not be acquired by prescriptive right unless they are transferred by the woman herself with the authorization of her guardian...

If anyone who has no direct heir dies intestate the nearest male agnate shall have the estate.

If there is not a male agnate the male clansmen shall have the estate.

Persons for whom[77] by will... a guardian is not given, for them... their male agnates shall be guardians.

C. THE REPEAL OF THE OPPIAN LAW

Livy, *History of Rome* XXXIV. 1-8 (abridged).

In 215 B.C., after its disastrous defeat by Hannibal at Cannae, Rome passed the Oppian law, an emergency measure which limited women's use of expensive goods. Twenty years later, the crisis having long-since passed, the law was repealed against the objections of many conservatives, here represented by the consul and champion of traditional values, Marcus Porcius Cato.

Among the troubles of great wars, either scarcely over or yet to come, something intervened which, while it can be told briefly, stirred up enough excitement to become a great battle. Marcus Fundanius and Lucius Valerius, the tribunes of the people, brought a motion to repeal the Oppian law before the people. Gaius Oppius had carried this law as tribune at the height of the Punic War, during the consulship of Quintus Fabius and Tiberius Sempronius. The law said that no woman might own more than half an ounce of gold nor wear a multicolored[78] dress nor ride in a carriage in the city or in a town within a mile of it, unless there was a religious festival. The tribunes, Marcus and Publius Junius Brutus, were in favor of the Oppian law and said that they would not allow its repeal. Many noble men came forward hoping to persuade or dissuade them; a crowd of men, both supporters and opponents, filled the Capitoline Hill. The matrons, whom neither counsel nor shame nor their husbands' orders could keep at home, blockaded every street in the city and every entrance to the Forum. As the men came down to the Forum, the matrons besought them to let them, too, have back the luxuries they had enjoyed before, giving as their reason that the republic was thriving and that everyone's private wealth was increasing with every day. This crowd of women was growing daily, for now they were even gathering from the towns and villages. Before long they dared go up and solicit the consuls, praetors, and other magistrates; but one of the consuls could not be moved in the least, Marcus Porcius Cato,[79] who spoke in favor of the law:

"If each man of us, fellow citizens, had established that the right and authority of the husband should be held over the mother of his own family, we should have less difficulty with women in general; now, at home our freedom is conquered by female fury, here in the Forum it is bruised and trampled upon, and, because we have not contained the individuals, we fear the lot. . . .

"Indeed, I blushed when, a short while ago, I walked through the midst of a band of women. Had not respect for the dignity and modesty of certain ones (not them all!) restrained me (so they would not be seen being scolded by a consul), I should have said, 'What kind of behavior is this? Running around in public, blocking streets, and speaking to other women's husbands! Could you not have asked your own husbands the same thing at home? Are you more charming in public with others' husbands than at home with your own? And yet, it is not fitting even at home (if modesty were to keep married women within the bounds of their rights) for you to concern yourselves with what laws are passed or repealed here.' Our ancestors did not want women to conduct any—not even private—business without a guardian; they wanted them to be under the authority of parents, brothers, or husbands; we (the gods help us!) even now let them snatch at the government and meddle in the Forum and our Assemblies. What are they doing now on the streets and crossroads, if they are not persuading the tribunes to vote for repeal? Give the reins to their unbridled nature and this unmastered creature, and hope that they will put limits on their own freedom; unless you do something yourselves, this is the least of the things imposed upon them either by custom or by law which they endure with hurt feelings. They want freedom, nay license (if we are to speak the truth), in all things.

"If they are victorious now, what will they not attempt? . . . As soon as they begin to be your equals, they will have become your superiors. . . .

"What honest excuse is offered, pray, for this womanish rebellion? 'That we might shine with gold and purple,' says one of them, 'that we might ride through the city in coaches on holidays and working-days, as though triumphant over the conquered law and the votes which we captured by tearing them from you; that there should be no limit to our expenses and our luxury.' ...

"The woman who can spend her own money will do so; the one who cannot will ask her husband. Pity that husband—the one who gives in and the one who stands firm! What he refuses, he will see given by another man. Now they publicly solicit other women's husbands, and, what is worse, they ask for a law and votes, and certain men give them what they want. You there, *you*, are easily moved about things which concern yourself, your estate, and your children; once the law no longer limits your wife's spending, you will never do it by yourself. Fellow citizens, do not imagine that the state which existed before the law was passed will return. A dishonest man is safer never accused than acquitted, and luxury, left alone, would have been more acceptable than it will be now, as when wild animals are first chafed by their chains and then released. I vote that the Oppian law should not, in the smallest measure, be repealed; whatever course you take, may all the gods make you happy with it."

After this, when the tribunes of the people, who had declared that they would oppose the motion to repeal, had added a few remarks along the same lines, Lucius Valerius spoke on behalf of the motion which he himself had brought:

"[Cato] used up more words castigating the women than he did opposing the motion, and he left in some uncertainty whether the women had done the deeds which he reproached on their own or at our instigation. I shall defend the motion, not ourselves, against whom the consul has hurled this charge, more for the words than for the reality of the accusation. He has called this assemblage 'secession' and sometimes 'womanish rebellion,' because the matrons have publicly asked you, in peacetime when the state is happy and prosperous, to repeal a law passed against them during the straits of war....

"What, may I ask, are the women doing that is new, having gathered and come forth publicly in a case which concerns them directly? Have they never appeared in public before this? Allow me to unroll your own *Origines*[80] before you. Listen to how often they have done so—always for the public good. From the very beginning—the reign of Romulus—when the Capitoline had been taken by the Sabines and there was fighting in the middle of the Forum, was not the battle halted by the women's intervention between the two lines? How about this? After the kings had been expelled, when the Volscian legions and their general, Marcius Coriolanus, had pitched camp at the fifth milestone, did not the matrons turn away the forces which would have buried the city? When Rome was in the hands of the Gauls, who ransomed it? Indeed the matrons agreed unanimously to turn their gold over to the public need. Not to go too far back in history, in the most recent war, when we needed funds, did not the widows' money assist the treasury? And when new gods were summoned to bring their power to our difficulties, was it not all the matrons who went to the sea to meet the Idaean Mother? You say these cases are different. I am not here to say they are the same; it is enough to prove that nothing new has been done. Indeed, as no one is amazed that they acted in situations affecting men and women alike, why should we wonder that they have taken action in a case which concerns themselves? What, after all, have they done? We have proud ears indeed, if, while masters do not scorn the appeals of slaves, we are angry when honorable women ask something of us. . . .

"Who then does not know that this is a recent law, passed twenty years ago? Since our matrons lived for so long by the highest standards of behavior without any law, what risk is there that, once it is repealed, they will yield to luxury? For if the law were an old one, or if it had been passed to restrain feminine license, there might be reason to fear that repeal would incite them. The times themselves will show you why the law was passed. Hannibal was in Italy, victorious at Cannae. Already he held Tarentum, Arpi, and Capua. He seemed on the verge of moving against Rome. Our allies had gone over to him. We had no reserve troops, no allies at sea to protect the fleet, no funds in the treasury. Slaves were being bought and armed, on condition that the price be paid their owners when the war was over. The contractors had declared that they would provide, on that same day of payment (after the war), the grain and other supplies the needs of war demanded. We were giving our slaves as rowers at our own expense, in proportion to our property rating. We were giving all our gold and silver for public use, as the senators had done first. Widows and children were donating their funds to the treasury. We were ordered to keep at home no more than a certain amount of wrought and stamped gold and silver. At a time like that were the matrons so taken up with luxury and fancy trappings that the Oppian law was needed to restrain them, when, since the rites of Ceres had been suspended because all the women were in mourning, the senate ordered mourning limited to thirty days? To whom is it not clear that poverty and misfortune were the authors of that law of yours, since all private wealth had to be turned over to public use, and that it was to remain in effect only as long as the reason for its writing did? . . .

"Shall it be our wives alone to whom the fruits of peace and tranquillity of the state do not come? . . . Shall we forbid only women to wear purple? When you, a man, may use purple on your clothes, will you not allow the mother of your family to have a purple cloak, and will your horse be more beautifully saddled than your wife is garbed? . . .

"[Cato] has said that, if none of them had anything, there would be no rivalry among individual women. By Hercules! All are unhappy and indignant when they see the finery denied them permitted to the wives of the Latin allies, when they see them adorned with gold and purple, when those other women ride through the city and they follow on foot, as though the power belonged to the other women's cities, not to their own. This could wound the spirits of men; what do you think it could do to the spirits of women, whom even little things disturb? They cannot partake of magistracies, priesthoods, triumphs, badges of office, gifts, or spoils of war; elegance, finery, and beautiful clothes are women's badges, in these they find joy and take pride, this our forebears called the women's world. When they are in mourning, what, other than purple and gold, do they take off? What do they put on again when they have completed the period of mourning? What do they add for public prayer and thanksgiving other than still greater ornament? Of course, if you repeal the Oppian law, you will not have the power to prohibit that which the law now forbids; daughters, wives, even some men's sisters will be less under your authority — never, while her men are sound, is a woman's slavery cast off; and even they hate the freedom created by widowhood and orphanage. They prefer their adornment to be subject to *your* judgment, not the law's; and you ought to hold them in *manus*[81] and guardianship, not slavery; you should prefer to be called fathers and husbands to masters. The consul just now used odious terms when he said 'womanish rebellion' and 'secession.' For there is danger—he would have us believe—that they will seize the Sacred Hill as once the angry plebeians did, or the Aventine. It is for the weaker sex to submit to whatever you advise. The more power you possess, all the more moderately should you exercise your authority."

When these speeches for and against the law had been made, a considerably larger crowd of women poured forth in public the next day; as a single body they besieged the doors of the Brutuses, who were vetoing their colleagues' motion, and they did not stop until the tribunes took back their veto. After that there was no doubt but that all the tribes would repeal the law. Twenty years after it was passed, the law was repealed.

D. THE JULIAN MARRIAGE LAWS

In 18 B.C., the Emperor Augustus turned his attention to social problems at Rome. Luxury and adultery were widespread. Among the upper classes, marriage was increasingly infrequent and, for couples who did marry, childlessness was common. Augustus was interested in raising both the morals and the numbers of the upper classes in Rome, and in increasing the population of native Italians in Italy. He enacted sumptuary laws, laws against adultery, and laws which encouraged marriage and children. The laws which regulated intermarriage between the classes are treated in the texts below.

The law against adultery (*lex Iulia de adulteriis coercendis*) made the offense a crime punishable by exile and confiscation of property. Fathers were permitted to kill daughters and their partners in adultery. Husbands could kill the partners under certain circumstances and were required to divorce adulterous wives. It is ironic that Augustus was eventually obliged to invoke this law against his own daughter, Julia, and to relegate her to the island of Pandateria.[82]

The Augustan social laws were badly received, and the emperor, years later, modified them. The *lex Papia Poppaea*, enacted in 9 A.D., softened slightly the rigidity of the earlier legislation. It takes its name from the two consuls of that year — both bachelors. While the laws were never formally repealed, they were never fully successful.

i. Dio Cassius, *Roman History*, LIV 16

He laid heavier assessments upon the unmarried men and women and on the other hand offered prizes for marriage and the begetting of children. And since among the nobility there were far more males than females, he allowed all [free men] who wished, except senators, to marry freedwomen, and ordered that their offspring should be held legitimate.

140

ii. Various legal sources, collected in *ADA*, pp. 166-98 (abridged)

The Julian Law provides as follows: No one who is or shall be a senator, or a son, grandson born of a son, or great-grandson born of a son's son of any one of these, shall knowingly and with malice aforethought have as betrothed or wife a freedwoman or any woman who herself or whose father or mother is or has been an actor. And no daughter of a senator or grandaughter born of a son or great-granddaughter born of a grandson (a son's son) shall knowingly and with malice aforethought be betrothed or married to a freedman or to a man who himself or whose father or mother is or has been an actor, and no such man shall knowingly and with malice aforethought have her as betrothed or wife.

Freeborn men are forbidden to marry a prostitute, a procuress, a woman manumitted by a procurer or procuress, one caught in adultery, one convicted in a public action, or one who has been an actress.

A freedwoman who is married to her patron shall not have the right of divorce... as long as the patron wants her to be his wife.

A man or wife can, by virtue of marriage, inherit a tenth of the other's estate. But if they have living children from a previous marriage, in addition to the tenth which they take by virtue of marriage they receive as many tenths as the number of children. Likewise a common son or daughter lost after the day of naming adds one tenth, and two lost after the ninth day add two tenths. Besides the tenth they can receive also the usufruct of a third part of the estate, and whenever they have children the ownership of the same part.

Sometimes a man or wife can inherit the other's entire estate, for example, if both or either are not yet of the age at which the law requires children—that is, if the husband is under twenty-five and the wife under twenty; or if both have while married passed the age prescribed by the Papian Law—that is, the man sixty, the woman fifty.... They enjoy testamentary freedom in each other's favor if they have obtained the "right of children" from the emperor, if they have a common son or daughter, or if they have lost a fourteen-year-old son or twelve-year-old daughter or two three-year-olds or three after the day of naming.... Likewise if the wife has a child by her husband within ten months after his death she takes the whole of his estate.

Sometimes they inherit nothing from each other, that is, if they contract a marriage contrary to the Julian and Papian-Poppaean Law (for example if anyone marries a woman of ill repute or a senator marries a freedwoman).

Bachelors also are forbidden by the Julian Law to receive inheritances or legacies.... Likewise by the Papian Law childless persons, precisely because they have no children, lose one half of inheritances and legacies.

The Julian Law exempted women from marriage for one year after the death of a husband and six months after a divorce; the Papian Law [raised these to] two years after the death of a husband and a year and six months after a divorce.[83]

E. ON PATRIA POTESTAS AND GUARDIANSHIP

i. Gaius, *Institutes* I. 97-117 and 136-137a

The jurists Gaius and Justinian give later interpretations of the concept of *patria potestas*, the power of the father over his own family, which was a fundamental principle of Roman law. Compare the laws given in the Twelve Tables (above, pp. 133-134).

Not only are the children of our bodies in our *potestas* according as we have stated, but also those whom we adopt. Adoption takes place in two ways, either by authority of the people or by the *imperium* of a magistrate, such as a praetor.... The former kind of adoption, that by authority of the people, can be performed nowhere but at Rome, whereas the latter kind is regularly performed in the provinces before the provincial governors. Further, females cannot be adopted by authority of the people, for this opinion has prevailed; but before a praetor or, in the provinces, before the proconsul or legate, females are regularly adopted.... But women cannot adopt by any method, for they do not hold even the children of their bodies in their *potestas*....

Let us proceed to consider persons who are in *manu* (hand, marital power), which is another right peculiar to Roman citizens. Now, while both males and females are found in *potestas*, only females can come under *manus*. Of old, women passed into *manus* in three ways, by *usus*, *confarreatio*, and *coemptio*.[84] A woman used to pass into *manus* by *usus* if she cohabited with her husband for a year without interruption, being as it were acquired by a usucapion of one year and so passing into her husband's family and ranking as a daughter. Hence it was provided by the Twelve Tables that any woman wishing not to come under her husband's *manus* in this way should stay away from him for three nights in each year and thus interrupt the *usus* of each year. But the whole of this institution has been in part abolished by statutes and in part obliterated by simple disuse. Entry of a woman into *manus* by *confarreatio* is effected by a kind of sacrifice offered to Jupiter Farreus, in which the spelt cake is employed, whence the name *confarreatio*. In the performance of this ceremony a number of acts and things are done, accompanied by special formal words, in the presence of 10 witnesses. This institution still exists at the present day. For the higher flamens, that is those of Jupiter, Mars, and Quirinus, and also the *rex sacrorum*, can only be chosen from those born of parents married by *confarreatio*; indeed, no person can hold the priesthood without being himself so married. Entry of a woman into *manus* by *coemptio* takes the form of a mancipation, that is a sort of imaginary sale: in the presence of not less than 5 witnesses, being Roman citizens above puberty, and of a scale-holder, the woman is bought by him into whose *manus* she is passing. It is, however, possible for a woman to make a *coemptio* not only with her husband, but also with a stranger; in other words, *coemptio* may be performed for either matrimonial or fiduciary purposes. A woman who makes a *coemptio* with her husband with the object of ranking as a daughter in his household is said to have made a *coemptio* for matrimonial purposes, while one who makes, whether with her husband or a stranger, a *coemptio* for some other object, such as that of evading a tutorship, is said to have done so for fiduciary purposes. What happens is as follows: a woman wishing to get rid of her existing tutors and to get another makes a *coemptio* with the *auctoritas* of her existing tutors; after that she is remancipated by her *coemptionator* to the person of her own choice and, having been manumitted *uindicta* by him, comes to have as her tutor the man by whom she has been manumitted. This person is called a fiduciary tutor, as will appear below. Formerly too fiduciary *coemptio* used to be performed for the purpose of making a will. This was at a time when women, with certain exceptions, had not the right to make a will unless they had made a *coemptio* and had been remancipated and manumitted. But the senate on the authority of the late emperor Hadrian has dispensed from this requirement of a *coemptio*.... But if a woman makes a fiduciary *coemptio* with her husband, she nevertheless acquires the position of his daughter. For it is the accepted view that, if for any reason whatever a wife be in her husband's *manus*, she acquires a daughter's rights.

We have still to explain what persons are *in mancipio* (bondage). All children, male or female, who are in a parent's *potestas* can be mancipated by him in just the same manner as slaves....

Also, women cease to be in their father's *potestas* by passing into *manus*. But in the case of the confarreate marriage of the wife of a *flamen* of Jupiter a decree of the senate passed on the proposal of Maximus and Tubero has provided that she is to be considered to be in *manus* only for sacral purposes, while for all other purposes she is to be treated as though she had not entered *manus*. On the other hand, a woman who enters *manus* by *coemptio* is freed from her father's *potestas*, and it makes no difference whether she be in her husband's or a stranger's *manus*, although only women who are in their husband's *manus* rank as daughters.

Women cease to be in *manus* in the same ways as those by which daughters are freed from their father's *potestas*. Thus, just as daughters pass out of their father's *potestas* by a single mancipation, so women in *manus* cease by a single mancipation to be in *manus*, and if manumitted from that mancipation become *sui iuris*. Between a woman who has made a *coemptio* with a stranger and one who has done so with her husband there is, however, this difference, that the former can compel her *coemptio* to remancipate her to the person of her choice, whereas the latter can no more compel her husband to do this than a daughter can compel her father. But, while a daughter, even if adoptive, is absolutely incapable of compelling her father, a woman in the *manus* of her husband can, if she has sent him notice of divorce, compel him to release her, just as though she had never been his wife.

ii. Justinian, *Institutes* I. 9

Our children whom we have begotten in lawful wedlock are in our power. Wedlock or matrimony is the union of male and female, involving the habitual intercourse of daily life. The power which we have over our children is peculiar to Roman

144

citizens and is found in no other nation. The offspring then of you and your wife is in your power, and so too is that of your son and his wife, that is to say, your grandson and granddaughter, and so on. But the offspring of your daughter is not in your power, but in that of its own father.

F. MARRIAGE AND INHERITANCE

i. Berlin Papyrus 1210; Alexandria, second century A.D.

The *idiologus*, the chief financial officer of Roman Egypt, administered the imperial account which consisted of funds acquired from means other than taxation (fines and confiscations, for example). The papyrus from which these extracts are taken contains a summary of the rules by which the *idiologus* carried out his duties. This document reveals fiscal oppression not only of women but of an entire province.

6. An Alexandrian, having no children by his wife, may not bequeath to her more than one quarter of his estate; if he does have children by her, her share may not exceed those of each son.

23. It is not permitted to Romans to marry their sisters or their aunts; it is permitted in the case of the daughter of brothers. Pardalas, however, confiscated the property when brothers and sisters married.

24. After death, the fiscus [i.e., the exchequer] takes the dowry given by a Roman woman over fifty to a Roman man under sixty.

26. And when a *Latina*[85] over fifty gives something to one over sixty it is likewise confiscated.

27. What is inherited by a Roman of sixty years, who has neither child nor wife, is confiscated. If he have a wife but no children and register himself, the half is conceded to him.

29. A free-born Roman woman who has an estate of 20,000 sesterces, so long as she is unmarried, pays a hundredth part annually; and a freedwoman who has an estate of 20,000 sesterces pays the same until she marries.

30. The inheritances left to Roman women possessing 50,000 sesterces, who are unmarried and childless, are confiscated.

31. It is permitted a Roman woman to leave her husband a tenth of her property; if she leaves more, it is confiscated.

32. Romans who have more than 100,000 sesterces, and are unmarried and childless, do not inherit; those who have less, do.

33. It is not permitted to a Roman woman to dispose of her property by will without a stipulated clause of the so-called *coemptio fiduciaria*.[86] A legacy left by a Roman woman to a Roman woman who is a minor is confiscated.

38. The children of a woman who is a citizen of Alexandria and an Egyptian man remain Egyptians but inherit from both parents.

39. When a Roman man or a Roman woman marries a citizen of Alexandria or an Egyptian, without knowledge [of the true status], the children follow the lower class.

46. To Roman men and citizens of Alexandria who married Egyptian women without knowledge [of their true status] it was granted, in addition to freedom from responsibility, also that the children follow the father's station.

52. It is permitted Roman men to marry Egyptian women.

53. Egyptian women married to ex-soldiers come under the clause of misrepresentation if they characterize themselves in business transactions as Roman women.

54. Ursus did not allow an ex-soldier's daughter who had become a Roman citizen to inherit from her mother if the latter was an Egyptian.

ii. P. Fam. Tebt. 22; 122 A.D.

Affidavits about the receipt of a final dowry payment, made fifteen years after a first installment of 500 drachmas. The text of the actual agreement[87] specifies that the woman is now 48, her cousin 52, her brothers 44 and 38, and her mother 75.

I, Didymarion, daughter of Heraclides, with my cousin Cronion son of Lusanius as guardian, agree that I have received from my brothers Valerius and Lysimachus 600 silver drachmas described under the terms of an agreement my father made with them on my behalf, under the terms of which (a) I shall not approach them for any transaction whatever made prior to the present day; (b) I have received the set of earrings (gold with genuine pearls weighing four quarters) and the cloak as specified. I, Cronion have written this on her behalf since she does not know letters.

I, Lysimachus son of Heraclides and my mother Didyme daughter of Lysimachus on my authority testify that a receipt has been made out to me, Lysimachus, and to Valerius for 600 drachmas, and that my mother Didyme has made a present to her daughter Didymarion of earrings and a purple cloak, and that she guarantees that she has kept unassigned and unencumbered the half share of the house and courtyard in Tebtunis which she turned over to her. I, Lysimachus, have written this for her since she does not know letters.

iii. P. Cattaoui III; second century A.D.

When Crotis argued through her lawyer Philoxenus that she was a citizen when she was living with Isidorus (who was a citizen) and that afterwards, when he had gone off as a soldier on campaign, she had by him a son Theodorus, about whom it is alleged that she neglected to file a birth certificate because it was clear that the son was his on the basis of an agreement which he wrote down in which he made him heir of his estate. After the will of Julius Martial [the Latin name of Isidorus], a soldier in the first Theban unit, was read, the judge Lupus conferred with his colleagues and stated: "It is impossible for a soldier on campaign to have a legitimate son, but he was within the law when he made him his heir in his will."

When Octavius Valens and Cassia Secunda came before the court in regard to one of the cases that had been postponed, the prefect Eudaemon, conferring with his court, stated: "Yesterday also, the moment the transcript of the honorable Heliodorus was read and the reason why the case had been postponed had been explained, it was evident that the mother of this child was pleading about a forbidden matter, and today also I declare to those of you who are disputing this issue that I am certain about the issues on which I passed judgment yesterday. When a man has entered the army, whether in a regiment or a tactical unit or in a company, a son born to him cannot be legitimate. Since he is not the lawful son of his father, who is an Alexandrian, he cannot be an Alexandrian. This child was born to Valens when he was on campaign with his unit. He is his bastard son. He cannot be enrolled in the citizenry of Alexandria." And he added: "Yesterday you said that you had other children. How old are they? When were they born?" Octavian Valens answered: "One was just born, the other is older." Eudaemon said: "The older one was born sometime while you were in the army?" Valens answered: "While I was with my unit, and so also was the younger child." Eudaemon said: "Realize that these children are in the same condition as your other son. Some

things cannot be changed." Valens said: "But if it were necessary for me to be out of town on business, you yourself would
order that I would receive justice through a trustee. How have
these children behaved unjustly?" Eudaemon said: "I have acted
in a straightforward manner explaining what I could do in detail.
.. Since you are attempting the impossible, neither this boy nor
your other sons can be citizens of Alexandria."

11. POLITICS

A. EARLY ROME

i. Aulus Gellius, *Attic Nights* X. 23.

A passage from a speech of Marcus Cato[88] on the mode of life and manners of
women of the olden time; and also that the husband had the right to kill his wife, if
he were taken in adultery.

Those who have written about the life and civilization of the
Roman people say that the women of Rome and Latium "lived
an abstemious life," that is, that they abstained altogether from
wine, which in the early language was called *temetum;* that it
was an established custom for them to kiss their kinsfolk for the
purpose of detection, so that, if they had been drinking, the odor
might betray them. But they say that the women were accustomed to drink the second brewing, raisin wine, spiced wine and
other sweet-tasting drinks of that kind. And these things are
indeed made known in those books which I have mentioned, but
Marcus Cato declares that women were not only censured but also
punished by a judge no less severely if they had drunk wine than
if they had disgraced themselves by adultery.

I have copied Marcus Cato's words from the oration entitled
On the Dowry, in which it is also stated that husbands had the
right to kill wives taken in adultery: "When a husband puts
away his wife," says he, "he judges the woman as a censor
would, and has full powers if she has been guilty of any wrong
or shameful act; she is severely punished if she has drunk wine;
if she has done wrong with another man, she is condemned to

death." Further, as to the right to put her to death it was thus written: "If you should take your wife in adultery, you may with impunity put her to death without a trial; but if you should commit adultery or indecency, she must not presume to lay a finger on you, nor does the law allow it."

ii. Valerius Maximus, *Memorable Deeds and Sayings* VI.3. 9-12.

Valerius Maximus, writing ca. 30 A.D., records some examples of husbands' punishment of wives in early Rome.

Egnatius Metellus [in Romulus' day] ... took a cudgel and beat his wife to death because she had drunk some wine. Not only did no one charge him with a crime, but no one even blamed him. Everyone considered this an excellent example of one who had justly paid the penalty for violating the laws of sobriety. Indeed, any woman who immoderately seeks the use of wine closes the door on all virtues and opens it to vices.

There was also the harsh marital severity of Gaius Sulpicius Gallus [consul in 166 B.C.]. He divorced his wife because he had caught her outdoors with her head uncovered: a stiff penalty but not without a certain logic. "The law," he said, "prescribes for you my eyes alone to which you may prove your beauty. For these eyes you should provide the ornaments of beauty, for these be lovely: entrust yourself to their more certain knowledge. If you, with needless provocation, invite the look of any one else, you must be suspected of wrongdoing."

Quintus Antistius Vetus felt no differently when he divorced his wife because he had seen her in public having a private conversation with a common freedwoman. For, moved not by an actual crime but, so to speak, by the birth and nourishment of one, he punished her before the sin could be committed, so that he might prevent the deed's being done at all, rather than punish it afterwards.

To these we should add the case of Publius Sempronius Sophus [consul in 268 B.C.] who disgraced his wife with divorce merely because she dared attend the games without his knowledge. And so, long ago, when the misdeeds of women were thus forestalled, their minds stayed far from wrongdoing.

B. SEMPRONIA: A CONSPIRATOR AGAINST THE STATE

Sallust, *The Conspiracy of Catiline* 24-25.

Catiline is said to have gained many adherents of every condition, including a number of women who in their earlier days had lived extravagantly on money that they obtained by prostituting themselves, and then, when advancing age reduced their incomes without changing their luxurious tastes, had run headlong into debt. These women, he thought, would do good service by acting as agitators among the city slaves and organizing acts of incendiarism; their husbands, too, could be either induced to join his cause, or be murdered.

Among their number was Sempronia, a woman who had committed many crimes that showed her to have the reckless daring of a man. Fortune had favored her abundantly, not only with birth and beauty, but with a good husband and children.[89] Well educated in Greek and Latin literature, she had greater skill in lyre-playing and dancing than there is any need for a respectable woman to acquire, besides many other accomplishments such as minister to dissipation. There was nothing that she set a smaller value on than seemliness and chastity, and she was as careless of her reputation as she was of her money. Her passions were so ardent that she more often made advances to men than they did to her. Many times already she had broken a solemn promise, repudiated a debt by perjury, and been an accessory to murder. At once self-indulgent and impecunious, she had gone headlong from bad to worse. Yet her abilities were not to be despised. She could write poetry, crack a joke, and converse at will with decorum, tender feeling, or wantonness; she was in fact a woman of ready wit and considerable charm.

C. WOMEN ORATORS

i. Valerius Maximus, *Memorable Deeds and Sayings* VII.3.

We must be silent no longer about those women whom neither the condition of their nature nor the cloak of modesty could keep silent in the Forum or the courts.

Amasia Sentia, a defendant, pled her case before a great crowd of people and Lucius Titius, the praetor who presided over the court (77 B.C.). She pursued every aspect of her defense diligently and boldly and was acquitted, almost unanimously, in a single hearing. Because she bore a man's spirit under the appearance of a woman, they called her *Androgyne*.

Gaia Afrania, the wife of the senator Licinius Buccio, a woman disposed to bring suits, always represented herself before the praetor: not because she had no advocates, but because her impudence was abundant. And so, by constantly plaguing the tribunals with such barking as the Forum had seldom heard, she became the best known example of women's litigiousness. As a result, to charge a woman with low morals, it is enough to cast up the name "Gaia Afrania" at her. She prolonged her life until Caesar's second consulship [48 B.C.] with Publius Servilius as his colleague; for it is better to record when such a monster died, rather than when it was born.

Hortensia, the daughter of Quintus Hortensius,[90] when the triumvirs burdened the matrons with a heavy tribute[91] and no man dared take their defense, pled their case before the triumvirs, both firmly and successfully. For by bringing back her father's eloquence, she brought about the remission of the greater part of the tax. Quintus Hortensius lived again in the female line and breathed in his daughter's words. If any of her male descendants had wished to follow her strength, the great heritage of Hortensian eloquence would not have come to an end in a woman's action.

ii. Quintilian, *Institutes of Oratory* I. 1.6.

As for parents, I should like them to be as well educated as possible, and I am not speaking just of fathers. We know that Cornelia, the mother of the Gracchi, contributed greatly to their eloquence, for the erudition of her speech has been handed down even to the present day in her letters. Laelia, too, daughter of Gaius [Laelius][92], is said to have brought back the elegance of her father's speech in her own; and the oration which Hortensia, Quintus' daughter, made before the triumvirs is read not merely as an honor to her sex.

iii. Hortensia's Speech
Appian, *Civil War* IV. 32-34.

The triumvirs addressed the people on this subject and pubished an edict requiring 1400 of the richest women to make a valuation of their property, and to furnish for the service of the war such portion as the triumvirs should require from each. It was provided further that if any should conceal their property or make a false valuation they should be fined, and that rewards should be given to informers, whether free persons or slaves. The women resolved to beseech the women-folk of the triumvirs. With the sister of Octavian and the mother of Antony they did not fail, but they were repulsed from the doors of Fulvia, the wife of Antony, whose rudeness they could scarce endure. They then forced their way to the tribunal of the triumvirs in the Forum, the people and the guards dividing to let them pass. There, through the mouth of Hortensia, whom they had selected to speak, they spoke as follows:

"As befitted women of our rank addressing a petition to you, we had recourse to the ladies of your households; but having been treated as did not befit us, at the hands of Fulvia, we have been driven by her to the Forum. You have already deprived us of our fathers, our sons, our husbands, and our brothers, whom you accused of having wronged you; if you take away our property also, you reduce us to a condition unbecoming our birth, our manners, our sex. If we have done you wrong, as you say our husbands have, proscribe us as you do them. But if we women have not voted any of you public enemies, have not torn down your houses, destroyed your army, or led another one against you; if we have not hindered you in obtaining offices and honors, why do we share the penalty when we did not share the guilt?

"Why should we pay taxes when we have no part in the honors, the commands, the state-craft, for which you contend against each other with such harmful results? 'Because this is a time of war,' do you say? When have there not been wars, and when have taxes ever been imposed on women, who are exempted by their sex among all mankind? Our mothers did once rise superior to their sex and made contributions when you were in danger of losing the whole empire and the city itself through the conflict with the Carthaginians. But then they contributed voluntarily, not from their landed property, their fields, their dowries, or their houses, without which life is not possible to free women, but only from their own jewellery, and even these not according to fixed valuation, not under fear of informers or accusers, not by force and violence, but what they themselves were willing to give. What alarm is there now for the empire or the country? Let war with the Gauls or the Parthians come, and we shall not be inferior to our mothers in zeal for the common safety; but for civil wars may we never contribute, nor ever assist you against each other! We did not contribute to Caesar or to Pompey. Neither Marius nor Cinna imposed taxes upon us. Nor did Sulla, who held despotic power in the state, do so, whereas you say that you are reestablishing the common wealth."

While Hortensia thus spoke the triumvirs were angry that women should dare to hold a public meeting when the men were silent; that they should demand from magistrates the reasons for their acts, and themselves not so much as furnish money while the men were serving in the army. They ordered the lictors to drive them away from the tribunal, which they proceeded to do until cries were raised by the multitude outside when the lictors desisted and the triumvirs said they would postpone till the next day the consideration of the matter. On the following day they reduced the number of women, who were to present a valuation of their property, from 1400 to 400, and decreed that all men who possessed more than 100,000 denarii both citizens and strangers, freedmen and priests, and men of all nationalities without a single exception, should (under the same dread of penalty and also of informers) lend them at interest a fiftieth part of their property and contribute one year's income to the war expenses.

D. HONORARY INSCRIPTIONS FROM THE PROVINCES

Inscriptions, which have been found by the thousands throughout the Roman Empire, are our principal source of information about people not important or influential enough to be mentioned by the historical writers. Public benefactors often recorded their good deeds in stone, or grateful recipients did it for them. Outstanding citizens were frequently immortalized in a statue accompanied by an explanatory inscription.

i. Pleket 13, 14, 15, 19.

The people of Arneae and vicinity, to Lalla daughter of Timarchus son of Diotimus, their fellow citizen, wife of Diotimus son of Vassus; priestess of the Emperor's cult and generous gymnasiarch, honored five times, chaste, cultivated, devoted to her husband and a model of all virtue, surpassing in every respect

he has glorified her ancestors' virtues with the example of her
wn character. [Erected] in recognition of her virtue and good
ill.

To Lalla of Arneae, daughter of Timarchus son of Diotimus,
Iasas, because she had set him free, set up this testimonial.

Timarchus of Arneae son of Diotimus, to Asë (who was also
alled Dimanthus), his daughter and daughter also of Pin-
armu, daughter of Diodotus, in loving remembrance. She has
lso been honored by the people: the people of Arneae and the
ntire vicinity honored with a gold wreath and a bronze statue
Asë (who was also called Dimanthus, daughter of Timarchus of
rneae son of Diotimus), a woman who was chaste and culti-
ated and who glorified the city and her family with praise for
er conduct, in recognition of her virtue and her reputation and
he admiring testimony of women in all respects.

The council and the people, to Flavia Publicia Nicomachis,
aughter of Dinomachus and Procle, benefactress of her parents
nd benefactress of her ancestors, founder of our city, president
or life, in recognition of her complete virtue.

ii. *CIL* VIII.23888; Africa, second/third century A.D.

The town council decreed a statue of Modia Quintia, daughter
f Quintus Modius Felix, perpetual priestess who, on account of
he honor of the priesthood, adorned the portico with marble
aving, coffered ceilings and columns, exceeding in cost her
riginal estimate with an additional contribution and quite apart
rom the statutory entry fee [for the priesthood] and also [built]
n aqueduct. By decree of the town council, [erected] with public
unds.

12. MEDICINE

A. ANATOMY

Galen, born and educated in Pergamum, the great Hellenistic seat of learning,
was both philosopher and physician, an eclectic dogmatist. He began his career
as a gladiators' doctor, but eventually became physician to the Emperor Marcus

154

Aurelius. His pathology was speculative and based on the doctrine that health depended on the balance of the four humors (black bile, yellow bile, blood, and phlegm), but he made significant contributions to diagnosis and prognosis. Some of his anatomical conclusions are based on inaccurate comparisons between animals, which he dissected, and humans, whom he did not.

Galen, *On the Usefulness of the Parts of the Body* XIV 6-7 (excerpts).

The female is less perfect than the male for one, principal reason — because she is colder, for if among animals the warm one is the more active, a colder animal would be less perfect than a warmer. A second reason is one that appears in dissecting. . . .

All the parts, then, that men have, women have too, the difference between them lying in only one thing, which must be kept in mind throughout the discussion, namely, that in women the parts are within [the body], whereas in men they are outside, in the region called the perineum. Consider first whichever ones you please, turn outward the woman's, turn inward, so to speak and fold double the man's, and you will find them the same in both in every respect. Then think first, please, of the man's turned in and extending inward between the rectum and the bladder. If this should happen, the scrotum would necessarily take the place of the uteri, with the testes lying outside, next to it on either side; the penis of the male would become the neck of the cavity that had been formed; and the skin at the end of the penis, now called the prepuce, would become the female pudendum [the vagina] itself. Think too, please of the converse, the uterus turned outward and projecting. Would not the testes [the ovaries] then necessarily be inside it? Would it not contain them like a scrotum? Would not the neck [the cervix], hitherto concealed inside the perineum but now pendent, be made into the male member? And would not the female pudendum, being a skin-like growth upon this neck, be changed into the part called the prepuce? It is also clear that in consequence the position of the arteries, veins, and spermatic vessels [the ductus deferentes and Fallopian tubes] would be changed too. In fact, you could not find a single male part left over that had not simply changed its position; for the parts that are inside in woman are outside in man. You can see something like this in the eyes of the mole, which have vitreous and crystalline humors and the tunics that surround these and grow out from the meninges, as I have said, and they have these just as much as animals do that make use of their eyes. The mole's eyes, however, do not open, nor do they project but are left there imperfect and remain like the eyes of other animals when these are still in the uterus. . . .

So too the woman is less perfect than the man in respect to the generative parts. For the parts were formed within her when she was still a fetus, but could not because of the defect in the heat emerge and project on the outside, and this, though making the animal itself that was being formed less perfect than one that is complete in all respects, provided no small advantage for the race; for there needs must be a female. Indeed, you ought not to think that our creator would purposely make half the whole race imperfect and, as it were, mutilated, unless there was to be some great advantage in such a mutilation.

Let me tell what this is. The fetus needs abundant material both when it is first constituted and for the entire period of growth that follows. Hence it is obliged to do one of two things; it must either snatch nutriment away from the mother herself or take nutriment that is left over. Snatching it away would be to injure the generant, and taking left over nutriment would be impossible if the female were perfectly warm; for if she were, she would easily disperse and evaporate it. Accordingly, it was better for the female to be made enough colder so that she cannot disperse all the nutriment which she concocts and elaborates. . . . This is the reason why the female was made cold, and the immediate consequence of this is the imperfection of the parts, which cannot emerge on the outside on account of the defect in the heat, another very great advantage for the continuance of the race. For, remaining within, that which would have become the scrotum if it had emerged on the outside was made into the substance of the uteri, an instrument fitted to receive and retain the semen and to nourish and perfect the fetus.

Forthwith, of course, the female must have smaller, less perfect testes, and the semen generated in them must be scantier, colder, and wetter (for these things too follow of necessity from the deficient heat). Certainly such semen would be incapable of generating an animal, and, since it too has not been made in vain, I shall explain in the course of my discussion what its use is: The testes of the male are as much larger as he is the warmer animal. The semen generated in them, having received the peak of concoction, becomes the efficient principle of the animal. Thus, from one principle devised by the creator in his wisdom, that principle in accordance with which the female has been made less perfect than the male, have stemmed all these things useful for the generation of the animal: that the parts of the female cannot escape to the outside; that she accumulates an excess of useful nutriment and has imperfect semen and a hollow instrument to receive the perfect semen; that since everything in the male is the opposite [of what it is in the female], the male member has been elongated to be most suitable for coitus and the excretion of semen; and that his semen itself has been made thick, abundant, and warm....

It is clear that the left testis in the male and the left uterus in the female receive blood still uncleansed, full of residues, watery and serous, and so it happens that the temperaments of the instruments themselves that receive [the blood] become different. For just as pure blood is warmer than blood full of residues, so too the instruments on the right side, nourished with pure blood, become warmer than those on the left.... Moreover, if this has been demonstrated and it has been granted that the male is warmer than the female, it is no longer at all unreasonable to say that the parts on the right produce males and those on the left, females. In fact, that is what Hippocrates meant when he said, "At puberty, whichever testis appears on the outside, the right, a male, the left, a female."[93] That is to say, when the generative parts first swell out and the voice becomes rougher and deeper — for this is what puberty is — Hippocrates bids us observe which of the parts is the stronger; for of course, those that swell out first and have a greater growth are the stronger.

B. THE REPRODUCTIVE TRACT

Soranus, *Gynecology* I (excerpts)

Soranus, a Greek from Ephesus in Asia Minor who practiced in Rome, approaches his topic with more sympathy and common sense than his colleagues, and, unlike other practitioners, includes in his account of gynecology all aspects of the female reproductive system, normal as well as abnormal.

Menstruation

One has to infer approaching menstruation from the fact that at the expected time of the period it becomes trying to move and there develops heaviness of the loins, sometimes pain as well, sluggishness, continual yawning, and tension of the limbs, sometimes also a flush of the cheeks which either remains or, having been dispersed, reappears after an interval; and in some cases approaching menstruation must be inferred from the fact that the stomach is prone to nausea and it lacks appetite. Menstruation which is about to occur for the first time must be inferred from the same signs but above all from the growth of the breasts which, broadly, takes place around the fourteenth year, and from the heaviness, irritation and pubescence in the region of the lower abdomen.

In women who have already menstruated often, each must be allowed to do according to her own custom. For some habitually take a rest, while others go on with moderate activities. But it is safer to rest and not to bathe especially on the first day. But in women who are about to menstruate no longer, their time for menstruation having passed, one must take care that the stoppage of the menses does not occur suddenly. For in regard to alteration, even if the body be changed for the better, all abruptness disturbs it through discomfort; for that which is unaccustomed is not tolerated, but is like some unfamiliar malaise. The methods we employ at the approach of the first menstruation must now be marshalled forth during the time when menstruation is about to cease; for that which is able to evoke the as yet absent excretion is even more able to preserve for some time menstruation which is still present. In addition, vaginal suppositories capable of softening and injections which have the [same] effect should be employed, together with all the remedies capable of rendering hardened bodies soft. But if the menstruation is too much for the strength of the patient, or again, if it is impeded by abnormal factors, then there is need for therapeutic measures which we shall elaborate in the section on "things abnormal."

Conception

One must judge the majority from the ages of fifteen to forty to be fit for conception, if they are not mannish, compact, and oversturdy, or too flabby and very moist. Since the uterus is similar to the whole [body], it will in these cases either be unable, on account of its pronounced hardness, easily to accept the attachment of the seed, or by reason of its extreme laxity and atony [let it fall again]. Furthermore they seem fit if their uteri are neither very moist or dry, nor too lax or constricted, and if they have their catharsis regularly, not through some moisture or ichors of various kinds, but through blood and of this neither too much nor, on the other hand, extremely little. Also those in whom the orifice of the uterus is comparatively far forward and lies in a straight line (for an orifice deviated even in its natural state and lying farther back in the vagina, is less suited for the attraction and acceptance of the seed).

The best time for fruitful intercourse is when menstruation is ending and abating, when urge and appetite for coitus are present, when the body is neither in want nor too congested and heavy from drunkenness and indigestion, and after the body has been rubbed down and a little food been eaten and when a pleasant state exists in every respect. (1) "When menstruation is ending and abating," for the time before menstruation is not suitable, the uterus already being overburdened and in an unresponsive state because of the ingress of material and incapable of carrying on two motions contrary to each other, one for the excretion of material, the other for receiving. (2) In order that the offspring may not be rendered misshapen, women must be sober during coitus because in drunkenness the soul becomes the victim of strange phantasies; this furthermore, because the offspring bears some resemblance to the mother as well not only in body but in soul.... (3) Together with these points it has already been stated that the best time is after a rubdown has been given and a little food been eaten. The food will give the inner turbulence an impetus towards coitus, the urge for intercourse not being diverted by appetite for food; while the rubdown will make it possible to lay hold of the injected seed more readily. For just as the rubdown naturally aids the distribution of food, it helps also in the reception and retention of the seed, yesterday's superfluities, as one may say, being unloaded, and the body thoroughly cleansed and in a sound state for its natural processes. Consequently, as the farmer sows only after having first cleansed the soil and removed any foreign material, in the same manner we too advise that insemination for the production of man should follow after the body has first been given a rubdown.

Contraception

A contraceptive differs from an abortive, for the first does not let conception take place, while the latter destroys what has been conceived.... And an expulsive some people say is synonymous with an abortive; others, however, say that there is a difference because an expulsive does not mean drugs but shaking and leaping.... For this reason they say that Hippocrates, although prohibiting abortives, yet in his book "On the Nature of the Child" employs leaping with the heels to the buttocks for the sake of expulsion.[94] But a controversy has arisen. For one party banishes abortives, citing the testimony of Hippocrates who says: "I will give to no one an abortive"; moreover, because it is the specific task of medicine to guard and preserve what has been engendered by nature. The other party prescribes abortives, but with discrimination, that is, they do not prescribe them when a person wishes to destroy the embryo because of adultery or out of consideration for youthful beauty; but only to prevent subsequent danger in parturition if the uterus is small and not capable of accommodating the complete development, or if the uterus at its orifice has knobby swellings and fissures, or if some similar difficulty is involved. And they say the same about contraceptives as well, and we too agree with them. And since it is safer to prevent conception from taking place than to destroy the fetus, we shall now first discourse upon such prevention.

For if it is much more advantageous not to conceive than to destroy the embryo, one must consequently beware of having sexual intercourse at those periods which we said were suitable for conception. And during the sexual act, at the critical moment of coitus when the man is about to discharge the seed, the woman must hold her breath and draw herself away a little, so that the seed may not be hurled too deep into the cavity of the uterus. And getting up immediately and squatting down, she should induce sneezing and carefully wipe the vagina all round; she might even drink something cold. It also aids in preventing conception to smear the orifice of the uterus all over before with old olive oil or honey or cedar resin or juice of the balsam tree, alone or together with white lead; or with a moist cerate containing myrtle oil and white lead; or before the act with moist alum, or with galbanum together with wine; or to put a lock of fine wool into the orifice of the uterus; or, before sexual relations to use vaginal suppositories which have the power to contract and to condense. For such of these things as are styptic, clogging, and cooling cause the orifice of the uterus to shut before the time of coitus and do not let the seed pass into its fundus. [Such, however, as are hot] and irritating not only do not allow the seed of the man to remain in the cavity of the uterus, but draw forth as well another fluid from it.

And we shall make specific mention of some. Pine bark, tanning sumach, equal quantities of each, rub with wine and apply in due measure before coitus after wool has been wrapped around; and after two or three hours she may remove it and have intercourse. Another: Of Cimolian earth, root of panax, equal quantities, rub with water separately and together, and when sticky apply in like manner. Or: Grind the inside of fresh pomegranate peel with water, and apply. Or: Grind two parts of pomegranate peel and one part of oak galls, form small suppositories and insert after the cessation of menstruation. Or: Moist alum, the inside of pomegranate rind, mix with water, and apply with wool. Or: Of unripe oak galls, of the inside of pomegranate peel, of ginger, of each 2 drachms, mold it with wine to the size of vetch peas and dry indoors and give before coitus, to be applied as a vaginal suppository. Or: Grind the flesh of dried figs and apply together with natron. Or: Apply pomegranate peel with an equal amount of gum and an equal amount of oil of roses. Then one should always follow with a drink of honey water. But one should beware of things which are very pungent, because of the ulcerations arising from them. And we use all these things after the end of menstruation....

Abortion

In order that the embryo be separated, the woman should have [more violent exercise], walking about energetically and being shaken by means of draught animals; she should also leap energetically and carry things which are heavy beyond her strength. She should use diuretic decoctions which also have the power to bring on menstruation, and empty and purge the abdomen with relatively pungent clysters; sometimes using warm and sweet olive oil as injections, sometimes anointing the whole body thoroughly therewith and rubbing it vigorously, especially around the pubes, the abdomen, and the loins, bathing daily in sweet water which is not too hot, lingering in the baths and drinking first a little wine and living on pungent food. If this is without effect, one must also treat locally by having her sit in a bath of a decoction of linseed, fenugreek, mallow, marsh mallow, and wormwood. She must also use poultices of the same substances and have injections of old oil, alone or together with rue juice or maybe with honey, or of iris oil, or of absinthium together with honey, or of panax balm or else of spelt together with rue and honey, or of Syrian unguent. And if the situation remains the same she must no longer apply the common poultices, but those made of meal of lupines together with ox bile and absinthium, [and she must use] plasters of a similar kind.

For a woman who intends to have an abortion, it is necessary for two or even three days beforehand to take protracted baths, little food and to use softening vaginal suppositories; also to abstain from wine; then to be bled and a relatively great quantity taken away. For the dictum of Hippocrates in the *Aphorisms*, even if not true in a case of constriction, is yet true of a healthy woman: "A pregnant woman if bled, miscarries." For just as sweat, urine or feces are excreted if the parts containing these substances slacken very much, so the fetus falls out after the uterus dilates. Following the venesection one must shake her by means of draught animals (for now the shaking is more effective on the parts which previously have been relaxed) and one must use softening vaginal suppositories. But if a woman reacts unfavorably to venesection and is languid, one must first relax the parts by means of sitz baths, full baths, softening vaginal suppositories, by keeping her on water and limited food, and by means of aperients and the application of a softening clyster; afterwards one must apply an abortive vaginal suppository. Of the latter one should choose those which are not too pungent, that they may not cause too great a sympathetic reaction and heat. And of the more gentle ones there exist for instance: Of myrtle, wallflower seed, bitter lupines equal quantities, by means of water, mold troches the size of a bean. Or: Of rue leaves 3 drachms, of myrtle 2 drachms and the same of sweet bay, mix with wine in the same way, and give her a drink. Another vaginal suppository which produces abortion with relatively little danger: Of wallflower, cardamom, brimstone, absinthium, myrrh, equal quantities, mold with water. And she who intends to apply these things should be bathed beforehand or made to relax by sitz baths; and if after some time she brings forth nothing, she should again be relaxed by sitz baths and for the second time a suppository should be applied. In addition, many different things have been mentioned by others; one must, however, beware of things that are too powerful and of separating the embryo by means of something sharp-edged, for danger arises that some of the adjacent parts be wounded. After the abortion one must treat as for inflammation.

C. HYSTERIA

i. Aretaeus, *On the Causes and Symptoms of Acute Diseases* II (excerpt).

Aretaeus of Cappadocia accepts the basic Hippocratic doctrines about hysteria but adds dramatic analogy to his account.

In the middle of the flanks of women lies the womb, a female viscus, closely resembling an animal; for it is moved of itself hither and thither in the flanks, also upwards in a direct line to below the cartilage of the thorax, and also obliquely to the right or to the left, either to the liver or spleen; and it likewise is subject to prolapsus downwards, and, in a word, it is altogether erratic. It delights, also, in fragrant smells, and advances towards them; and it has an aversion to fetid smells, and flees from them; and, on the whole, the womb is like an animal within an animal.

When, therefore, it is suddenly carried upwards, and remains above for a considerable time, and violently compresses the intestines, the woman experiences a choking, after the form of epilepsy, but without convulsions. For the liver, diaphragm, lungs and heart are quickly squeezed within a narrow space; and therefore loss of breathing and of speech seems to be present. And, moreover, the carotids are compressed from sympathy with the heart, and hence there is heaviness of head, loss of sensibility, and deep sleep.

And in women there also arises another affection resembling this form, with sense of choking and loss of speech, but not proceeding from the womb; for it also happens to men, in the manner of catalepsy. But those from the uterus are remedied by fetid smells, and the application of fragrant things to the female parts; but in the others these things do no good; and the limbs are moved about in the affection from the womb, but in the other affection not at all. Moreover, voluntary and involuntary tremblings...but from the application of a pessary to induce abortion, powerful congelation of the womb, the stoppage of a copious hemorrhage, and such like.

If, therefore, upon the womb's being moved upwards, she begin to suffer: there is sluggishness in the performance of her offices, prostration of strength, atony, loss of the faculties of her knees, vertigo (and the limbs sink under her), headache, heaviness of the head, and the woman is pained in the veins on each side of the nose.

But if they fall down they have heartburn ... in the hypochondriac regions; flanks empty, where is the seat of the womb; pulse intermittent, irregular, and failing; strong sense of choking; loss of speech and of sensibility; respiration imperceptible and indistinct; a very sudden and incredible death, for they have nothing deadly in their appearance; in color like that of life, and for a considerable time after death they are more ruddy than usual; eyes somewhat prominent, bright, not entirely fixed, but yet not very much turned aside.

But if the uterus be removed back to its seat before the affection come to a conclusion, they escape the suffocation. When the belly rumbles there is moisture about the female parts, respiration thicker and more distinct, a very speedy rousing up from the affection, in like manner as death is very sudden; for as it readily ascends to the higher regions, so it readily recedes. For the uterus is buoyant, but the membranes, its supporters, are humid, and the place is humid in which the uterus lies; and, moreover, it flees from fetid things, and seeks after sweet; wherefore it readily inclines to this side and to that, like a log of wood, and floats upwards and downwards. For this reason the affection occurs in young women, but not in old. For in those in whom the age, mode of life, and understanding is more mobile, the uterus also is of a wandering nature; but in those more advanced in life, the age, mode of living, understanding, and the uterus are of a steady character. Wherefore this suffocation from the womb accompanies females alone.

But the affections common to men happen also to the uterus, such as inflammation and hemorrhage, and they have the common symptoms; namely, fever, asphexy, coldness, loss of speech. But in hemorrhage the death is even more sudden, being like that of a slaughtered animal.

ii. Aretaeus, *Therapeutics of Acute Diseases* II (excerpt).

The uterus in women has membranes extended on both sides at the flanks, and also is subject to the affections of an animal in smelling; for it follows after fragrant things as if for pleasure, and flees from fetid and disagreeable things as if for dislike. If, therefore, anything annoy it from above, it protrudes even beyond the genital organs. But if any of these things be applied to the os, it retreats backwards and upwards. Sometimes it will go to this side or to that—to the spleen and liver, while the membranes yield to the distension and contraction like the sails of a ship.

It suffers in this way also from inflammation; and it pro-

trudes more than usual in this affection and in the swelling of
its neck; for inflammation of the fundus inclines upwards; but
if downwards to the feet, it protrudes externally, a troublesome
painful and unseemly complaint, rendering it difficult to walk
to lie on the side or on the back, unless the woman suffer from
inflammation of the feet. But if it mount upwards, it very speed
ily suffocates the woman, and stops the respiration as if with a
cord, before she feels pain, or can scream aloud, or can cal
upon the spectators, for in many cases the respiration is firs
stopped, and in others the speech. It is proper, then, in these
cases, to call the physician quickly before the patient die. Should
you fortunately arrive in time and ascertain that it is inflamma
tion, you must open a vein, especially the one at the ankle, and
pursue the other means which prove remedial in suffocation with
out inflammation: ligatures of the hands and feet so tight as to
induce torpor; smelling to fetid substances—liquid pitch, hairs
and wool burnt, the extinguished flame of a lamp, and castor
since, in addition to its bad smell, it warms the congealed
nerves. Old urine greatly rouses the sense of one in a death-like
state, and drives the uterus downwards. Wherefore we must
apply fragrant things on pessaries to the region of the uterus—
any ointment of a mild nature, and not pungent to the touch
nard, or Egyptian bacchar, or the medicine from the leaves of
the malabathrum, the Indian tree, or cinnamon pounded with
any of the fragrant oils. These articles are to be rubbed into the
female parts. And also an injection of these things is to be
thrown into the uterus. The anus is to be rubbed with applica
tions which dispel flatus; and injections of things not acrid, but
softening, viscid, and lubricant, are to be given to the expulsion
of the feces solely, so that the region of the uterus may be
emptied—with the juice of marsh mallow, or of fenugreek, but
let melilot or marjoram be boiled along with the oil. But, if the
uterus stands in need of support rather than evacuation, the
abdomen is to be compressed by the hands of a strong woman, or
of an expert man, binding it round also with a roller, when you
have replaced the part, so that it may not ascend upwards again
Having produced sneezing, you must compress the nostrils; for
by the sneezing and straining, in certain cases, the uterus has
returned to its place. We are to blow into the nostrils also some
of the root of soapwort, or of pepper, or of castor. We are also to
apply the instrument for dry-cupping to the thighs, loins, the
ischiatic regions, and groins, in order to attract the uterus. And

moreover, we are to apply it to the spine, and between the scapulae, in order to relieve the sense of suffocation. But if the feeling of suffocation be connected with inflammation, we may also scarify the vein leading along the pubes, and abstract plenty of blood.... Should the patient partially recover, she is to be seated in a decoction of aromatics, and fumigated from below with fragrant perfumes. Also before a meal, she is to drink of castor, and a little quantity of the hiera with the castor. And if relieved, she is to bathe, and at the proper season is to return to her accustomed habits; and we must look to the woman that her menstrual discharges flow freely.

iii. Soranus, *Gynecology* III. 26, 28, 29.

Hysterical suffocation has been named after both the affected organ and one symptom, viz. suffocation. But its connotation is: obstructed respiration together with aphonia and a seizure of the senses caused by some condition of the uterus. In most cases the disease is preceded by recurrent miscarriages, premature birth, long widowhood, retention of menses and the end of ordinary childbearing or inflation of the uterus. When an attack occurs, sufferers from the disease collapse, show aphonia, labored breathing, a seizure of the senses, clenching of the teeth, stridor, convulsive contraction of the extremities (but sometimes only weakness), upper abdominal distention, retraction of the uterus, swelling of the thorax, bulging of the network of vessels of the face. The whole body is cool, covered with perspiration, the pulse stops or is very small. In the majority of cases they recover quickly from the collapse and usually recall what has happened; head and tendons ache and sometimes they are even deranged....

[The disease] is of the constricted and violent class and exists both in an acute and chronic form; therefore the treatment must be suitable to these characteristics. During the initial stage one should lay the patient down in a room which is moderately warm and bright and, without hurting her, rouse her from the collapsed state by moving the jaw, placing warm compresses all over the middle of her body, gently straightening out all the cramped parts, restraining each extremity, and warming all the cool parts by the touch of [the] bare hands. Then one should wash the face with a sponge soaked in warm water, for sponging the face has a vitalizing effect.

If, however, the state of aphonia persists, we also use dry cupping over the groin, pubes, and the neighboring regions; then we put on covers of soft clean wool. We also moisten these parts freely with sweet olive oil, keeping it up for some time, and swathe each extremity in wool (for this conducts the relaxation from the extremities toward the center). Then we instill warm water into the opened jaws, and afterwards honey water too, and prescribe movement in a hammock. When the initial stage has ended we bleed, provided that weakness does not prevent it, or it is not long since food was given. Afterwards we give an injection of warm, sweet olive oil, moisten the parts, offer warm water as a mouthwash and drink, and make her abstain from food until the third day. On this day we first rub the patient down and afterwards we offer gruel-like food and give this from now on, every second day, until the dangerous condition regarding the uterus has safely subsided. [But every day] we use poultices like those prescribed for women who suffer from painful menstruation and apply hot sponge baths and relaxing sitz baths, the material for which we have mentioned above, and suppositories made of fat, marrow, fenugreek, mallow, and oil of lilies or henna oil, and injections by means of a clyster of olive oil or oil mixed with water, particularly if feces are retained (for the excrement bruises the adjacent uterus). When the condition has abated we make use of wax salves and suppositories of a relatively high emollient power, then we give varied food, later on a bath, and finally wine.

But the majority of the ancients and almost all followers of the other sects have made use of ill-smelling odors (such as burnt hair, extinguished lamp wicks, charred deer's horn, burnt wool, burnt flock, skins, and rags, castoreum with which they anoint the nose and ears, pitch, cedar resin, bitumen, squashed bed bugs, and all substances which are supposed to have an oppressive smell) in the opinion that the uterus flees from evil smells. Wherefore they have also fumigated with fragrant substances from below, and have approved of suppositories of spikenard and storax, so that the uterus fleeing the first-mentioned odors, but pursuing the last-mentioned, might move from the upper to the lower parts. Besides, Hippocrates made some of his patients drink a decoction of cabbage, others asses' milk; and he believing that the uterus is twisted like the intestines are in intestinal obstruction, inserted a small pipe and blew air into the vagina by means of a blacksmith's bellow, thus causing dilation. Dioles, however, in the third book *On Gynecology*, pinches the nostrils, but opens the mouth and applies a sternutative; moreover, with the hand he pushes the uterus toward the lower parts by pressing upon the hypochondriac region; and applies warm fomentations to the legs. Mantias gives castoreum and bitumen in wine to drink and if the arousal is imminent, he orders playing on the flute and drumming. Xenophon proposes torchlight and prescribes the making of greater noise by whetting and beating metal plates. And Asclepiades applies a sternutative, constricts the hypochondriac region with bandages and strings of gut, shouts loudly, blows vinegar into the nose, allows sexual intercourse during remissions, drinking of water [and pouring cold water over the head]. We, however, censure all these men who start by hurting the inflamed parts and cause torpor by the effluvia of ill-smelling substances. For the uterus does not issue forth like a wild animal from the lair, delighted by fragrant odors and fleeing bad odors; rather it is drawn together because of the stricture caused by the inflammation. Also upsetting the stomach, which suffers from sympathetic inflammation, with toxic and pungent potions makes trouble. Forcing air by means of the smith's bellows into the vagina—this inflation makes the uterus even more tense, which is already rendered sufficiently tense by reason of the inflammation. Moreover, the use of sternutatives, through their shaking effects and the pungency of the drugs, produces a metasyncrisis in chronic conditions, thus aggravating the condition of the patient who during the initial stage needs not force but gentleness. Sounds and the noise of metal plates have an overpowering effect and irritate those who are made sensitive by inflammation. At any rate, even many healthy persons have been given headaches by such sounds. Vinegar blown in is also harmful, for just as external inflammations, so internal inflammations are increased by every astringent. Furthermore, it is injurious to constrict externally with strings or bandages the inflamed uterus which cannot even bear a poultice without feeling it burdensome, because of the intensification caused by the pressure. And drinking of water is not only not helpful but sometimes even noxious, since the patient needs strengthening, not metasyncrisis; moreover, metasyncrisis is produced again by switching to diluted wine. Intercourse causes atony in everybody and is therefore not appropriate; for without giving any advantage it affects the body adversely by making it atonic. Pouring cold water over the head in order to stop aphonia is obviously a technical mistake. For if the body is rendered dense

by the cold, the arousal necessarily becomes more difficult to accomplish on account of the increased inflammation.

iv. Celsus, *On Medicine* VI.27 and V.21.

From the womb of a woman, also, there arises a violent
malady; and next to the stomach this organ is affected the most
by the body, and has the most influence upon it. At times it
makes the woman so insensible that it prostrates her as if by
epilepsy. The case, however, differs from epilepsy, in that the
eyes are not turned nor is there foaming at the mouth nor
spasm of sinews; there is merely stupor. In some women this
attack recurs at frequent intervals and lasts throughout life.
When this happens, if there is sufficient strength, bloodletting
is beneficial; if too little, wet cups should be applied to the
groins. If she lies prostrate for a long while, or if she has done
so at other times, hold to her nostrils an extinguished lamp
wick, or some other of these materials which I have referred to
as having a specially fetid odor to arouse the woman.[95] For the
same end, affusion with cold water is also effectual. And there
is benefit from rue pounded up in honey, or from a wax-salve
made up with cyprus oil or from hot moist plasters of some sort
applied to the external genitals as far as the pubes. At the same
time also the hips and the backs of the knees should be rubbed.
Then when she has come to herself, she should be cut off from
wine for a whole year, even if a similar attack does not recur.
Friction should be applied daily to the whole body, but particularly to the abdomen and behind the knees. Food of the middle
class[96] should be given: every third or fourth day mustard is to
be applied over the hypogastrium until the skin is reddened. If
induration persists, a convenient emollient appears to be bitter
sweet steeped in milk, then pounded and mixed with white wax
and deer marrow in iris oil, or suet of beef or goat mixed with
rose oil. Also there should be given in draught either castory, or
git,[97] or dill. If the womb is not healthy, it is cleaned with
square rushes; but if it is actually ulcerated a wax-salve is made
with rose oil, mixed with fresh lard and white of egg, and
applied to it, or else white of egg mixed with rose oil, with
pounded rose-leaves added to give it consistence. When painful
the womb should be fumigated from below with sulphur. But if
excessive menstruation is doing harm to the woman, the remedy
is to scarify and cup the groins, or even to apply cups under the

reasts. If the menstrual discharge is bad, the following medicaments are to applied to evoke blood, costmary, pennyroyal, white
violet, parsley, catmint and savory and hyssop. Let her include
what is suitable in her diet: leeks, rue, cummin, onion, mustard,
or any other acrid vegetable. If blood bursts out from the nose at a
time when it should do so from the genitals, the groins are to be
scarified and cupped, repeating this every thirtieth day for three
or four months, then you may be sure that this affection has been
cured. But if there is no show of blood, you may be sure that there
are pains coming in the head. Then blood is to be let from the
arms, and you have given relief at once.

*

But there are other useful compositions, such as those which
are introduced into women from below, the Greeks call them
pessoi [pessaries]. Their characteristic is that the component
medicaments are taken up in soft wool, and this wool is inserted
into the genitals.

A pessary for inducing menstruation contains 2/3 of a denarius[98] soda, added to two Caunean figs; or garlic seeds are
pounded, a little myrrh added, and these are mixed with Susine
lily ointment; or the pulp of a wild cucumber is diluted in
woman's milk.

To mollify the womb a yolk of egg, fenugreek, rose-oil and
saffron are mixed together. Or 1/6 denarius elaterium, the same
quantity of salt, and 6 denarii of black bryony berries are taken
up with honey.

The pessary invented by Boethus consists of saffron and tur-
pentine resin, 4 denarii each, 1/3 denarius myrrh, 1 denarius
rose-oil, 1 1/6 denarii calf's suet, 2 denarii wax, mixed together.

But against inflammations of the womb the composition of
Numenius is the best; it consists of 1/4 denarius saffron, 1
denarius wax, 8 denarii butter, 12 denarii goose-fat, 2 yolks of
egg boiled, and of rose-oil less than 1 cyathus.[99]

If the fetus is dead, to render its expulsion easier, pomegranate rind should be rubbed up in water and so used.

If a woman is liable to fits owing to genital disease, snails are
to be burnt with their shells and pounded up together; then
honey added to them.

If a woman does not conceive, lion's fat is to be softened by
rose-oil.

v. Galen, *On Prognosis* 6.

I was called in to see a woman who was stated to be sleepless at night and to lie tossing about from one position into another. Finding she had no fever, I made a detailed inquiry into everything that had happened to her, especially considering such factors as we know to cause insomnia. But she either answered little or nothing at all, as if to show that it was useless to question her. Finally, she turned away, hiding herself completely by throwing the bedclothes over her whole body, and laying her head on another small pillow, as if desiring sleep.

After leaving I came to the conclusion that she was suffering from one of two things: either from a melancholy dependent on black bile, or else trouble about something she was unwilling to confess. I therefore deferred till the next day a closer investigation of this. Further, on first arriving, I was told by her attendant maid that she could not at present be seen; and on returning a second time, I was told the same again. So I went yet a third time, but the attendant asked me to go away, as she did not want her mistress disturbed. Having learned, however, that when I left she had washed and taken food in her customary manner, I came back the next day and in a private conversation with the maid on one subject and another I found out exactly what was worrying the patient. And this I discovered by chance.

After I had diagnosed that there was no bodily trouble, and that the woman was suffering from some mental uneasiness, it happened that, at the very time I was examining her, this was confirmed. Somebody came from the theatre and said he had seen Pylades dancing. Then both her expression and the color of her face changed. Seeing this, I applied my hand to her wrist, and noticed that her pulse had suddenly become extremely irregular. This kind of pulse indicates that the mind is disturbed; thus it occurs also in people who are disputing over any subject. So on the next day I said to one of my followers that, when I paid my visit to the woman, he was to come a little later and announce to me, "Morphus is dancing to-day." When he said this, I found that the pulse was unaffected. Similarly also on the next day, when I had an announcement made about the third member of the troupe, the pulse remained unchanged as before. On the fourth evening I kept very careful watch when it was announced that Pylades was dancing, and I noticed that the pulse was very much disturbed. Thus I found out that the woman was in love with Pylades, and by careful watch on the succeeding days my discovery was confirmed.

Similarly too I diagnosed the case of a slave who administered the household of another wealthy man, and who sickened in the same way. He was concerned about having to give an account of his expenses, in which he knew that there was a considerable sum wanting; the thought of this kept him awake, and he grew thin with anxiety. I first told his master that there was nothing physically wrong with the old man, and advised an investigation to be made as to whether he feared his master was about to ask an account of the sums he had entrusted to him, and for this reason was worried, knowing that a considerable amount would be found wanting. The master told me I had made a good suggestion, so in order to make the diagnosis certain, I advised him to do as follows: he was to tell the slave to give him back all the money he had in hand, lest, in the event of his sudden death, it should be lost, owing to the administration passing into the hands of some other servant whom he did not know: for there would be no use asking for an account from such a one. And when the master said this to him, he felt sure he would not be questioned. So he ceased to worry, and by the third day had regained his natural physical condition.

Now what was it that escaped the notice of previous physicians when examining the aforesaid woman and the aforesaid slave? For such discoveries are made by common inductions if one has even the smallest acquaintance with medical science. I suppose it is because they have no clear conception of how the body tends to be affected by mental conditions. Possibly also they do not know that the pulse is altered by quarrels and alarms which suddenly disturb the mind.

D. A DEATH FROM CHOKING

Peek 1293; Samë, first/second century A.D.

This inscription will not hold you long beside the road. Stop, and depart after you have learned who I am. My name is Laudice, Samë my country, my husband Alcimus, a daughter, my mother with her grey hair—all I (short-lived) leave to the light of the sun. I was not burned with fever, I was not killed by disease or by sorrows, but my throat, which devoured a fish, silently choked off my breathing.

172

E. WOMEN PHYSICIANS

i. Pleket 12; Tlos (Lycia), first century A.D.

Antiochus, daughter of Diodotus of Tlos, awarded special rec ognition by the council and the people of Tlos for her experience in the healing art, has set up this statue of herself.

ii. Pleket 26; Neoclaudopolis (Asia), second/third century A.D.

You rush off to be with the gods, Domnina, and forget your husband. You have raised your body to the heavenly stars. Men will say that you have not died but that the gods stole you away because you saved your native fatherland from disease. Good bye, and rejoice in the Elysian fields. But you have left pain and funeral lamentations behind for your loved ones.

iii. *CIL VI.* 7581 (= *ILS* 7804) and 9619; Rome, first/second century A.D.

To my holy goddess. To Primilla, a physician, daughter of Lucius Vibius Melito. She lived forty-four years, of which thirty were spent with Lucius Cocceius Apthorus without a quarrel. Apthorus built this monument for his best, chaste wife and for himself.

To Terentia Nice, freedwoman of Terentia Prima the physi- cian. Mussius Antiochus and Mussia Dionysia, her children, put this up for their well-deserving mother.[100]

13. DAILY LIFE

A. MIDWIVES

i. Soranus, *Gynecology* I (excerpts). Second century A.D.

A unique account of the elaborate professional skill involved in an exclusively female profession.

A suitable person ... must be literate in order to be able to comprehend the art through theory too: she must have her wits about her so that she may easily follow what is said and what is happening: she must have a good memory to retain the imparted instructions (for knowledge arises from memory of what has been grasped). She must love work in order to persevere through all vicissitudes (for a woman who wishes to acquire such vast knowledge needs manly patience). She must be respectable since people will have to trust their household and the secrets of their lives to her and because to women of bad character the semblance of medical instruction is a cover for evil scheming. She must not be handicapped as regards her senses since there are things which she must see, answers which she must hear when questioning, and objects which she must grasp by her sense of touch. She needs sound limbs so as not to be handicapped in the performances of her work and she must be robust, for she takes a double task upon herself during the hardship of her professional visits. Long and slim fingers and short nails are necessary to touch a deep lying inflammation without causing too much pain. This skill, however, can also be acquired through zealous endeavor and practice in her work. . . .

We call a person the best midwife if she is trained in all branches of therapy (for some cases must be treated by diet, others by surgery, while still others must be cured by drugs); if she is moreover able to prescribe hygienic regulations for her patients, to observe the general and the individual features of the case, and from this to find out what is expedient, not from the causes or from the repeated observations of what usually occurs or something of the kind. Now to go into detail: she will not change her methods when the symptoms change, but will give her advice in accordance with the course of the disease: she will be unperturbed, unafraid in danger, able to state clearly the reasons for her measures, she will bring reassurance to her patients, and be sympathetic. And, it is not absolutely essential for her to have borne children, as some people contend, in order that she may sympathize with the mother, because of her experience with pain; for [to have sympathy] is not more characteristic of a person who has given birth to a child. She must be robust on account of her duties but not necessarily young as some people maintain, for sometimes young persons are weak whereas on the contrary older persons may be robust. She will be well disciplined and always sober, since it is uncertain when she may be summoned to those in danger. She will have a quiet disposition, for she will have to share many secrets of life. She must not be greedy for money, lest she give an abortive wickedly for payment; she will be free from superstition so as not to overlook salutary measures on account of a dream or omen or some customary rite or vulgar superstition. She must also keep her hands soft, abstaining from such woolworking as may make them hard, and she must acquire softness by means of oint ments if it is not present naturally. Such persons will be the best midwives.

ii. Epitaphs of Midwives
CIL VI. 6647, 9720, 9721; Rome, first century A.D.

The nomenclature and status-indications of midwives in the inscriptions suggest that, in some cases, they began their careers at an early age in slavery, but continued to practice (and to own slaves themselves) after receiving their free dom. Some of the stones were dedicated by the midwives' slaves.[101]

To Hygia (goddess of health). (The tomb) of Flavia Sabina midwife. She lived thirty years. Marius Orthrus and Apollonius (put this up) to (Apollonius') dearest wife.

To Claudia Trophima, midwife. Titus Cassius Trophimus, her son, to his most gentle mother, and Tiberius Cassius Trophimi anus to his grandmother, and to their descendants, (put this up). She lived seventy-five years and five months.

Gaius Grattius Plocamus, freedman of Hilara the midwife from the Esquiline Hill.

B. WET NURSES

i. Soranus, *Gynecology* II (excerpts)

To be sure, other things being equal, it is better to feed the child with maternal milk, for this is more suited to it, and the mothers become more sympathetic towards the offspring, and it is more natural to be fed from the mother after parturition just as before parturition. But if anything prevents it one must choose the best wet nurse, lest the mother grows prematurely old, having spent herself through the daily suckling....

One should choose a wet nurse not younger than twenty nor older than forty years, who has already given birth twice or thrice, who is healthy, of good habitus, of large frame, and of a good color. Her breasts should be of medium size, lax, soft and unwrinkled, the nipples neither big nor too small and neither too compact nor too porous and discharging milk overabundantly. She should be self-controlled, sympathetic and not ill-tempered, a Greek, and tidy. And for each of these points the reasons are as follows:

She should be in her prime because younger women are ignorant in the rearing of children and their minds are still somewhat careless and childish; while older ones yield a more watery milk because of the atony of the body. In women in their prime, however, every natural function is at its highest. She should already have given birth twice or thrice, because women with their first child are as yet unpracticed in the rearing of children and have breasts whose structure is still infantile, small and too compact; while those who have delivered often have nursed children often and, being wrinkled, produce thin milk which is not at its best. [She should be healthy because healthful] and nourishing milk comes from a healthy body, unwholesome and worthless milk from a sickly one; just as water which flows through worthless soil is itself rendered worthless, spoiled by the qualities of its basin. And she should be of good habitus, that is, fleshy and strong, not only for the same reason, but also lest she easily become too weak for hard work and nightly duties with the result that the milk also deteriorates. Of large frame: for everything else being equal, milk from large bodies is more nourishing. Of a good color: for in such women bigger vessels carry the material up to the breasts so that there is more milk. And her breasts should be of medium size: for small ones have little milk, whereas excessively large ones have more than is necessary so that if after nursing the surplus is retained it will be drawn out by the newborn when no longer fresh, and in some way already spoiled. If, on the other hand, it is all sucked out by other children or even other animals, the wet nurse will be completely exhausted. . . .

The wet nurse should be self-controlled so as to abstain from coitus, drinking, lewdness, and any other such pleasure and incontinence. For coitus cools the affection toward the nursling by the diversion of sexual pleasure and moreover spoils and diminishes the milk or suppresses it entirely by stimulating menstrual catharsis through the uterus or by bringing about conception. In regard to drinking, first the wet nurse is harmed in soul as well as in body and for this reason the milk also is spoiled. Secondly, seized by a sleep from which she is hard to awaken, she leaves the newborn untended or even falls down upon it in a dangerous way. Thirdly, too much wine passes its quality to the milk and therefore the nursling becomes sluggish and comatose and sometimes even afflicted with tremor, apoplexy, and convulsions, just as suckling pigs become comatose and stupefied when the sow has eaten drugs. [She should be] sympathetic and affectionate, that she may fulfill her duties without hesitation and without murmuring. For some wet nurses are so lacking in sympathy towards the nursling that they not only pay no heed when it cries for a long time, but do not even arrange its position when it lies still; rather, they leave it in one position so that often because of the pressure the sinewy parts suffer and consequently become numb and bad. Not ill-tempered: since by nature the nursling becomes similar to the nurse and accordingly grows sullen if the nurse is ill-tempered, but of mild disposition if she is even-tempered. Besides, angry women are like maniacs and sometimes when the newborn cries from fear and they are unable to restrain it, they let it drop from their hands or overturn it dangerously. For the same reason the wet nurse should not be superstitious and prone to ecstatic states so that she may not expose the infant to danger when led astray by fallacious reasoning, sometimes even trembling like mad. And the wet nurse should be tidy-minded lest the odor of the swaddling clothes cause the child's stomach to become weak and it lie awake on account of itching or suffer some ulceration subsequently. And she should be a Greek so that the infant nursed by her may become accustomed to the best speech.

At the most she should have had milk for two or three months. For very early milk, as we have said, is thick of particles and is hard to digest, while late milk is not nutritious, and is thin. But some people say that a woman who is going to feed a male must have given birth to a male, if a female, on the other hand, to a female. One should pay no heed to these people, for they do not consider that mothers of twins, the one being male and the other female, feed both with one and the same milk. And in general, each kind of animal makes use of the same nourishment, male as well as female; and this is [no] reason at all for the male to become more feminine or for the female to become more masculine. One should, on the other hand, provide several wet nurses for children who are to be nursed safely and successfully. For it is precarious for the nursling to become accustomed to one nurse who might become ill or die, and then, because of the change of milk, the child sometimes suffers from the strange milk and is distressed, while sometimes it rejects it altogether and succumbs to hunger.

ii. Engagement of a Wet Nurse
Berlin papyrus 1107; 13 B.C.

To Protarchus from Isidora daughter of . . ., having with her as guardian her brother Eutychides son of . . ., and from Didyma daughter of Apollonius, Persian, having with her as guardian her brother Ischyrion son of Apollonius, Persian of the Epigone. Didyma agrees to nurse and suckle, outside at her own home in the city, with her own milk pure and untainted, for a period of sixteen months from Pharmouthi of the current 17th year of Caesar, the foundling infant slave child . . . called . . . which Isidora has given out to her, receiving from her, Isidora, as wages for milk and nursing ten silver drachmas and two cotyls of oil every month. So long as she is duly paid she shall take proper care both of herself and of the child, not injuring her milk nor sleeping with a man nor becoming pregnant nor suckling another child, and whatever things of the child she receives or is entrusted with she shall keep safe and shall give back when demanded or else forfeit the value of each except in the case of manifest loss, on proof of which she shall be exempted. Didyma has forthwith received from Isidora by hand from the house oil for the first three months, Pharmouthi, Pachon, and Pauni. She shall not cease nursing before the end of the time, and if she breaks the agreement in any way she shall forfeit the wages which she has already received and those which she may have received besides, increased by one half, with damages and expenses, and shall moreover pay 500 drachmas and the prescribed fine, Isidora having the right of execution upon the person of Didyma and all her property as if by legal decision, all assurances which she may produce and all resort to protection being invalid. If she fulfils every condition, Isidora shall deliver to her the monthly wages as stated above for the remaining thirteen months and shall not remove the child before the end of the time, or she herself shall pay the like penalty. Didyma shall visit Isidora every month regularly on four separate days bringing the child to be inspected by her. We request [ratification]. (Signed) I, Isidora, agree on the above terms. I, Eutychides, have professed myself guardian of my sister and have written for her as she is illiterate. I, Didyma, agree on the above terms. I, Ischyrion, have professed myself guardian of my sister and have written for her, as she is illiterate. (Docketed) Isidora's [agreement]. The 17th year of Caesar . . .

iii. Receipt for Wages for Nursing
Oxyrhynchus papyrus 91; 187 A.D.

Chosion son of Sarapion son of Harpocration, his mother being Sarapias, of Oxyrhynchus, to Tanenteris daughter of Thonis son of Thonis, her mother being Zoilous, of the said city with her guardian Demetrius son of Horion and Arisone, of the said city, greeting. I acknowledge that I have received from you through Heliodorus and his fellow supervisors of the bank at the Serapeum by Oxyrhynchus, for which Epimachus issued the promise of payment, 400 silver drachmas of Imperial coin for nurse's wages, oil, clothing, and all other expenses of the two years for which my slave Sarapias nursed your daughter Helena, styled as daughter of her male parent, whom you have received back after having been weaned and treated with every attention, and that I neither make nor will make any claim upon you nor will take any proceedings about this or about any other matter whatsoever up to the present day. This receipt is valid. The 28th year of the Emperor Caesar Marcus Aurelius Commodus Antoninus Pius Felix Augustus Armeniacus Medicus Parthicus Sarmaticus Germanicus Maximus Britannicus, Phaophi 15. (Signed) I, Chosion son of Sarapion, have received the 400 drachmas forming the nurse's wages, and I make no claim as stated above. I, Tanenteris daughter of Thonis, with my guardian Demetrius son of Horion, assent, and I have received back my daughter as stated above. I, Plution son of Hermes, have written for them, as they are illiterate.

C. CARE OF CHILDREN AND PROPERTY

i. Hamburg papyrus 86; second century A.D.

Ptolema to Antas her brother greeting. You write to Longinus (?) to look out for the prefect. Lo, the prefect has gone up. If you extricate yourself successfully, come here quickly before the prefect, in order that we may be able to have the youngster examined. All the fields are in good condition. The southern basin of the seventeen arurae has been sold for the use of the cattle. Your cattle have eaten one arura and gone off to Pansoue. All the land there has been given over to the cattle. The west of the vegetable plot has been given over for grass-cutting. We have sold the grass in the cleruchies, excepting the six eastern basins, for 112 drachmas. Grass is exceedingly (?) cheap. Three arurae were bought for you through Vetranius for 130 drachmas for growing grass, and they have been sold through him again for the use of sheep for 68 drachmas. Longinus and Sarapion and all at home salute you. Vibius has gone off to Psenuris to sell the corn. Your people are all well. Goodbye. Mecheir 30.

ii. Oxyrhynchus papyrus 930; second/third century A.D.

...do not hesitate to write to me about anything which you require from here. I was grieved to learn from the daughter of our teacher Diogenes that he had gone down the river; for my mind was easy with regard to him, as I knew that he intended to look after you to the best of his power. I took care to send and inquire about your health and to learn what you were reading. He said it was the 6th book, and he testified at large to the conduct of your attendant. So now, my child, you and your attendant must take care to have you placed under a suitable teacher. Many salutations from your sisters and the children of Theonis, whom the evil eye shall not harm, and from all our friends by name. Salute from me your esteemed attendant Eros ... (Addressed) ... to her son Ptolemaeus.

iii. Italian Society papyrus 1080; third century A.D.

Diogenis to her brother Alexander greeting. In accordance with your instructions to Taamois about a house for us to move into, we found the one which we let go before moving over to Agathinus. The house is beside the Iseum, adjoining the house of Claudianus.... We move into it in Phamenoth. I wish you to know that I received from Bottus a hundred and twenty drachmas. I have sent you ... of purple dye by Sarapiacus. The letter which you forwarded to me to deliver to Bolphius I have delivered. Many saluations to the little Theon. Eight toys have been brought for him by the lady to whom you told me to give your salutations, and these I have forwarded to you.... (Addressed) To Aurelius Alexander.

D. AN APPRENTICESHIP AGREEMENT

Oxyrhynchus papyrus 1647; second century A.D.

An agreement between Platonis (also called Ophelia) daughter of Horion, of the city of Oxyrhynchus, with her full brother Plato as guardian, and Lucius son of Ision and Tisasis, of Aphrodisium in the Small Oasis: Platonis (also called Ophelia) has apprenticed to Lucius her slave Thermuthion, who is under age, to learn the weaver's trade, for four years starting at the beginning of the coming month Tubi of the present year, during which time he shall feed and clothe the girl and bring her to her instructor every day from sunrise to sunset so that she can perform all the duties assigned to her by him that are relevant to the aforesaid trade; her pay for the first year to be 8 drachmas a month, for the second similarly twelve, for the third sixteen, for the fourth twenty. The girl is to have each year eighteen days off for festivals, but if she does no work or is sick for some days, she is to remain with her instructor for an equal number of days at the end of her time of service. The instructor is to pay for trade taxes and expenses.

E. A DIET

Plutarch, *Natural Phenomena* VI.913.

That dew has a natural erosive property is evidenced by its making fat people thinner. At any rate fat women imagine that by soaking up some dew on cloths or soft flocks of wool they cause their excess flesh to melt away.

F. WOMEN PAINTERS

Pliny, *Natural History* XXXV. 40.

Women, too, have been painters. Timarete, the daughter of

Micon, painted a Diana on a panel of the very archaic painting in Ephesus. Irene, daughter and student of Cratinus, painted a girl at Eleusis, a Calypso, the old juggler Theodorus, and the dancer Alcisthenes. Aristarete, daughter and pupil of Nearchus, painted an Asclepius. Iaia of Cyzicus, who never married, worked in Rome during the youth of Marcus Varro.[102] She used both the painter's brush and, on ivory, the graving tool. She painted women most frequently, including a panel picture of an old woman in Naples, and even a self-portrait for which she used a mirror. No one's hand was quicker to paint a picture than hers; so great was her talent that her prices far exceeded those of the most celebrated painters of her day, Sopolis and Dionysius, whose works fill the galleries. A certain Olympias, too, was a painter. About her we know only that Autobulus was her student.

G. WOMEN IN THE SERVICE OF THE IMPERIAL HOUSEHOLD (EPITAPHS)

CIL VI. 8958, 5539, 8959, 9037 (= *ILS* 1784, 1786, 1786a, 1788) 8977, 8949.)

To Juno. (The tomb) of Dorcas, hairdresser of Julia Augusta,[103] born a slave (in the imperial house) on Capri. Lycastus, polling-clerk, her fellow-freedman, (put this up) for his dearest wife and for himself.

To Paezusa, hairdresser of Octavia, daughter of Caesar Augustus (Claudius [41-54 A.D.]), who lived eighteen years. Philetus, silver-slave of Octavia, daughter of Caesar Augustus (Claudius), put this up for his dearest wife and for himself.

To the gods of the dead. To Telesphoris, who lived twenty-five years, three months, and eleven days, hairdresser of Domitia (wife) of (the Emperor) Domitian [81-96 A.D.]. Theopompus (put this up) for his wife.

Extricata, seamstress of Octavia, daughter of (Claudius) Augustus, lived twenty years.

(The tomb) of Antonia Thallusa, freedwoman of the Emperor, a midwife.

To Julia [...]sia, freedwoman of the deified Empress,[104] a midwife.

H. OCCUPATIONS OF SLAVES AND FREEDWOMEN (EPITAPHS)

CIL VI. 9884, 6357, 9980, 9727, 9730, 9732, 33892, 9523, 9540, 9892, 9801 (= *ILS* 7567, 7435b, 7428, 7420, 7419, 7420a, 7760, 7400, 7397, 7600, 7500), 9496-8, 9758. Rome, first century B.C./A.D.

Titus Thoranius Savius, freedman of Titus, (erected this monument) for himself and for Matia Prima, freedwoman of Gaia,[105] his wife, a seamstress from Six Altars.[106] She lived forty-six years.

Phyllis, Statilia's seamstress, (dedicated this stone) to Sophrus, her deserving husband.

To Italia, dressmaker of Cocceia Phyllis. She lived twenty years. Acastus, her fellow-slave, put up (this stone) because she was poor.

To the gods of the dead. Polydeuces dedicated this to the well-deserving Cypare, a hairdresser. [This marble plaque is decorated with a roughly engraved comb and hairpin.]

Gnome, handmaiden of Pieris, a hairdresser, was buried on January 28 of the year of Caesar (Augustus') thirteenth consulship, when Marcus Plautius Silvanus was his colleague [2 B.C.].

Psamate, Furia's hairdresser, lived nineteen years. Mithridates, baker of Thorius Flaccus, put up (this stone).[107]

Sacred to the gods of the dead. To Hapate, a Greek stenographer, who lived twenty-five years. Pittosus put this up for his sweetest wife.

Pyrrhe, scribe of Rubria Helvia. Publius Rubrius Optatus (dedicated this) to his wife.

Grapte, secretary of Egnatia Maximilla.[108] Gaius Egnatius Arogus (dedicated this) to his dearest wife.

Thymele, Marcella's silk-slave.

Aurelia Nais, freedwoman of Gaius, fishmonger in the warehouses of (the Emperor) Galba. Gaius Aurelius Phileros, freedman of Gaius, and Lucius Valerius Secundus, freedman of Lucius, (dedicated this altar).

Crecusa, the wool-weigher.

To the gods of the dead. (The tomb) of Irene the wool-weigher. She lived twenty-eight years. Olympus put this up for his well-deserving wife.

To the gods of the dead. (The tomb) of Julia Soter, a wool-weigher. She lived eighty years. Marcus Julius Primus, Julia Musa, Julia Thisbe, Julia Ampliata, and Julia Romana put this up.

Urbana, the teacher. She lived twenty-five years.

I. CALPURNIA AND PLINY THE YOUNGER

Pliny the Younger, *Letters* IV. 19, VI. 4 and 7, VII. 5, VIII. 10.

Calpurnia, Pliny's third wife, was an orphan and several years Pliny's junior. She was a native of Comum in northern Italy, Pliny's home town.

To Calpurnia Hispulla, his wife's aunt and nearest living female relative

You are a model of family affection, and loved your excellent and devoted brother as dearly as he loved you; you love his daughter as if she were your own, and, by filling the place of the father she lost, you are more than an aunt to her. I know then how glad you will be to hear that she has proved herself worthy of her father, her grandfather and you. She is highly intelligent and a careful housewife, and her devotion to me is a sure indication of her virtue. In addition, this love has given her an interest in literature: she keeps copies of my works to read again and again and even learn by heart. She is so anxious when she knows that I am going to plead in court, and so happy when all is over! (She arranges to be kept informed of the sort of reception and applause I receive, and what verdict I win in the case.) If I am giving a reading she sits behind a curtain near by and greedily drinks in every word of appreciation. She has even set my verses to music and sings them, to the accompaniment of her lyre, with no musician to teach her but the best of masters, love.

All this gives me the highest reason to hope that our mutual happiness will last for ever and go on increasing day by day, for she does not love me for my present age nor my person, which will gradually grow old and decay, but for my aspirations to fame; nor would any other feelings be suitable for one brought up by your hands and trained in your precepts, who has seen only what was pure and moral in your company and learned to love me on your recommendation. For you respected my mother like a daughter, and have given me guidance and encouragement since my boyhood; you always foretold that I should become the man I am now in the eyes of my wife. Please accept our united thanks for having given her to me and me to her as if chosen for each other.

To Calpurnia

Never have I complained so much about my public duties as I do now. They would not let me come with you to Campania in search of better health, and they still prevent me from following hard on your heels. This is a time when I particularly want to be with you, to see with my own eyes whether you are gaining in strength and weight, and if the pleasures of your holiday and the luxuries of the district are doing you no harm. Indeed, I should worry when you are away even if you were well, for there are always anxious moments without news of anyone one loves dearly, and, as things are, I have the thought of your health as well as your absence to alarm me with fluctuating doubts and fears. I am full of forebodings of every imaginable disaster, and like all nervous people dwell most on what I pray fervently will not happen. So do please think of my anxiety and write to me once or even twice a day—I shall worry less while I am reading your letters, but my fears will return as soon as I have finished them.

To Calpurnia

You say that you are feeling my absence very much, and your only comfort when I am not there is to hold my writings in your hand and often put them in my place by your side. I like to think that you miss me and find relief in this sort of consolation. I, too, am always reading your letters, and returning to them again and again as if they were new to me—but this only fans the fire of my longing for you. If your letters are so dear to me, you can imagine how I delight in your company; do write as often as you can, although you give me pleasure mingled with pain.

To Calpurnia

You cannot believe how much I miss you. I love you so much, and we are not used to separation.[109] So I stay awake most of the night thinking of you, and by day I find my feet carrying me (a true word, carrying) to your room at the times I usually visited you; then finding it empty I depart, as sick and sorrowful as a lover locked out. The only time I am free from this misery is when I am in court and wearing myself out with my friends' lawsuits. You can judge then what a life I am leading, when I find my rest in work and distraction in troubles and anxiety.

To Calpurnius Fabatus, his wife's grandfather

I know how anxious you are for us to give you a great-grand-child, so you will be all the more sorry to hear that your grand-daughter has had a miscarriage. Being young and inexperienced she did not realize she was pregnant, failed to take proper pre-cautions, and did several things which were better left undone. She has had a severe lesson, and paid for her mistake by seri-ously endangering her life; so that although you must inevitably feel it hard for your old age to be robbed of a descendant already on the way, you should thank the gods for sparing your granddaughter's life even though they denied you the child for the present. They will surely grant us children later on, and we may take hope from this evidence of her fertility though the proof has been unfortunate.

I am giving you the same advice and encouragement as I use on myself, for your desire for great-grandchildren cannot be keener than mine for children. Their descent from both of us should make their road to office easy; I can leave them a well-known name and an established ancestry, if only they may be born and turn our present grief to joy.[110]

J. A WEDDING INVITATION

Oxyrhynchus papyrus 111; third century A.D.

Herais requests your company at dinner in celebration of the marriage of her children at her house tomorrow, the fifth, at nine o'clock.

K. AN ITALIAN BENEFACTRESS

CIL X.6328 = *ILS* 6278. Tarracina, second century A.D.

Caelia Macrina left money for the construction of the building to which this inscription was originally attached, and at the same time endowed an alimentary fund (i.e., to provide cash grants for food) for 200 children of her city. Alimen-tary grants could be either private or governmental, and were customarily larger for boys than for girls. Caelia follows this pattern but is slightly more generous to girls than was usual. The shorter period allowed for girls to receive support reflects their younger age at marriage (often 13 or 14 years old).

Caelia Macrina, daughter of Gaius, by her will ordered 300,000 sesterces to be used [for the construction of this building]. She left ... sesterces for its decoration and maintenance. To the people of Tarracina, in memory of her son Macer, she left 1,000,000 sesterces, so that the income from the money might be given to 100 boys [and to 100 girls] under the title of "alimenta": 5 denarii [= 20 sesterces] each month to each citizen boy up to the age of 16, and 4 denarii [= 16 sesterces] each month to each citizen girl up to the age of 14, so that 100 boys and 100 girls might always be receiving (the grant) in succession.

14. RELIGION

A. VESTAL VIRGINS

Plutarch, *Life of Numa* 9-10.

The goddess of the hearth, Vesta, was served by six virgins, whose duty it was to keep the sacred fire which took the place of a cult statue. Vesta's temple was a round building in the Roman Forum.

The office of Pontifex Maximus, or chief priest, was to declare and interpret the divine law, or, rather, to preside over sacred rites; he not only prescribed rules for public ceremony, but regulated the sacrifices of private persons, not suffering them to vary from established custom, and giving information to every one of what was requisite for purposes of worship or supplication. He was also guardian of the Vestal Virgins, the institution of whom, and of their perpetual fire, was attributed to Numa,[111] who, perhaps, fancied the charge of pure and uncorrupted flames would be fitly entrusted to chaste and unpolluted persons, or that fire, which consumes but produces nothing, bears an analogy to the virgin state. In Greece, wherever a perpetual holy fire is kept, as at Delphi and Athens, the charge of it is

committed, not to virgins, but widows past the time of marriage.
.. Some are of opinion that these vestals had no other business
than the preservation of this fire; but others conceive that they
were keepers of other divine secrets concealed from all but
themselves. Gegania and Verenia, it is recorded, were the names
of the first two virgins consecrated and ordained by Numa;
Canuleia and Tarpeia succeeded; Servius afterwards added two,
and the number of four has continued to the present time.

The statutes prescribed by Numa for the vestals were these:
that they should take a vow of virginity for the space of thirty
years, the first ten of which they were to spend in learning their
duties, the second ten in performing them, and the remaining
ten in teaching and instructing others. Thus the whole term
being completed, it was lawful for them to marry, and, leaving
the sacred order, to choose any condition of life that pleased
them; but this permission few, as they say, made use of; and in
cases where they did so, it was observed that their change was
not a happy one but accompanied ever after with regret and
melancholy; so that the greater number, from religious fears
and scruples, forbore and continued to old age and death in the
strict observance of a single life.

For this condition he compensated by great privileges and
prerogatives; as that they had power to make a will in the
lifetime of their father; that they had a free administration of
their own affairs without guardian or tutor, which was the
privilege of women who were the mothers of three children;[112]
when they go abroad, they have the fasces carried before them;
and if in their walks they chance to meet a criminal on his way
to execution, it saves his life, upon oath made that the meeting
was an accidental one and not concerted or of set purpose. Any
one who presses upon the chair on which they are carried, is put
to death. If these vestals commit any minor fault, they are
punishable by the high priest only, who scourges the offender,
sometimes with her clothes off, in a dark place, with a curtain
drawn between; but she that has broken her vow is buried alive
near the gate called Collina, where a little mound of earth
stands inside the city, reaching some little distance, called in
Latin *agger*; under it a narrow room is constructed, to which a
descent is made by stairs; here they prepare a bed, light a lamp,
and leave a small quantity of victuals, such as bread, water, a
pail of milk; and some oil; so that body which had been consecrated and devoted to the most sacred service of religion might

not be said to perish by such a death as famine. The culprit herself is put in a litter, which they cover over, and tie her down with cords on it, so that nothing she utters may be heard. They then take her to the Forum; all people silently go out of the way as she passes, and such as follow accompany the bier with solemn and speechless sorrow; and indeed, there is not any spectacle more appalling, nor any day observed by the city with greater appearance of gloom and sadness. When they come to the place of execution, the officers loose the cords, and then the high priest, lifting his hands to heaven, pronounces certain prayers to himself before the act; then he brings out the prisoner, being still covered, and placing her upon the steps that lead down to the cell, turns away his face with the rest of the priests; the stairs are drawn up after she has gone down, and a quantity of earth is heaped up over the entrance to the cell, so as to prevent it from being distinguished from the rest of the mound. This is the punishment of those who break their vow of virginity.

B. BACCHIC RITES

The worship of the god Dionysus spread through Italy from the Greek cities of the South and was particularly popular among the lower classes and slaves.[11] While the exaggerated reports of orgiastic rites were shocking to conservative Romans, far more alarming was the organizational nature of this new religion. Secret societies of any sort, and especially of the lower classes, always held for the Romans the threat of sedition. The senate's decree which follows applied to all Italy and placed strict limitations on the worship of Bacchus, though it did not prohibit it entirely.

CIL I².581. 186 B.C.

The consuls Quintus Marcius, son of Lucius, and Spurius Postumius, son of Lucius, consulted the Senate on October 7 in the Temple of Bellona. Marcus Claudius, son of Marcus, Lucius Valerius, son of Publius, and Quintus Minucius, son of Gaius assisted in drafting the decree.

Regarding the Bacchanalia the senators proposed to issue a decree as follows to those who are allied with us: "No one of them shall have a place devoted to the worship of Bacchus: and if there are any who say that they have a need for such a place they shall appear in Rome before the urban praetor; and when he pleas of these men have been heard, our Senate shall make a ecision regarding these matters, provided that not less than 100 enators are present when the matter is discussed. No Roman itizen or man of Latin rights or anyone of the allies shall ssociate with the Bacchae, unless they have appeared before he urban praetor and he has given permission, in accordance vith the opinion of the Senate, delivered while not less than 100 enators were present when the matter was discussed." The roposal passed.

"No man shall be priest of, nor shall any man or woman be naster of, such an organization; nor shall anyone of them have common fund; nor shall anyone appoint any man or woman to e master of such an organization or to act as master; nor ereafter shall anyone take common oath with them, shall make ommon vows, shall make stipulations with them, nor shall any- ne give them surety or shall take surety from them. No one hall perform their rites in secret; nor shall anyone perform heir rites in public, in private, or outside the city, unless he has ppeared before the urban praetor and he has given permission, n accordance with the opinion of the Senate, delivered while ot less than 100 senators were present when the matter was liscussed." The proposal passed.

"No one in a company of more than five persons altogether, nen and women, shall perform such rites; nor in that company hall more than two men or three women be present, unless it is n accordance with the opinion of the urban praetor and the enate, as has been written above."

You shall publish these decrees in public assembly for not less han three market days, that you may know the opinion of the enate. For the opinion of the senators is as follows: "If there re any persons who act contrary to what has been written bove, it is our opinion that a proceeding for a capital offense nust be made against them"; and you shall inscribe this on a ronze tablet, for thus the Senate voted was proper; and you hall order it to be posted where it can be read most easily; and, s has been written above, you shall provide within ten days fter these tablets have been delivered to you that those places levoted to the worship of Bacchus shall be dismantled, if there re any such, except in case something sacred is concerned in he matter.

C. WITCHCRAFT

Many papyri and tablets survive to testify to a pervasive faith, among all strata of society, in the efficacy of magic. Although both men and women were practitioners, sexual motives were considered particularly unnatural in females, who are portrayed in such works as Apuleius' *Golden Ass* as capable of murdering children and husband to attain their evil desires. Such things at least were believed to have happened in real life: cf. the epitaph for Iucundus (*CIL* VI 19747 = *ILS* 8522, Rome, ca. 20 A.D.): "As I was approaching my fourth birthday I was seized and put in the ground, when I could have been sweet to my mother and father. A witch (*saga*) stole me away, her hand everywhere cruel. While she is on earth she can also harm you and your children; guard them, parents, lest sorrow be driven into your hearts." Horace composed a dramatic poem about a similar event: a young boy is killed to provide ingredients for a love charm to bring back Varus, the lover of the witch Canidia; the text follows.

i. Horace, *Epodes* 5

"Oh, by all the gods in the sky who rule earth and the human race, what does this noise mean, why are all of you looking at me savagely? I beg you, by your children, if you ever called on Lucina[114] and she came to bring you successful childbirth—by this purple band on my toga, insignia of innocent childhood; by Jupiter, who will not approve of this—why are you looking at me like a step-mother, like a wild animal facing a spear?"

This is what the boy said in protest, with his lips trembling. He stood there (they had torn off his children's insignia), a young body, the sort that would soften the sacrilegious heart of a Thracian. Canidia, who had twined little snakes in her dishevelled hair, gave orders to burn in her witch's fire wild fig trees uprooted from tombs and funeral cypresses, eggs dipped in the blood of foul frogs, a night owl's feather, herbs from Iolchus[115] and Spain with its rich poisons, and bones torn from the mouth of a hungry bitch.

Now Sagana, with her skirts tied up, sprinkles water from Lake Avernus[116] through the whole house, with her rough hair standing on end, like a sea-urchin or some bristling wild boar. Vera, who lacks any conscience, had been digging up the ground with thick hoes, groaning with the effort, so the boy could be placed in the ditch and die from watching, throughout the long day, meals brought in two and three times—only his face would remain unburied, like a swimmer hanging in water by his chin. All this so his marrow could be cut out and his liver dried, to make a love charm, once his eyeballs had melted away from staring at the food.

Folia of Ariminum was there also, with her man's lust—so the
resort town of Naples and all the neighboring towns believed—
she can bring down the stars and the moon from the sky with
her Thessalian incantantions. Then Canidia, gnawing her nails—
what did she say (or not say?):
"Oh faithful witnesses to my deeds, Night and Diana, you who
rule the silent time, when the secret rites are enacted, come to
me now, and turn your divine anger on my enemy's house.
While wild beasts lie hidden in the treacherous woods, relaxed
in sweet slumber, that old man, whom everyone laughs at, my
over Varus—have Subura's[117] dogs bark at him—he has been
rubbed with an ointment, the most perfect my hands have yet
made. What has happened? Why does my cruel poison work less
well than barbarian Medea's, the poisons she used when she
went into exile, after taking revenge on her royal rival, high
Creon's daughter, when the robe she prepared, a gift steeped in
poison, carried off the new bride in fire? No herb, no root
hidden in inaccessible places has escaped me. He is lying asleep
on his couch, forgetting all of his lovers. But no! He's free to
move around, thanks to an incantation by some more knowledgeable poisoner! No, Varus, I won't use ordinary potions.
You'll regret what you've done; you'll come back to me, and
your devotion to me will return with no help from Marsian
spells.[118] I'll prepare a stronger potion, made stronger because
you disdain me. You'll see heaven sinking beneath the sea,
below the earth's surface, before you'll fail to burn with love for
me, just like pitch in dark flames."
After she said this the boy stopped trying (as he had earlier)
to mollify the sacrilegious women with kind words and, uncertain how he should break the silence, he threw out Thyestean
curses: "Your magic poisons don't have the power to invert
right and wrong, to stop a man's vengeance. I'll pursue you with
curses; no sacrifice can atone for my angry curse. No, when I
die the death you have determined, I'll come as a Fury by
night,[119] as a shade I'll find your face with my hooked talons,
the gods of the Dead[120] have this power, and I'll set on your
restless hearts and drive your sleep off in terror. People will
pursue you in turn and hit you with stones, you dirty old hags,
and the wolves and the birds on the Esquiline hill[121] will scatter
your unburied remains—a sight my parents (who alas will survive me)[122] will not fail to enjoy."

ii. *CIL* VI.20905; Rome, first century A.D.

An epitaph set up by a father to his daughter, with a curse added against the girl's mother, Acte, who had left him.

To the gods of the dead, the tomb of Junia Procula, daughter of Marcus. She lived eight years, eleven months, five days. She left in sorrow her unhappy father and mother. Marcus Junius Euphrosynus put up this altar for himself and_____e [the name has been erased].

You, may your daughter's bones and your parents' rest together without you. Whatever you have done to us, may you get the same yourself. Believe me, you will be witness to your (fate): here are inscribed the marks of eternal shame of Acte, a freedwoman, a treacherous, tricky, hard-hearted poisoner. (I leave her) a nail and a hempen rope to fasten about her neck and burning pitch to sear her evil heart. Manumitted gratis, she went off with an adulterer, cheated her patron, and took away his servants, a maid and a boy, as he lay in bed, leaving him a lonely, despoiled man, broken-hearted. And the same curse (i, laid upon) Hymnus and those who went away with Zosimus.

iii. *ILS* 8751; late second/third century A.D.

Tabellae defixionum ("curse tablets") usually give the names of the victim and the author of the curse (although that is omitted here) and list the parts of the body to be affected by the malediction. The reason for the curse is often given, but frequently, as here, omitted. This text, written on a thin sheet of lead, was discovered in a cinerary urn in a tomb north of Rome along with the cremated woman's remains.

Rufa Publica: her hands, her teeth, her eyes, her arms, her belly, her tits, her chest, her bones, her marrow, her belly, her legs, her mouth, her feet, her forehead, her nails, her fingers, her belly, her navel, her cunt, her womb, her groin; I curse Rufa Publica on these tablets.

D. PRIESTESSES

i. Pleket 11; Phocaea, first century A.D.

The tribe of the Teuthades to Flavia Ammion, daughter of Moschus, who is called Aristion, high priestess of Asia of the temple in Ephesus, president, twice awarded a crown, and sacred judge of the games at Bassalia, wife of Flavius Hermocrates, for her excellence and decorous life and her holiness.

ii. *CIL* X.810, 811, 813; A. Maiuri, *Pompeii* p. 83; first century A.D.

Eumachia was priestess and prominent citizen of the city of Pompeii. She was patroness of the guild of fullers (cleaners, dyers, and clothing makers), one of the most influential trade-guilds of the city because of the importance of the wool industry in Pompeii's economy. Although her ancestry was humble, the fortune she inherited from her father, a brick manufacturer, enabled her to marry into one of Pompeii's older families. She provided the fullers with a large and beautiful building which was probably used as the guild's headquarters.

Over each of the two entrances to the Building of Eumachia in the Civil Forum (the dedication refers to the Emperor Tiberius and his mother, Livia, whose statue was found inside the building):

Eumachia, daughter of Lucius (Eumachius), public priestess, in her own name and that of her son, Marcus Numistrius Fronto, built with her own funds the porch, covered passage, and colonnade and dedicated them to Concordia Augusta and to Pietas.

On the base of a statue (now in the Naples Museum) of Eumachia, with her head veiled as a priestess:

To Eumachia, daughter of Lucius, public priestess, the fullers (dedicated this statue).

On her tomb in the cemetery outside the Porta Nuceria:

Eumachia, daughter of Lucius, (built this) for herself and for her household.

iii. Pleket 18; Aphrodisias, second century A.D.

The council and the people and the senate honor with first-rank honors Tata, daughter of Diodorus son of Diodorus son of Leon, reverend priestess of Hera for life, mother of the city, who became and remained the wife of Attalus son of Pythias, who earned the right to wear a wreath, herself a member of an illustrious family of the first rank, who, as priestess of the imperial cult a second time, twice supplied oil for athletes in hand-bottles, filled most lavishly from basins for the better part of the night as well (as in the day), who earned the right to wear a wreath, who sacrificed throughout the year for the health of the imperial family, who held banquets for the people many times with couches provided for the public, who herself, for dances and plays, imported the foremost performers in Asia and displayed them in her native city (and the neighboring cities could also come to the display of the performance), a woman who spared no expense, who loved honor, glorious in virtue and chastity.

iv. Pleket 25; Syros, second/third century A.D.

The resolution of the prytaneis approved by the council and the people: Whereas Berenice, daughter of Nicomachus, wife of Aristocles son of Isidorus, has conducted herself well and appropriately on all occasions, and after she was made a magistrate unsparingly celebrated rites at her own expense for god and men on behalf of her native city, and after she was made priestess of the heavenly and holy goddesses Demeter and Kore and celebrated their rites in a holy and worthy manner, gave up her life—meanwhile she had raised her own children; Voted to commend the span of this woman's lifetime, to crown her with the gold wreath which in our fatherland is customarily used to crown good women. The man who inscribes this stone is to write on her tomb this announcement: the people of Syros crown Berenice daughter of Nicomachus with a gold crown in recognition of her virtue and their good will towards her.

v. Pleket 29; Thasos, late Empire.

Good fortune. The council honors Flavia Vibia Sabina, most noteworthy high priestess, and because of her ancestors uniquely mother of the council: she is the first and only woman to have for life honor equal to those of the councilmen.

E. CHRISTIANITY

Christianity was, for the Romans, another foreign religion (in this case an offshoot of Judaism) to be regarded with suspicion. Like the cult of Bacchus the Christian religion brought members of the lower classes together in assemblies, which was particularly worrisome to the authorities. Christians were also victims of wildly exaggerated stories and false accusations based upon misinterpretation: incest and cannibalism, for example. Still, the Roman concern was for security of the state; the opposition to Christianity was not theological.

i. Paul of Tarsus on Women

From The New English Bible. © The Delegates of the Oxford University Press
and The Syndics of the Cambridge University Press 1961, 1970. Reprinted by
permission.)

I Corinthians 7:1-16, 25-40, 11:2-16, 14:34-35

And now for the matters you wrote about.

It is a good thing for a man to have nothing to do with
women; but because there is so much immorality, let each man
have his own wife and each woman her own husband. The
husband must give the wife what is due to her, and the wife
equally must give the husband his due. The wife cannot claim
her body as her own; it is her husband's. Equally, the husband
cannot claim his body as his own; it is his wife's. Do not deny
yourselves to one another, except when you agree upon a temporary abstinence in order to devote yourselves to prayer; afterwards you may come together again; otherwise, for lack of self-
control, you may be tempted by Satan.

All this I say by way of concession, not command. I should
like you all to be as I am myself; but everyone has the gift God
has granted him, one this gift and another that.

To the unmarried and to widows I say this: it is a good thing
they stay as I am myself; but if they cannot control themselves, they should marry. Better be married than burn with
vain desire.

To the married I give this ruling, which is not mine but the
Lord's: a wife must not separate herself from her husband; if
she does, she must either remain unmarried or be reconciled to
her husband; and the husband must not divorce his wife.

To the rest I say this, as my own word, not as the Lord's: if a
Christian has a heathen wife, and she is willing to live with him,
he must not divorce her; and a woman who has a heathen
husband willing to live with her must not divorce her husband.
For the heathen husband now belongs to God through his Christian wife, and the heathen wife through her Christian husband.
Otherwise your children would not belong to God, whereas in
fact they do. If on the other hand the heathen partner wishes
for a separation, let him have it. In such cases the Christian
husband or wife is under no compulsion; but God's call is a call
to live in peace. Think of it: as a wife you may be your husband's salvation; as a husband you may be your wife's salvation.

However that may be, each one must order his life according
to the gift the Lord has granted him and his condition when

God called him. That is what I teach in all our congregations.
Was a man called with the marks of circumcision on him? Let
him not remove them. Was he uncircumcised when he was
called? Let him not be circumcised. Circumcision or uncircumci-
sion is neither here nor there; what matters is to keep God's
commands. Every man should remain in the condition in which
he was called. Were you a slave when you were called? Do not
let that trouble you; but if a chance of liberty should come, take
it. For the man who as a slave received the call to be a Christian
is the Lord's freedman, and, equally, the free man who received
the call is a slave in the service of Christ. You were bought at a
price; do not become slaves of men. Thus each one, my friends,
is to remain before God in the condition in which he received
his call.

On the question of celibacy, I have no instructions from the
Lord, but I give my judgement as one who by God's mercy is fit
to be trusted.

It is my opinion, then, that in a time of stress like the present
this is the best way for a man to live—it is best for a man to be
as he is. Are you bound in marriage? Do not seek a dissolution.
Has your marriage been dissolved? Do not seek a wife. If, however, you do marry, there is nothing wrong in it; and if a virgin
marries, she has done no wrong. But those who marry will have
pain and grief in this bodily life, and my aim is to spare you.

What I mean, my friends, is this. The time we live in will not
last long. While it lasts, married men should be as if they had
no wives; mourners should be as if they had nothing to grieve
them, the joyful as if they did not rejoice; buyers must not
count on keeping what they buy, nor those who use the world's
wealth on using it to the full. For the whole frame of this world
is passing away.

I want you to be free from anxious care. The unmarried man
cares for the Lord's business; his aim is to please the Lord. But
the married man cares for worldly things; his aim is to please
his wife; and he has a divided mind. The unmarried or celibate
woman cares for the Lord's business; her aim is to be dedicated
to him in body as in spirit; but the married woman cares for
worldly things; her aim is to please her husband.

In saying this I have no wish to keep you on a tight rein. I am
thinking simply of your own good, of what is seemly, and of
your freedom to wait upon the Lord without distraction.

But if a man has a partner in celibacy and feels that he is not behaving properly towards her, if, that is, his instincts are too strong for him; and something must be done, he may do as he pleases; there is nothing wrong in it; let them marry. But if a man is steadfast in his purpose, being under no compulsion, and has complete control of his own choice; and if he has decided in his own mind to preserve his partner in her virginity, he will do well. Thus, he who marries his partner does well, and he who does not will do better.

A wife is bound to her husband as long as he lives. But if the husband die, she is free to marry whom she will, provided the marriage is within the Lord's fellowship. But she is better off as she is; that is my opinion, and I believe that I too have the Spirit of God....

I commend you for always keeping me in mind, and maintaining the tradition I handed on to you. But I wish you to understand that, while every man has Christ for his Head, woman's head is man, as Christ's Head is God. A man who keeps his head covered when he prays or prophesies brings shame on his head; a woman, on the contrary, brings shame on her head if she prays or prophesies bare-headed: it is as bad as if her head were shaved. If a woman is not to wear a veil she might as well have her hair cut off; but if it is a disgrace for her to be cropped and shaved, then she should wear a veil. A man has no need to cover his head, because man is the image of God, and the mirror of his glory, whereas woman reflects the glory of man. For man did not originally spring from woman, but woman was made out of man; and man was not created for woman's sake, but woman for the sake of man; and therefore it is woman's duty to have a sign of authority on her head, out of regard for the angels. And yet, in Christ's fellowship woman is as essential to man as man to woman. If woman was made out of man, it is through woman that man now comes to be; and God is the source of all.

Judge for yourselves: is it fitting for a woman to pray to God bare-headed? Does not Nature herself teach you that while flowing locks disgrace a man, they are a woman's glory? For her locks were given for covering.

However, if you insist on arguing, let me tell you, there is no such custom among us, or in any of the congregations of God's people....

As in all congregations of God's people, women should not address the meeting. They have no license to speak, but should keep their place as the law directs. If there is something they

want to know, they can ask their own husbands at home. It is
shocking thing that a woman should address the congregation.

I Timothy 2:8-14

It is my desire, therefore, that everywhere prayers be said b
the men of the congregation, who shall lift up their hands wit
a pure intention, excluding angry or quarrelsome thought:
Women again must dress in becoming manner, modestly an
soberly, not with elaborate hair-styles, not decked out with gol
or pearls, or expensive clothes, but with good deeds, as befit
women who claim to be religious. A woman must be a learner
listening quietly and with due submission. I do not permit
woman to be a teacher, nor must woman domineer over man
she should be quiet. For Adam was created first, and Eve after
wards; and it was not Adam who was deceived; it was the woma
who, yielding to deception, fell into sin.

ii. Martyrs

Acts of the Christian Martyrs 8. 2-10

In 203 Septimius Severus banned conversion to either Judaism or Christianit
and, as a result of this ban, Saint Perpetua was martyred.

A number of young catechumens were arrested, Revocatu
and his fellow slave Felicitas, Saturninus and Secundulus, an
with them Vibia Perpetua, a newly married woman of goo
family and upbringing. Her mother and father were still aliv
and one of her two brothers was a catechumen like herself. Sh
was about twenty-two years old and had an infant son at th
breast. (Now from this point on the entire account of her ordea
is her own, according to her own ideas and in the way that sh
herself wrote it down.)

While we were still under arrest (she said) my father out o
love for me was trying to persuade me and shake my resolution
"Father," said I, "do you see this vase here, for example, o
waterpot or whatever?"

"Yes, I do," said he.

And I told him: "Could it be called by any other name tha
what it is?"

And he said: "No."

"Well, so too I cannot be called anything other than what
am, a Christian."

At this my father was so angered by the word "Christian" that he moved towards me as though he would pluck my eyes out. But he left it at that and departed, vanquished along with his diabolical arguments.

For a few days afterwards I gave thanks to the Lord that I was separated from my father, and I was comforted by his absence. During these few days I was baptized, and I was inspired by the Spirit not to ask for any other favor after the water but simply the perseverance of the flesh. A few days later we were lodged in the prison; and I was terrified, as I had never before been in such a dark hole. What a difficult time it was! With the crowd the heat was stifling; then there was the extortion of the soldiers; and to crown all, I was tortured with worry for my baby there.

Then Tertius and Pomponius, those blessed deacons who tried to take care of us, bribed the soldiers to allow us to go to a better part of the prison to refresh ourselves for a few hours. Everyone then left that dungeon and shifted for himself. I nursed my baby, who was faint from hunger. In my anxiety I spoke to my mother about the child, I tried to comfort my brother, and I gave the child in their charge. I was in pain because I saw them suffering out of pity for me. These were the trials I had to endure for many days. Then I got permission for my baby to stay with me in prison. At once I recovered my health, relieved as I was of my worry and anxiety over the child. My prison had suddenly become a palace, so that I wanted to be there rather than anywhere else.

Then my brother said to me: "Dear sister, you are greatly privileged; surely you might ask for a vision to discover whether you are to be condemned or freed."

Faithfully I promised that I would, for I knew that I could speak with the Lord, whose great blessings I had come to experience. And so I said: "I shall tell you tomorrow." Then I made my request and this was the vision I had.

I saw a ladder of tremendous height made of bronze, reaching all the way to the heavens, but it was so narrow that only one person could climb up at a time. To the sides of the ladder were attached all sorts of metal weapons: there were swords, spears, hooks, daggers, and spikes; so that if anyone tried to climb up carelessly or without paying attention, he would be mangled and his flesh would adhere to the weapons.

At the foot of the ladder lay a dragon of enormous size, and it would attack those who tried to climb up and try to terrify them from doing so. And Saturus was the first to go up, he who was later to give himself up of his own accord. He had been the builder of our strength, although he was not present when we were arrested. And he arrived at the top of the staircase and he looked back and said to me: "Perpetua, I am waiting for you But take care; do not let the dragon bite you."

"He will not harm me," I said, "in the name of Christ Jesus."

Slowly, as though he were afraid of me, the dragon stuck his head out from underneath the ladder. Then, using it as my first step, I trod on his head and went up.

Then I saw an immense garden, and in it a grey-haired man sat in shepherd's garb; tall he was, and milking sheep. And standing around him were many thousands of people clad in white garments. He raised his head, looked at me, and said: ". am glad you have come, my child."

He called me over to him and gave me, as it were, a mouthful of the milk he was drawing; and I took it into my cupped hands and consumed it. And all those who stood around said: "Amen!" At the sound of this word I came to, with the taste of something sweet still in my mouth. I at once told this to my brother, and we realized that we would have to suffer, and that from now on we would no longer have any hope in this life.

A few days later there was a rumor that we were going to be given a hearing. My father also arrived from the city, worn with worry, and he came to see me with the idea of persuading me.

"Daughter," he said, "have pity on my grey head—have pity on me your father, if I deserve to be called your father, if I have favored you above all your brothers, if I have raised you to reach this prime of your life. Do not abandon me to be the reproach of men. Think of your brothers, think of your mother and your aunt, think of your child, who will not be able to live once you are gone. Give up your pride! You will destroy all of us! None of us will ever be able to speak freely again if anything happens to you."

This was the way my father spoke out of love for me, kissing my hands and throwing himself down before me. With tears in his eyes he no longer addressed me as his daughter but as a woman. I was sorry for my father's sake, because he alone of all my kin would be unhappy to see me suffer.

I tried to comfort him saying: "It will all happen in the prisoner's dock as God wills; for you may be sure that we are not left to ourselves but are all in his power."

And he left me in great sorrow.

One day while we were eating breakfast we were suddenly hurried off for a hearing. We arrived at the forum, and straight away the story went about the neighborhood near the forum and a huge crowd gathered. We walked up to the prisoner's dock. All the others when questioned admitted their guilt. Then, when it came my turn, my father appeared with my son, dragged me from the step, and said: "Perform the sacrifice—have pity on your baby!"

Hilarianus the governor, who had received his judicial powers as the successor of the late proconsul Minucius Timinianus, said to me: "Have pity on your father's grey head; have pity on your infant son. Offer the sacrifice for the welfare of the emperors."

"I will not", I retorted.

"Are you a Christian?" said Hilarianus.

And I said: "Yes, I am."

When my father persisted in trying to dissuade me, Hilarianus ordered him to be thrown to the ground and beaten with a rod. I felt sorry for father, just as if I myself had been beaten. I felt sorry for his pathetic old age.

Then Hilarianus passed sentence on all of us: we were condemned to the beasts, and we returned to prison in high spirits. But my baby had got used to being nursed at the breast and to staying with me in prison. So I sent the deacon Pomponius straight away to my father to ask for the baby. But father refused to give him over. But as God willed, the baby had no further desire for the breast, nor did I suffer any inflammation; and so I was relieved of any anxiety for my child and of any discomfort in my breasts.

Some days later when we were all at prayer, suddenly while praying I spoke out and uttered the name Dinocrates. I was surprised; for the name had never entered my mind until that moment. And I was pained when I recalled what had happened to him. At once I realized that I was privileged to pray for him. I began to pray for him and to sigh deeply for him before the Lord. That very night I had the following vision. I saw Dinocrates coming out of a dark hole, where there were many others with him, very hot and thirsty, pale and dirty. On his face was the wound he had when he died.

Now Dinocrates had been my brother according to the flesh; but he had died horribly of cancer of the face when he was seven years old, and his death was a source of loathing to everyone. Thus it was for him that I made my prayer. There was a great abyss between us: neither could approach the other. Where Dinocrates stood there was a pool full of water; and its rim was higher than the child's height, so that Dinocrates had to stretch himself up to drink. I was sorry that, though the pool had water in it, Dinocrates could not drink because of the height of the rim. Then I woke up, realizing that my brother was suffering. But I was confident that I could help him in his trouble; and I prayed for him every day until we were transferred to the military prison. For we were supposed to fight with the beasts at the military games to be held on the occasion of the emperor Geta's birthday. And I prayed for my brother day and night with tears and sighs that this favor might be granted me.

On the day we were kept in chains, I had this vision shown to me. I saw the same spot that I had seen before, but there was Dinocrates all clean, well dressed, and refreshed. I saw a scar where the wound had been; and the pool that I had seen before now had its rim lowered to the level of the child's waist. And Dinocrates kept drinking water from it, and there above the rim was a golden bowl full of water. And Dinocrates drew close and began to drink from it, and yet the bowl remained full. And when he had drunk enough of the water, he began to play as children do. Then I awoke, and I realized that he had been delivered from his suffering.

Some days later, an adjutant named Pudens, who was in charge of the prison, began to show us great honor, realizing that we possessed some great power within us. And he began to allow many visitors to see us for our mutual comfort.

Now the day of the contest was approaching, and my father came to see me overwhelmed with sorrow. He started tearing the hairs from his beard and threw them on the ground; he then threw himself on the ground and began to curse his old age and to say such words as would move all creation. I felt sorry for his unhappy old age.

The day before we were to fight with the beasts I saw the following vision. Pomponius the deacon came to the prison gates and began to knock violently. I went out and opened the gate for him. He was dressed in an unbelted white tunic, wearing elaborate sandals. And he said to me: "Perpetua, come; we are waiting for you."

Then he took my hand and we began to walk through rough

and broken country. At last we came to the amphitheater out of breath, and he led me into the center of the arena.

Then he told me: "Do not be afraid. I am here, struggling with you." Then he left.

I looked at the enormous crowd who watched in astonishment. I was surprised that no beasts were let loose on me; for I knew that I was condemned to die by the beasts. Then out came an Egyptian against me, of vicious appearance, together with his seconds, to fight with me. There also came up to me some handsome young men to be my seconds and assistants.

My clothes were stripped off, and suddenly I was a man. My seconds began to rub me down with oil (as they are wont to do before a contest). Then I saw the Egyptian on the other side rolling in the dust. Next there came forth a man of marvellous stature, such that he rose above the top of the amphitheater. He was clad in a beltless purple tunic with two stripes (one on either side) running down the middle of his chest. He wore sandals that were wondrously made of gold and silver, and he carried a wand like an athletic trainer and a green branch on which there were golden apples.

And he asked for silence and said: "If this Egyptian defeats her he will slay her with the sword. But if she defeats him, she will receive this branch." Then he withdrew.

We drew close to one another and began to let our fists fly. My opponent tried to get hold of my feet, but I kept striking him in the face with the heels of my feet. Then I was raised up into the air and I began to pummel him without as it were touching the ground. Then when I noticed there was a lull, I put my two hands together linking the fingers of one hand with those of the other and thus I got hold of his head. He fell flat on his face and I stepped on his head.

The crowd began to shout and my assistants started to sing psalms. Then I walked up to the trainer and took the branch. He kissed me and said to me: "Peace be with you, my daughter!" I began to walk in triumph towards the Gate of Life.[123] Then I awoke. I realized that it was not with wild animals that I would fight but with the Devil, but I knew that I would win the victory. So much for what I did up until the eve of the contest. About what happened at the contest itself, let him write of it who will.

Acts of the Christian Martyrs 22

When the Emperor Diocletian became ill in 303, a sacrifice for his health was required of all citizens, and those who did not cooperate were executed.

Since the advent and the presence on earth of our Lord and Saviour Jesus Christ, the greater the grace of the men of old, so much the greater was the victory of holy men. For instead of those visible enemies, we have now begun to crush enemies that cannot be seen with bodily eyes, and the invisible substance of the demons has been handed over to the flames by pure and holy women who were full of the Holy Spirit. Such were the three saintly women who came from the city of Thessalonica, the city that the inspired Paul celebrated when he praised its faith and love, saying, *Your faith in God has gone out to every place.*[124] And elsewhere he says, *Of charity for your brothers I have no need to write to you; for you yourselves have learned from God to love one another.*[125]

When the persecution was raging under the Emperor Maximian, these women, who had adorned themselves with virtue, following the precepts of the Gospel, abandoned their native city, their family, property, and possessions because of their love of God and their expectation of heavenly things, performing deeds worthy of their father Abraham. They fled the persecutors, according to the commandment, and took refuge on a high mountain. There they gave themselves to prayer: though their bodies resided on a mountain top, their souls lived in heaven.[126]

At any rate, they were here captured and brought to the official who was conducting the persecution, that, by thus fulfilling the rest of the divine commands and loving their Master even unto death, they might weave for themselves the chaplet of immortality. Of these girls one had preserved the shining purity of her baptism according to the holy prophet who said: *You will wash me and I shall be whiter than snow,*[127] and she was called Chionê ["snow"]. The second girl possessed the gift of our God and Saviour within herself and manifested it to everyone according to the word, *My peace I give you,*[128] and she was called Irenê ["peace"] by everyone. The third girl possessed the perfection of the Gospel, loving God with her whole heart and her neighbor as herself, in accord with the holy Apostle who says, *The aim of our charge is love,*[129] and she was appropriately named Agapê ["love"]. When these three girls were brought before the magistrate and refused to sacrifice, he sentenced them to the fire, in order that thus by a short time in the fire they might overcome those that are devoted to fire, that is, the Devil and all his heavenly host of demons, and, attaining the incorruptible crown of glory, they might endlessly praise along with the angels the God who had showered this grace upon them. The record that was taken down in their case is the material of our account.

The prefect Dulcitius was sitting on the tribunal, and the court clerk Artemisius spoke: "With your permission, I shall read the charge which was sent to your *genius* by the *stationarius*,[130] here present, in connection with the parties in court."

"You may read it," said the prefect Dulcitius. And the charge was duly read: "To you, my lord, greetings from Cassander, *beneficiarius*.[131] This is to inform you, Sir, that Agatho, Irenê, Agapê, Chionê, Cassia, Philippa, and Eutychia refuse to eat sacrificial food, and so I have referred them to your genius."

"What is this insanity," said the prefect Dulcitius, "that you refuse to obey the order of our most religious emperors and Caesars?" And turning to Agatho, he said: "When you came to the sacrifices, why did you not perform the cult practices like other religious people?"

"Because I am a Christian," said Agatho.

The prefect Dulcitius said: "Do you still remain in the same mind today?"

"Yes," said Agatho.

The prefect Dulcitius said: "What do you say, Agapê?"

"I believe in the living God," replied Agapê, "and I refuse to destroy my conscience."

"What do you say, Irenê?" asked the prefect Dulcitius. "Why did you disobey the command of our lords the emperors and Caesars?"

"Because of my fear of God," said Irenê.

"What do you say, Chionê?" asked the prefect.

"I believe in the living God," replied Chionê, "and I refuse to do this."

The prefect said: "And how about you, Cassia?"

"I wish to save my soul," said Cassia.

The prefect said: "Are you willing to partake of the sacrificial meat?"

"I am not," said Cassia.

"The prefect said: "And what say you, Philippa?"

"I say the same," said Philippa.

"What do you mean, the same?" said the prefect.

Said Philippa: "I mean, I would rather die than partake."

"Eutychia," said the prefect, "what do you say?"

"I say the same," said Eutychia; "I would rather die."

The prefect said: "Do you have a husband?"

"He is dead," said Eutychia.

"When did he die?" asked the prefect.

"About seven months ago," said Eutychia.

The prefect said, "How is it then that you are pregnant?"

Eutychia said: "By the man whom God gave me."

The prefect said: "But how can you be pregnant when you say your husband is dead?"

Eutychia said: "No one can know the will of almighty God. So God willed it."

The prefect said: "I urge Eutychia to cease this madness and to return to sound reason. What do you say? Will you obey the imperial command?"

"No, I will not," said Eutychia. "I am a Christian, a servant of almighty God."

The prefect said: "Since Eutychia is pregnant, she shall be kept meanwhile in jail." Then he added: "What say you, Agapê? Will you perform all the actions which religious persons perform in honor of our lords the emperors and Caesars?"

Agapê replied: "It is not at all in Satan's power. He cannot move my reason; it is invincible."

The prefect said: "What say you, Chionê?"

Chionê said: "No one can change my mind."

The prefect said: "Do you have in your possession any writings, parchments, or books of the impious Christians?"

Chionê said: 'We do not, Sir. Our present emperors have taken these from us."

"Who was it who gave you this idea?" asked the prefect.

"God almighty," said Chionê.

The prefect said: "Who was it who counselled you to commit such folly?"

"It was almighty God", answered Chionê, "and his only begotten Son, our Lord Jesus Christ."

The prefect Dulcitius said: "It is clear to all that you are all liable to the crime of treason against our lords the emperors and Caesars. But seeing that you have persisted in this folly for such a long time, in spite of strong warnings and so many decrees, sanctioned by stern threats, and have despised the command of our lords the emperors and Caesars, remaining in this impious name of Christian, and seeing that even today when you were ordered by the soldiers and officials to deny your belief and signify this in writing, you refused—therefore you shall receive the punishment appropriate for you."

Then he read the sentence written on a sheet: "Whereas Agapê and Chionê have with malicious intent acted against the divine decree of our lords the Augusti and Caesars, and whereas they adhere to the worthless and obsolete worship of the Christians which is hateful to all religious men, I sentence them to be burned." Then he added: "Agatho, Irenê, Cassia, Philippa, and Eutychia, because of their youth are to be put in prison in the meanwhile."

After the most holy women were consumed in the flames, the saintly girl Irenê was once again brought before the court on the following day. Dulcitius said to her: "It is clear from what we have seen that you are determined in your folly, for you have deliberately kept even till now so many tablets, books, parchments, codices, and pages of the writings of the former Christians of unholy name; even now, though you denied each time that you possessed such writings, you did show a sign of recognition when they were mentioned. You are not satisfied with the punishment of your sisters, nor do you keep before your eyes the terror of death. Therefore you must be punished.

"It would not, however, seem out of place to show you some measure of mercy: if even now you would be willing to recognize the gods you will be released from all danger and punishment. Now what do you say? Will you do the bidding of our emperors and Caesars? Are you prepared to eat the sacrificial meats and to sacrifice to the gods?"

"No," said Irenê, "I am not prepared, for the sake of the God almighty who *has created heaven and earth and the seas and all that is in them*.[132] For those who transgress the word of God there awaits the great judgement of eternal punishment."

The prefect Dulcitius said: "Who was it that advised you to retain those parchments and writings up to the present time?"

"It was almighty God," said Irenê, "who bade us to love him unto death. For this reason we did not dare to be traitors, but we chose to be burned alive or suffer anything else that might happen to us rather than betray the writings."

The prefect said: "Was anyone else aware that the documents were in the house where you lived?"

"No one else", said Irenê, "saw them, save almighty God who knows all things. But no stranger. As for our own relatives, we considered them worse than our enemies, in fear that they would denounce us. Hence we told no one."

"Last year," said the prefect, "when this edict of our lords the emperors and Caesars was first promulgated, where did you hide?"

"Wherever God willed," said Irenê. "We lived on the mountains, in the open air, as God is my witness."

"Whom were you living with?" asked the prefect.

Irenê answered: "We lived out of doors in different places among the mountains."

The prefect said: "Who supplied you with bread?"

Irenê answered: "God, who supplies all men."

"Was your father aware of this?" asked the prefect.

Irenê answered: "I swear by almighty God, he was not aware; he knew nothing at all about it."

"Were any of your neighbors aware of this?" asked the prefect.

Irenê answered: "Go and question our neighbors, and inquire about the area to see whether anyone knew where we were."

The prefect said: "Now after you returned from the mountain where you had been, as you say, were any persons present at the reading of these books?"

Irenê answered: "They were in our house and we did not dare to bring them out. In fact, it caused us much distress that we could not devote ourselves to them night and day as we had done from the beginning until that day last year when we hid them."

Dulcitius the prefect said: "Your sisters, in accordance with my commands in their regard, have received their sentence. Now you were guilty even before you ran away and before you concealed these writings and parchments, and hence I do not wish you to die immediately in the same way. Instead I sentence you to be placed naked in the brothel with the help of the public notaries of this city and of Zosimus the executioner; and you will receive merely one loaf of bread from our residence, and the notaries will not allow you to leave."

And so, after the notaries and the slave Zosimus, the executioner, were brought in, the prefect said: "Be it known to you that if ever I find out from the troops that this girl was removed from the spot where I have ordered her to be even for a single instant, you will immediately be punished with the most extreme penalties. The writings we have referred to, in the cabinets and chests belonging to Irenê, are to be publicly burned."

After those who were put in charge had taken the girl off to the public brothel in accordance with the prefect's order, by the grace of the Holy Spirit which preserved and guarded her pure and inviolate for the God who is the lord of all things, no man dared to approach her or so much as tried to insult her in speech. Hence the prefect Dulcitius called back this most saintly girl, had her stand before the tribunal, and said to her: "Do you still persist in the same folly?"

But Irenê said to him: "It is not folly, but piety."

"It was abundantly clear from your earlier testimony," said the prefect Dulcitius, "that you did not wish to submit religiously to the bidding of the emperors; and now I perceive that you are persisting in the same foolishness. Therefore you shall pay the appropriate penalty."

He then asked for a sheet of papyrus and wrote the sentence against her as follows: "Whereas Irenê has refused to obey the command of the emperors and to offer sacrifice, and still adheres to a sect called the Christians, I therefore sentence her to be burned alive, as I did her two sisters before her."

After this sentence had been pronounced by the prefect, the soldiers took the girl and brought her to a high place, where her sisters had been martyred before her. They ignited a huge pyre and ordered her to climb up on it. And the holy woman Irenê, singing and praising God, threw herself upon it and so died. It was in the ninth consulship of Diocletian Augustus, in the eighth of Maximian Augustus, on the first day of April, in the kingship of our Lord Christ Jesus, who reigns for ever, with whom there is glory to the Father with the Holy Spirit for ever. Amen.

iii. Gnosticism
Irenaeus, *Against Heresies* I.13.1-5.

Irenaeus, a second-century bishop of Lugdunum (Lyons), in describing the initiation of a woman into a Gnostic sect, emphasizes as the most dangerous aspects of this heretical cult its appeal to women and the priest Marcus' use of magic tricks. The important role played by a female essence (grace) in the ritual, a characteristic of Gnostic Christian belief, is significantly absent from the conversion literature of the "right-thinking" or orthodox church in this period.[133]

There is another of those among them who prides himself on being an improver of his master's teaching. His name is Marcus, and he is knowledgeable in magical deceit, by means of which he has led astray many men and not a few women and has induced them to turn to him as to one possessed of great skill and who has received a great power from the invisible and ineffable regions, an actual precursor of the Antichrist. . . .

Over a cup mixed with wine he pretends to pray and, whilst greatly prolonging the invocation, he contrives that it should appear purple and red so that Grace, who belongs to the company of those who are superior to all things, may seem to be dropping her blood into that cup by means of his invocation, and that those present should fervently desire to taste of that cup in order that the Grace called hither by that magician may let (her blood) flow into them. Again, he gives to women cups already mixed and full, and bids them offer thanks in his presence. When this is done, he produces another cup much larger than the one over which the deluded woman has given thanks, and he then pours from the smaller one over which she has given thanks into the one which he has brought forward—which was much larger—and at the same time he speaks as follows: "May Grace who is before all things, who is beyond thought and description, fill thine inner man and multiply in thee her knowledge, sowing the mustard seed in good soil." By saying such things and by making the wretched woman deranged, he appears as a wonder-worker, when the larger cup is filled from the smaller one to such an extent that it actually overflows. By doing other things like this he has deceived many and drawn them into following him.

It is clearly recognizable that he has a demon too residing in him, by means of which he appears to be able to prophesy and to enable [the women] whom he counts worthy to be partakers of his Grace to prophesy as well. He concerns himself in particular with women, especially with those of high rank, the elegantly attired and wealthy, whom he frequently attempts to lead astray by flattering them and saying, "I desire to make thee a partaker of my Grace, since the Father of all doth continually behold thy angel before his face[134]. The place of thy greatness is ever in us: we must come together. First, receive from me and through Grace. Adorn theyself as a bride who expects her bridegroom, that thou mayest be what I am, and I what thou art. Receive in they bride-chamber the seed of light. Receive from me the bridegroom, and give him a place, and have a place in him. Behold, Grace has descended upon thee; open thy mouth and prophesy." But if the woman replies, "I have never prophesied before, nor can I prophesy," then, for the second time, he offers some prayers to bewilder the deluded woman, and says to her, "Open thy mouth and speak whatever comes to thee, and thou shalt prophesy." And the woman, deluded and puffed up by what has been said, and excited by the expectation that she is about to prophesy, takes the risk, and with her heart pounding abnormally she utters ridiculous nonsense, anything that happens to come into her head, idly and audaciously, for she is stimulated by a vain spirit..., henceforth considers herself as a prophetess, and thanks Marcus who has shared with her his Grace. She tries to repay him, not only with the gift of her possessions—by which means he has collected a great amount of money—but also by physical intercourse, prepared as she is to be united with him in everything in order that she, with him, may enter into the One....

Moreover, that this man Marcus, with the intention of degrading their bodies, administers love-potions and aphrodisiacs to some of these women, even if not to all of them, they have frequently confessed after they have returned to the church of God; and that they were physically abused by him, and that they had loved him with violent passion.

iv. The Advantages of Celibacy
St. Jerome, *Against Jovinianus* 47

In the process of marshalling evidence against marriage (and women) the priest Jerome, who often appears to be more concerned with making an effective case than with historical accuracy, cites an otherwise unknown treatise on marriage by Aristotle's successor Theophrastus (fourth century B.C.). Such treatises had been in circulation since the late fifth century B.C., and it is interesting that even in the context of Christian theology Greek and Roman misogyny did not lose its currency.

A book *On Marriage*, worth its weight in gold, passes under the name of Theophrastus.[135] In it the author asks whether a wise man marries. And after laying down the conditions—that the wife must be fair, of good character, and honest parentage, the husband in good health and of ample means, and after saying that under these circumstances a wise man sometimes enters the state of matrimony, he immediately proceeds thus: "But all these conditions are seldom satisfied in marriage. A wise man therefore must not take a wife. For in the first place his study of philosophy will be hindered, and it is impossible for anyone to attend to his books and his wife. Matrons want many things, costly dresses, gold, jewels, great outlay, maid-servants, all kinds of furniture, litters and gilded coaches. Then come lectures the livelong night: she complains that one lady goes out better dressed than she: that another is looked up to by all: 'I am a poor despised nobody at the ladies' assemblies.' 'Why did you ogle that creature next door?' 'Why were you talking to the maid?' 'What did you bring from the market?' 'I am not allowed to have a single friend, or companion.' She suspects that her husband's love goes the same way as her hate. There may be in some neighboring city the wisest of teachers; but if we have a wife we can neither leave her behind, nor take the burden with us. To support a poor wife, is hard: to put up with a rich one, is torture.

"Notice, too, that in the case of a wife you cannot pick and choose: you must take her as you find her. If she has a bad temper, or is a fool, if she has a blemish, or is proud, or has bad breath, whatever her fault may be—all this we learn after marriage. Horses, asses, cattle, even slaves of the smallest worth, clothes, kettles, wooden seats, cups, and earthenware pitchers, are first tried and then bought: a wife is the only thing that is not shown before she is married, for fear she may not give satisfaction. Our gaze must always be directed to her face, and we must always praise her beauty: if you look at another woman, she thinks that she is out of favor. She must be called my lady, her birthday must be kept, we must swear by her health and wish that she may survive us, respect must be paid to the nurse, to the nursemaid, to the father's slave, to the foster-child, to the handsome hanger-on, to the curled darling who manages her affairs, and to the eunuch who ministers to the safe indulgence of her lust: names which are only a cloak for adultery.

"Upon whomsoever she sets her heart, they must have her love though they want her not. If you give her the management of the whole house, you must yourself be her slave. If you reserve something for yourself, she will not think you are loyal to her; but she will turn to strife and hatred, and unless you quickly take care, she will have the poison ready. If you introduce old women, and soothsayers, and prophets, and vendors of jewels and silken clothing, you imperil her chastity; if you shut the door upon them, she is injured and fancies you suspect her. But what is the good of even a careful guardian, when an unchaste wife cannot be watched, and a chaste one ought not to be? For necessity is but a faithless keeper of chastity, and she alone really deserves to be called pure, who is free to sin if she chooses. If a woman be fair, she soon finds lovers; if she be ugly, it is easy to be wanton. It is difficult to guard what many long for. It is annoying to have what no one thinks worth possessing. But the misery of having an ugly wife is less than that of watching a comely one. Nothing is safe, for which a whole people sighs and longs. One man entices with his figure, another with his brains, another with his wit, another with his open hand. Somehow, or sometime, the fortress is captured which is attacked on all sides.

"Men marry, indeed, so as to get a manager for the house, to solace weariness, to banish solitude; but a faithful slave is a far better manager, more submissive to the master, more observant of his ways, than a wife who thinks she proves herself mistress if she acts in opposition to her husband, that is, if she does what pleases her not what she is commanded. But friends, and servants who are under the obligation of benefits received, are better able to wait upon us in sickness than a wife who makes us responsible for her tears (she will sell you enough to make a deluge for the hope of a legacy); who boasts of her anxiety, yet drives her sick husband to the distraction of despair. But if she herself feels ill, we must fall sick with her and never leave her bedside. Or if she be a good and agreeable wife (how rare a bird she is!), we have to share her groans in childbirth, and suffer torture when she is in danger."[136]

A wise man can never be alone. He has with him the good men of all time, and turns his mind freely wherever he chooses. What is inaccessible to him in person he can embrace in thought. And, if men are scarce, he converses with God. He is never less alone than when alone.

Notes

1. See W. A. Meeks, *History of Religion* 13 (1974) 167-168.

2. Aphrodite's promise closely resembles the type of binding formula used in magical incantations. See *Papyri Graecae Magicae*, ed. K. Preisendanz, I, pp. 122-124.

3. In the Greek there is more emphasis on imagination—the "I" of the poem (a female, but not necessarily Sappho herself) says "he seems to me to be like one of the gods." See M. R. Lefkowitz, "Critical Stereotypes and the Poetry of Sappho," *Greek, Roman, and Byzantine Studies* 14 (1973) 113-123.

4. Sappho's simile describes not just the moon's beauty but its sustaining effect on whatever its light touches. The implication is that her absent friend will similarly beautify and nourish everyone in her new environment. In a poem written for a chorus of girls by a male poet, Alcman of Sparta (seventh century B.C.), the sun is used simply as a metaphor of pre-eminence, stressing physical appearance, "I sing Agido's light. I see her as the sun; Agido testifies that it shines on us" (l. 39-43). Alcman also has his girls speak openly of their sexual attraction to each other. Agido is compared to the dream-horse whose appearance connotes sexual release; see G. Nagy, "Phaethon, Sappho's Phaon, and the White Rocks of Leucas," *Harvard Studies in Classical Philology* 77 (1973) 137-148. Another girl, Hagesichora, whose hair is like "unmixed gold" (52-54), "wears me out" (*teirei*, as if denoting specifically post-orgasmic sensation); see S. Pomeroy, *Goddesses, Whores, Wives, and Slaves*, p. 55. But in Alcman, unlike Sappho, there is no reference to the emotional and aesthetic benefits of such relationships.

5. A bogy-woman who was thought to kill children because she had lost her own.

6. For a female, death before marriage was considered particularly wasteful. For other examples in extant inscriptions, see R. Lattimore, *Themes in Greek and Latin Epitaphs*, pp. 189-192.

7. The Greeks admired verisimilitude; cf. what the women say about the tableau of Adonis and Aphrodite in Theocritus *Idylls* 15 (below, pp. 88-90). The two women in Herodas, *Mimes* 4 are equally effusive.

8. Tyrant of Athens 527-510 B.C., son of Pisistratus.

9. The whole story may be an aetion (or fictional narrative explanation) for this transvestite ritual and the strange law cited below. Cf. Plutarch's account (*Theseus* 7) of the origin of the Athenian transvestite Oschophoria.

10. Euripides, *Bacchae* 1236.

11. Cf. also the enigmatic Roman inscription (*CIL* VI. 29149, tr. R. Lattimore, *op. cit.*, p. 280), "To my dear wife, with whom I lived two years, six months, three days, ten hours. On the day of her death I gave thanks to god and man."

12. On political reasons for suppressing mourning, see M. Alexiou, *The Ritual Lament in Greek Tradition*, pp. 21-23.

13. The four classes of Athenian society at this time were: (1) Pentacosiomedimni, "500-measure men," who had an income of 500 measures of grain or wine. (2) Knights, who were able to bring a horse to the army and had an income of 300 measures. (3) Zeugitae, "yoke men," who could own a yoke of oxen and had an income of 200 measures. (4) Thetes, "serfs," who had either no land or an income of less than 200 measures.

14. For laws on rape and property rights, see the Laws of Gortyn, in N. Lewis, ed., *Greek Historical Documents: The Fifth Century B.C.*, pp. 93-103.

15. 373/2 B.C., thirty years or more before the present trial.

16. Until it could be determined whether she was slave or free. The Polemarch was the archon in charge of suits involving foreign residents.

17. Sophocles, *Ajax* 293.

18. For a detailed discussion of women in Sparta and the ancient sources, see H. Michell, *Sparta.*

19. The legendary giver of the Spartan constitution, seventh century B.C.

20. *Republic* 458 D.

21. According to Diogenes Laertius (VII. 33), the philosopher Zeno (333-261 B.C.), foun-

der of Stoicism, suggested in his Utopia that wives be shared and that men and women dress alike, covering no part of the body completely.

22. A *lesche* is a public building or meeting-place. Here it may be the tribe's headquarters.

23. Cf. Apollo's argument in Aeschylus, *Eumenides* 658-661, which wins the case for Orestes:

> The mother is no parent of that which is called her child, but only nurse of the new-planted seed that grows. The parent is he who mounts. A stranger she preserves a stranger's seed, if no god interfere. (Tr. R. Lattimore)

24. In the Hippocratic Corpus (*On the Nature of the Child* 20), baldness is also attributed to excess fluid.

25. The authorship of the writings collected in the Hippocratic Corpus is uncertain, to say the least. It is unlikely that Hippocrates himself wrote any of them.

26. The flute-girl's gymnastics would not have aborted a healthy pregnancy, but they helped eject more quickly an early defective embryo (or "blood mole") that would soon have been miscarried in the normal course of events. The embryo was of course much older than six days. See A. Guttmacher's note in T. H. Ellinger, *Hippocrates on Intercourse and Pregnancy*, pp. 113-117.

27. The idea is to induce a substitute pregnancy, by using the Egyptian beans the Pythagoreans would not eat, because they believed that they could house human souls.

28. "Womb" here translates the plural in Greek. Since human dissection was not practiced, doctors inferred that the human uterus was similar to the bicornuate uterus of domestic animals. See A. Guttmacher, in T. H. Ellinger, *op. cit.*, p. 128.

29. Cf. the modern notion of a "tipped uterus," a "disease" which mainly afflicts older married women and whose cure involves frequent manual examination by a physician (usually, of course, male).

30. Cf. also the letter of Perictione on the "harmonious woman," quoted in S. Pomeroy, *Goddesses, Whores, Wives, and Slaves*, pp. 134-136.

31. The ultimate proof; cf. Glycon's praise for his wife Panthia (below p. 111), "You bore me children completely like myself."

32. Cf. Cicero's emphasis on the luxury of Clodia's household, below p. 000.

33. But even religious festivals could provide opportunity for misconduct. Thus, Simaetha below, p. 99) meets Delphis at the Thesmophoria of Artemis.

34. Cf. the Athenian law against excessive mourning (above, p. 19) and the public reaction to Dionysiac ritual (below, pp. 188-189).

35. Also his wife, following an Egyptian custom.

36. See especially I. M. Lewis, *Ecstatic Religion*, p. 101.

37. Cf. the description of the women worshippers of Dionysus in Euripides' *Bacchae* (esp. 134-166), rushing through the mountains, freed from the constraints of home and domestic life.

38. The story of how Demeter managed to get her daughter back for at least some of the time from Death, her husband, is a story of the meaning of motherhood and of the continuation of life through the daughter-mother bond. See M. Arthur, "Politics and Pomegranates: An Interpretation of the Homeric Hymn to Demeter," forthcoming in *Arethusa*.

39. The parents/masters of this household are P. Larcius Nicia and Saufeia Thalea, both former slaves themselves. They had two sons, L. Larcius Rufus and P. Larcius Brocchus. Horaea, a former slave in the household, married Brocchus. She took the family name Larcia, not when she married, but when she received her freedom.

40. The ceremonial torch which would have lit her wedding now lights her funeral.

41. In Aeschylus' *Agamemnon* (416-419) the chorus comments on the inadequacy of a statue as substitute for Menelaus' real wife Helen. Admetus, in Euripides' *Alcestis*, promises his dying wife that he will put a likeness of her in his bed, so that he can embrace and caress it and hold it in his arms, "so that I will seem to hold my dear wife in my arms even though I am not holding her" (348-354), a speech that illustrates how much emphasis he places on her physical presence.

42. A play on the word *potestas* which means "power."

43. Cornelia, perhaps the most illustrious example of Roman motherhood, was the daugh-

ter of Scipio Africanus and mother of Tiberius and Gaius Sempronius Gracchus. Aristo
crats, the Gracchi were champions of popular reform. Both were killed as a result o
political violence in 133 and 122 B.C.

44. Gaius Aurelius Cotta was an orator. He was exiled from Rome but returned with Sull
(the dictator) and became consul in 75 B.C.

45. Martial, *Epigrams* 1.13, also records these words: When chaste Arria handed t
Paetus the sword which she had drawn from her own breast, she said, "If you believe me
the wound which I have made does not hurt, but, the wound which you are going to make
that one, Paetus, hurts me."

46. This, in fact, happened. Thrasea Paetus was a member of the "Stoic opposition" t
Nero and was condemned to death in 66 A.D. He persuaded his wife, the younger Arria, no
to follow her mother's example, but to live for their daughter Fannia. See Tacitus, *Annal*
XVI.34 for the story.

47. It would appear that Arria was given a sort of divine status in popular belief. Cf. fo
example, this verse from a woman's epitaph from Anagnia in Latium (*CIL* X.5920 = *IL*
6261):

A paragon has died; mourn, maidens!
Oppia is no more, Oppia has been taken from Firmus.
Receive this soul and, Arria, increase it by the
Roman sacred number, and you, Laodamia, by the Greek.

The mythical Laodamia, like the historical Arria, took her own life for her husband.

48. Fannia was the second wife of Helvidius Priscus, a fervent Stoic and a member, alon,
with Thrasea Paetus, of the "Stoic opposition" to Nero.

49. The first occasion was in 66 A.D. because of his association with Thrasea. He was abl
to return after Nero died, and he became praetor in 70. Vespasian relegated him for hi
opposition, and he was killed outside of Italy, possibly by order of the Emperor Titus. See A
N. Sherwin-White, *The Letters of Pliny*, pp. 424-425.

50. Nonetheless Arria did accompany her daughter into exile.

51. This Helvidius was Fannia's stepson, her husband's son by his first wife. An ex-consul
he has condemned to death, possibly for his associations, in 93 A.D. by the Empero
Domitian.

52. Minicius Fundanus, consul in 107 A.D. The girl's epitaph was found in the famil
tomb outside Rome (*CIL* VI.16631 = *ILS* 1030): "To the gods of the dead. The tomb o
Minicia Marcella, daughter of Fundanus. She lived twelve years, eleven months, sever
days."

53. Because of his influence over her husband. Confidant of his fellow African, the
Emperor Septimius Severus, Plautianus became Prefect of the Praetorian Guard and, in
202, the father-in-law of Caracalla. In 203 he became Geta's colleague in the consulship. In
205, an unhappily married Caracalla arranged his fall from grace.

54. See K. A. Geffcken, *Comedy in the Pro Caelio* on Cicero's use of ridicule to discredi
Clodia.

55. This is the "Lesbia" of Catullus. She was the sister of Publius Clodius Pulcher
Cicero's bitter enemy. Her husband was Quintus Caecilius Metellus Celer (consul in 6
B.C.).

56. Gnaeus Domitius Calvinus, the praetor who presided over the trial.

57. Appius Claudius Caecus ("blind"), consul in 307 and 296 B.C. An aristocrat, he
championed the lower classes and built the first aqueduct in Rome and the major highway
the Via Appia.

58. A spa on the Bay of Naples known for luxury and loose living. "The mere mention o
Baiae [in the *Pro Caelio*] contributed effectively to the impression of Clodia's immoralit
which Cicero was striving to establish." J. H. D'Arms, *Romans on the Bay of Naples*, p. 43.

59. From a comic playwright, perhaps Caecilius Statius (d. 168 B.C.).

60. W. W. Tarn, *Cambridge Ancient History*, vol. X, p. 111.

61. 41 B.C. Antony summoned her to Tarsus in Asia Minor, accusing her of aiding
Cassius, one of the murderers of Caesar.

62. Plutarch probably uses this term in derogation. Cleopatra was of Macedonian descen
and had no Egyptian blood.

63. The infamous Empress Messalina, mother of Octavia and Brittanicus. She was later put to death for conspiracy against Claudius.

64. The "triumphs" are those of her father Scipio Africanus, the hero of the Second Punic War. Cf. above, p. 121.

65. Cf. below, p. 150, Valerius Maximus of Gaia Afrania.

66. At the Floralia, a particularly joyous festival in honor of the goddess Flora, celebrated from April 28 to May 3. See Ovid, *Fasti* V. 331 ff.

67. Cf. below, p. 137.

68. Queen of Carthage, lover of Aeneas. She committed suicide when he abandoned her.

69. Eclipses of the moon, thought by some to be caused by witchcraft, were met with loud noises to dispel the accompanying evil spirits.

70. A reference to the short tunic worn by men.

71. Palaemon, a freedman, was a grammarian of the early first century A.D.

72. This sacred marriage, known as *confarreatio*, was exclusively for patricians. The pontifex maximus and the chief priest of Jupiter (*flamen dialis*) were present along with ten witnesses. Only a very elaborate ceremony (*diffarreatio*) could dissolve the marriage. Other types of marriage, *conventio in manum* or *coemptio* and *usus*, existed in the early period. *Coemptio* placed the wife under the husband's power (*manus*—literally "hand"), by a mock sale, as his chattel. Under *usus*, a wife could free herself from her husband's power by leaving his house for three nights of the year.

73. This most likely refers to contraception and abortion. Divorce for sterility appears to have been first allowed in 235 B.C. (Aulus Gellius, *Attic Nights* 17.21.44). During the Empire, when marriage by *usus* was the norm, divorce required only notification. Complex laws concerning the disposition of the dowry operated to prevent ill-considered divorce.

74. Repudiation (*repudium*, different from *divortium* which required mutual consent) involved a formula which included the words, "Handle your own property for yourself." Either the husband or the wife could repudiate the other. The dowry, managed by the husband during the marriage, returned to the wife when the marriage ended, whether by repudiation or divorce.

75. Twenty-five was a woman's age of majority, but not of independence. She was either under her father's power (*potestas*) or her husband's (*manus*), or, lacking both, under that of a tutor (*tutela*). On Vestal Virgins, see below, p. 186.

76. In Roman civil law at this time the family is the agnatic, the father's side; the mother's side is called the cognate.

77. Boys 7-14, girls 7-12, and women who were not under a father's or husband's power.

78. This refers particularly to purple, a very expensive dye obtained from certain shell-fish. It was a sign of luxury. The togas of magistrates and wealthy youths (*togae praetextae*) were adorned with a purple stripe.

79. Marcus Porcius Cato "Censorius"—Cato the Elder (234-149 B.C.). He was the quintessential conservative and champion of traditional morality. Among his acts as censor in 184 B.C. was the taxation of luxury. He deplored and fought vainly against the acceptance of anything Greek into Roman life.

80. Cato's history of early Rome.

81. See above, notes 72, 75.

82. For an interesting fictional account of Julia's exile and the events which led to it, see John Williams, *Augustus*.

83. An interpretation of the law by the Stoic Musonius Rufus (first century A.D.): "The rulers forbade women to abort and attached a penalty to those who disobeyed; secondly they forbade them to use contraceptives on themselves and to prevent pregnancy; finally they established honors for both men and women who had many children, and made childlessness punishable." (M. K. Hopkins, *CQ* 15 [1965] 72.)

84. See above, note 72.

85. I.e., a woman possessing Latin rights, halfway between those of aliens and those of citizens.

86. "As to making a will . . . women not only had to have guardian's authorization but, until Hadrian, also had to go through a complicated rigmarole of changing guardians by

coemptio." J. A. Crook, *Law and Life of Rome*, p. 120, Cf. above, p. 142.

87. For a translation of the formal legal agreement, see *P. Fam. Tebt.* 22, pp. 76-77.

88. See above, note 79.

89. Her husband was Decimus Junius Brutus, consul in 77 B.C. Her son, Decimus Brutus, was one of the assassins of Julius Caesar.

90. Quintus Hortensius Hortalus (114-50 B.C.) was one of the Republic's most famous orators. He was consul in 69 B.C., and was a great forensic rival of Cicero.

91. 42 B.C. The triumvirs, Octavian, Antony and Lepidus, levied this tax to help pay for the war against Brutus and Cassius.

92. Nicknamed *Sapiens*, "the wise." Laelius was a hero of the Third Punic War and consul in 140 B.C.

93. *On Common Diseases* 6.6.21.

94. See above p. 64, *On the Nature of the Child* 13.

95. The list of ingredients (in another context, III. 20.1) consists of: burning pitch, unscoured wool, pepper, hellebore, castoreum, vinegar, garlic, onion.

96. Celsus (II. 18) defines foods of the middle class as nourishment for moderately strong people, relatively easy to digest, e.g., plant roots and bulbs, rabbit, birds (smaller than a flamingo), all unsalted fish, small whole salted fish, pork feet and brains, vinegar, and wine.

97. Nigella sativa, melanthium, melanospermum or black cumin. Its seeds were used both as a spice and as a medication for various ills.

98. The denarius, or dram, was a measure of weight equal to one-seventh of an *uncia* (one-twelfth of a Roman pound). The pound equalled about 333 metric grams, the denarius about 4 grams. (Metric equivalents from LCL.)

99. The *cyathus* was a liquid measure equivalent to about 42cc.

100. Women from all social classes seem to have been doctors. Primilla may be presumed to have been freeborn. Freedwomen doctors include Minucia Asste (*CIL* VI.9615) and Venuleia Sosis (*CIL* VI.9617). Melitine (*CIL* VI.6851) may have been a slave.

101. For some other epitaphs of midwives, see *CIL* VI.6325 (Secunda, a slave), 8192 (Sallustia Athenais, freedwoman), and 9723 (Publicia Aphe, a 21-year-old freedwoman).

102. 116-27 B.C. A scholar and politician whose extant writings were on agriculture and the Latin language.

103. That is, Livia, wife of Augustus and mother of the Emperor Tiberius. She received the name Julia Augusta by order of Augustus' will (14 A.D.), so this inscription must date after that year.

104. The empress is Livia (above, note 103). She was deified by Claudius in 41 A.D.

105. The designation Gaia (abbreviated Ɔ) refers to any woman, regardless of her actual name. This might be translated "freedwoman of a woman."

106. An unspecified area of the city.

107. The stone is Augustan. Thorius Flaccus was proconsul of the province of Bithynia under Augustus.

108. Grapte's mistress is herself noteworthy. According to Tacitus (*Annals* XV.71), she accompanied her husband, Glitius Gallus, into the exile imposed by Nero. She was possessed of a large personal fortune which was subsequently taken away from her, both of which circumstances, Tacitus says, "increased her glory."

109. One writer disposes of this sentiment thus: "What he seems most to have loved in Calpurnia was her admiration for his writings, and we soon come to the conclusion that he was readily consoled for the absences he complains of by the pleasure of polishing the phrases in which he so gracefully deplores them." J. Carcopino, *Daily Life in Ancient Rome*, p. 89, who adds the evidence from IX.36: Pliny slept alone and first thing in the morning summoned his secretary, not his wife.

110. Pliny and Calpurnia never were able to have children.

111. Numa Pompilius, the second king of Rome (715-673 B.C.).

112. The *ius trium liberorum* or "right of three children" was part of the Augustan marriage legislation (cf. above, p. 139). A mother of three children (four if a freedwoman) was released from *tutela*, or guardianship.

113. See also Livy, *History of Rome*, XXXIX.8-18.

114. An epithet of Juno as goddess of childbirth.

115. A town in Thessaly, known for witchcraft. Cf. *Odes* 1.27.21.

116. A volcanic lake in Campania, thought to be the entrance to the underworld.

117. The Subura was a crowded, dirty section of Rome between the Viminal and Esquiline Hills. Though it was notorious for containing many brothels, it also contained respectable merchants and residents.

118. The Marsi inhabited the mountains east of Rome. They practiced magic, but it was, apparently, not strong enough for Canidia.

119. That is, an avenger.

120. The Manes were the spirits of the dead or the gods of the underworld. It is the Manes who are invoked on many tombstones.

121. The land outside the Esquiline Gate (on the east side of the city) was used as a cemetery for paupers. Unlike other Roman corpses of this period, those placed here were not cremated, hence the reference to limbs. It is interesting to note that Maecenas, Horace's patron, built his villa in this area: cf. Horace, *Satires* I.8.

122. A letter of the second/third century A.D. (Oxyrhynchus papyrus 1761) contains the statement, "From the time that you went away we have searched your excrement, since we want to see you." Excretions from the dead are used in magic ritual: cf. *Papyri Graecae Magicae* I. 1396, 1441.

123. Arenas had two gates, the Porta Sanavivaria (Gate of Life) for gladiators who survived, and the Porta Libitina (Gate of Death). On the political significance of her death, see M. R. Lefkowitz, "The Motivations for St. Perpetua's Martyrdom," *Journ. Amer. Acad. of Religion* 44 (1976) 417-421 and G. E. M. de Ste. Croix, "Why were the Early Christians Persecuted," *Past and Present* 26 (1963) 6-37.

124. I Thess. 1:8.

125. I Thess. 4:9.

126. Cf. Matt. 10:23. In Euripides' *Bacchae* the women's being "on the mountain" is also contrued as a serious social threat (e.g., 217-220).

127. Ps. 51:7.

128. John 14:27.

129. I Tim. 1:5.

130. A guard or police officer.

131. A staff-officer sometimes with police duties.

132. Acts 4:24.

133. On the role of women in Gnostic cults, see E. H. Pagels, "What Became of God the Mother? Conflicting Images of God in Early Christianity," *Signs* 2.2(1976) 293-303.

134. Matt. 18:10.

135. The fragment of "Theophrastus" has also been attributed to Seneca (frag. 13, 47 ff.). The anthologist Stobaeus preserves some theoretical abstracts from ethical treatises for and against marriage by Antiphon the Sophist (fifth century B.C., 87 B 49 Diels-Kranz), and the Hellenistic Neopythagoreans (collected in Thesleff), and the Stoics Antipater (first century B.C.) and Hierocles (first century A.D.).

136. Cf. Antiphon (note 135): "It is not clear that a wife, if she is to his mind, gives her husband no less cause for love and pain than he does to himself, for the health of two bodies, the acquisition of two livelihoods, and for respectability and honor? Suppose children are born: then all is full of anxiety, and the youthful spring goes out of the mind, and the countenance is no longer the same" (tr. K. Freeman, *Ancilla to the Pre-Socratic Philosophers*, pp. 149-150).

Empresses. A. Turquoise cameo; Roman, first century A.D. The portraits show Livia, Augustus' wife, and her son Tiberius, Augustus' step-son and successor. Because the gem, unlike a coin, was not intended for mass circulation, the scene is more informal and intimate but does not lack political overtones. Livia was notoriously ambitious for Tiberius to become emperor. (Courtesy, Museum of Fine Arts, Boston)

B. Reverse of an *aureus* (gold coin) of the emperor Septimus Severus; 202 A.D. Septimius (whose portrait appears on the obverse of the coin) secured his rule after a brief period of civil war. This coin, which shows his wife Julia Domna and their sons Caracalla (left) and Geta (right), makes the political statement that all is well in the emperor's house: through his family, the emperor will ensure the dynasty and prevent political violence from recurring at his death. The legend, which a modern politician might render "Happy days are here again," can be taken to mean "Future generations of Severans will bring happiness to the Empire." See pp. 121-123 for the nightmare that the dream became. (Courtesy of the American Numismatic Society, New York)

Index